THE ENGLISH COUNTRY HOUSE

FROM THE ARCHIVES OF
COUNTRY LIFE

MARY MIERS

Dear Jerry + Family ~
With our best wishes!!!
Graham + Lori

From the Archives
of Country Life

THE
ENGLISH
COUNTRY
HOUSE

NEW YORK

FOR MY PARENTS,
DOUGLAS AND RICHENDA
MIERS, IN THE YEAR OF
THEIR GOLDEN
WEDDING.

First published in the United States
of America in 2009
by Rizzoli International Publications, Inc.
300 Park Avenue South, New York, NY 10010

www.rizzoliusa.com

© 2009 by Country Life
Text © 2009 by Mary Miers

2009 2010 2011 2012 / 10 9 8 7 6 5 4 3 2 1

Designed and typeset by Dalrymple
Printed in China

Page 1: A door at Cold Ashton Manor,
Gloucestershire

Page 2: Sheringham Hall, Norfolk, which was
designed and built by Humphry Repton and
his son John Adey Repton in 1812–18 for
Abbot Upcher, and remained in the Upcher
family until it was acquired by the National
Trust in 1987.

Right: Robert Adam's entrance hall at Syon
House, Middlesex, with its coffered apse and
classical detail providing a fine setting for Luigi
Valadier's bronze cast of *The Dying Gladiator*.

Endpapers: Fynedon Gothic, ca. 1790,
Hamilton Weston Wallpapers

ISBN-13: 978-0-8478-3057-2

*Library of Congress Cataloging-in-Publication
Data*

Miers, Mary.
    The English country house : from the
archives of Country life / Mary Miers. -- 1st ed.
        p. cm.
ISBN 0-8478-3057-8 (hardcover)
1. Country homes--England. 1. Country life
(London, England) 11. Title.
    NA7562.M53 2009
    728.80942--dc22

009019573

Contents

The English Country House

THE English country house is an extraordinary phenomenon that lies at the very heart of England's history and cultural life. That it is associated with such an iconic image and continues to be a source of dreams and aspiration owes much to the London-based journal *Country Life*, which, since it was established in 1897, has featured a different country house in each weekly issue and advertised many hundreds more in its property pages.

The magazine's founder was Edward Hudson, a self-made man who shared many characteristics with his typical reader: a successful, bourgeois businessman tied to a job in the city but seduced by the idea of owning a house in the country, and in particular by the weathered beauty of England's

[OPPOSITE] *A glimpse of the south front of Canons Ashby, Northamptonshire, taken from the lower garden in 1921. On the right of the early-eighteenth-century doorcase is an Elizabethan window, with an earlier window above.*

[LEFT] *Biddesden House, Wiltshire, with its three distinctive round windows or oeils de boeuf over the entrance. The house dates from 1712; this photograph was taken in 1938, soon after it had been bought and renovated by Bryan Guinness (later the 2nd Lord Moyne) and his first wife, Diana Mitford.*

*Montacute House, Somerset,
begun around 1589.*

old manor houses. As the owner of a printing firm, Hudson had access to the latest printing techniques, and so *Country Life* was able to illustrate its early articles with evocative black and white photographs that presented an enticingly romantic vision of rural England that was to have a consuming and widespread appeal. A selection of these images is featured on the pages of this introduction, many of them by A. E. Henson, who worked for *Country Life* from 1918 to 1959.

No other publication has succeeded in promoting so far afield such an enduring image of a domestic ideal—I have even found a stash of old *Country Life*s in a mountain ranch high up in the Ecuadorian Andes. Over the years the magazine has featured many fine foreign residences, but its principal focus has always been Britain, and by far the majority of houses featured in its pages have been English. Even today, the list of suitable candidates awaiting publication is endless, and the property pages never cease to amaze readers for their seemingly limitless supply of beautiful houses seeking a new owner. The continuing success of the magazine is evidence that the country house is still very much alive and in demand. For sheer number and diversity of fine examples, no other country can compete.

As a result of its famous series of beautifully illustrated and authoritative articles, *Country Life* has amassed an astonishing archive of photography and scholarship that provides a fascinating record of changing tastes and approaches to the country house and its garden over the past century. This book is illustrated almost entirely with images from the famous Country

Life Picture Library, many of them by leading photographers of their day.

You will find here not the great stately piles and ducal palaces whose names are familiar across the world—although their influence is frequently acknowledged and some are illustrated in the appendix. Instead, this book provides an *entré* to the sort of houses to which *Country Life* has had privileged access over the years, many of which are still private homes, often occupied by descendants of the families that built them. Spanning more than seven centuries, these houses were nearly all built as an expression of status at the centre of a landed estate, many interpreting the mainstream architectural trends of the day with their own distinctive provincial character. They celebrate that rich seam of English domestic architecture that reflects, through a variety of material and design, the diversity of the English landscape and its regional traditions of craftsmanship. Some of the more modest-sized houses were built by country squires and merchants rather than aristocrats and industrial plutocrats—houses such as Daneway, Stepleton, and Castle Godwyn, whose charming detail mixes pretension with naïveté, and whose architects and craftsmen are often unrecorded—and they represent the typical homes of the English gentry.

Other houses featured here, of varying status and grandeur, were built by an intriguing assortment of patrons, ranging from merchants and courtiers such as Sir Henry Fermor of East Barsham and Sir Richard Weston of

Upton House, Gloucestershire, of 1752.

Sutton Place, eager to flaunt their rank and loyalty to the monarch, and reckless aristocrats such as the 2nd Earl Verney of Claydon, who had "a brace of tall negroes with silver French-horns behind his coach and six . . . blowing very joyfully to behold and see," to Victorian industrialists such as the paint and varnish manufacturer Samuel Theodore Mander, and the high-minded, church-going patriarch William Gibbs of Tyntesfield, who made his money importing guano from Peru.

Many houses in the book illustrate the influences of the Grand Tour, a period in a young gentleman's education that involved travelling to the Continent to see the classical sites of Rome and Greece, to visit great palaces and art collections and meet artists and dealers, before returning home laden with art and antiquities. Some, like Thomas Worsley of Hovingham, became so well-versed in the principles of architecture that they designed their own country houses, or at least directed the works, as did Joseph Townsend at Honingham and William Holbech at Farnborough. These enlightened patrons belonged to the eighteenth-century tradition of amateur gentleman architects, whose modern-day equivalents might be Anthony Sykes of Bellamont or Sebastian de Ferranti of Henbury.

The sixty-two houses described in the main part of this book have featured in *Country Life* since the 1980s, when it started printing photographs in colour. The principal sources for the text were the accompanying articles, whose authors (see page 481), must be credited with much of the information. In addition, six essays by leading architectural historians set the houses into their wider context, elucidating on their changing role and function, interior decoration, collections, associated buildings, gardens and landscapes, and the influence of the English country house in America.

It is never entirely satisfactory to describe a building without showing its plan, but this book adopts *Country Life*'s current policy of omitting room plans for reasons of privacy and security.

Most houses are impossible to place exclusively into one specific period or style, having evolved over centuries of changing circumstances and taste. They are arranged here in loosely chronological order according to their most significant architectural phase. John Martin Robinson and Geoffrey Tyack's essays describe the arrangement of the medieval house and its ensemble of courtyards and dependent buildings, and the function and symbolism of its internal spaces. The book starts with houses such as Stokesay Castle and Cothay Manor, which are entered through a gatehouse, a structure that can be traced back to late Anglo-Saxon times. The gatehouse created an imposing entrance to the complex, leading into an outer court filled with storehouses, stables, brew house, and other domestic ranges. The house itself was

A. E. Henson's 1924 photograph of St. Catherine's Valley in the Cotswolds, viewed from the roof terrace of Cold Ashton Manor, which Col. Reggie Cooper restored in the 1920s. Country Life's architectural writer H. Avray Tipping described the gateway arch through which the house is approached as "the first English exposition of the Vitruvian rule."

entered through a porch, often, as at East Barsham, an echo of the gatehouse on a smaller scale.

Dominating the life of these houses, and by far the largest and most important structure, was the great hall, a fine example of which can be seen at Stokesay. Usually rising to full height, and with an open timber roof, this was the communal space at the heart of the medieval house, where, until the twelfth century, the entire household would eat and sleep. By the thirteenth century, hooded chimneypieces were replacing central open fires, and the lord and his family and guests were accommodated in suites of private chambers or "lodgings." But as late as the seventeenth century, the hall remained the central feature of house plans, albeit by this time more symbolic than functional in purpose. At Jacobean Chastleton House, for example, the conventional arrrangement of the medieval hall is still in evidence, with the main entrance at one end leading into an internal corridor known as the screens passage, off which led the service quarters. At the opposite end, a low dais often lit by an oriel window indicated the position of the lord's "high table." Although the original function of the hall has been forgotten, this ancient domestic space survived in many houses, later perhaps furnished as a billiard or sitting room. Even in modern houses it is echoed in the usual arrangement of the front door leading into a central space commonly known as the hall.

The introduction to England in the fifteenth century of the technology to mass-produce brick precipitated a flowering of brick architecture. Sometimes, as at Sutton Place and East Barsham Manor, fine terra-cotta ornament was introduced to enrich the brickwork. Elaborate chimneys shaped with cut and moulded bricks became a particularly distinctive feature of both brick and timber-framed Tudor houses. Skilled timber construction continued to flourish, particularly in areas of poor building stone, where various techniques of building with mud and clay were also prevalent. Chalk regions, such as East Anglia, produced flints, which, cut in half or "knapped," were widely used to face buildings, often combined decoratively with brick. In Suffolk, buildings constructed of inferior materials were often rendered over with decorative plasterwork known as pargetting. In other parts of the country, notably along the rich seam of Oolitic limestone that runs in a great band from Lincolnshire to Dorset, dynasties of skilled masons embellished their beautiful golden-grey buildings with exuberant carved stone ornament. Few countries so small possess such a range of different building traditions; the variety of England's vernacular architecture is a testament to the remarkable diversity of its geology.

Under the influence of Renaissance architecture, Elizabethan houses became increasingly symmetrical, often built to an E plan enclosing three sides of a courtyard, with mullioned and transomed windows larger and more regularly spaced. Gatehouses and entrance towers survived as symbols of martial power, and the bones of the medieval plan prevailed, though there was now a greater number of withdrawing apartments and the hall

was relegated to servants' use. Each room in the progression of chambers, from the hall at the most public end, to the bed chamber at the end of the sequence, had its own hierarchy and level of privacy. The most important was the great chamber, a room of splendid furnishings and display reserved for grand eating and dancing. Situated on the first floor, it was linked to the hall by a ceremonial staircase. The parlour, generally located off the high end of the hall, was used for more informal entertaining. Larger houses of the sixteenth and seventeenth centuries had a long gallery on their top floor, used for exercising and various recreational activities, as well as often doubling as a picture gallery and serving as a link between the two ends of the house. Chastleton in the Cotswolds has one of the most memorable surviving long galleries.

Classical forms first appeared in English houses around 1500, although often distorted and used with unsophisticated enthusiasm as a means of decoration rather than a logical system for designing entire buildings. Jacobean houses became highly elaborated, with exuberant skylines and a profusion of heraldic, allegorical, classical, and biblical ornament carved into their façades, overmantels, chimneypieces, and any other available surface. All this was employed to proclaim the wealth, rank, and lineage of their competitive owners, as well as their learning and moral well-being. Colour abounded: woodwork was painted and gilded, and walls and furniture were smothered in tapestries and embroidered textiles.

But the first quarter of the seventeenth century also witnessed a reaction against Jacobean mannerism with its surfeit of allusory ornament, and a more literate use of the classical language emerged. Inigo Jones (1573–1652) was the key architectural figure at this period. His earliest designs in the Italian Renaissance manner were for the sets of court masques, often staged in collaboration with Ben Jonson. In 1615 he was appointed Surveyor General of the King's Works, and most of his architectural commissions came from the immediate circle of the court, the Banqueting House in Whitehall of 1619–22 being the most famous surviving example.

Jones had made several visits to the Continent, including France and Italy, and so had seen the monuments of classical antiquity firsthand. He also looked at buildings and collected drawings by the Italian architect Andrea Palladio (1508–1580), whose I Quattro Libri dell'Architettura of 1570 set out the rules of classical architecture first drawn up by Vitruvius in 50 BC. The rediscovery of this architectural language in sixteenth-century Italy initiated a wave of change that, over the next few centuries, would extend throughout Europe and beyond.

Jones fused the lessons he had learned from Palladio and his pupil Scamozzi (he met the latter in Vicenza in 1614), with those of Serlio and contemporary French designers, and adapted them to the very different climate and conditions of England. The sophistication of his architecture stood in complete contrast to the work of his contemporaries, and it was not easily absorbed by regional master builders, although Lodge Park in

[OPPOSITE, CLOCKWISE FROM TOP LEFT]

The octagonal dovecote at Nymans in Sussex (see page 402), which overlooks the stone-arched doorway to the forecourt on the west wing. It was built for Maud and Leonard Messel by Sir Walter Tapper in 1928.

Deanery Garden, Berkshire, the perfect exemplar of Sir Edwin Lutyens's Old English style. The house was built in 1899–1901 for Edward Hudson, founder of Country Life.

A view through one of the delicately patterned Mogul-style windows to the orangery at Sezincote, Gloucestershire, a house built by S. P. Cockerell for his brother in ca. 1805.

The Elizabethan manor house of Levens Hall, Westmorland, showing its rare surviving early-eighteenth-century garden as it appeared in 1926.

Gloucestershire is a striking early example of a provincial building conversant with the latest developments in the capital.

Jones's Queen's House at Greenwich, begun in 1616, was England's first Palladian house, but it would be nearly a century before Palladianism would exercise its far-reaching influence across Britain. In the interim years of civil war followed by the Restoration and the reign of Queen Anne, a more conservative architecture prevailed: less intellectual, exuding a warm sense of domestic comfort and solidity. A form of house conceived by Jones in the 1630s and developed by architects such as Sir Roger Pratt (whose rebuilding of Coleshill in Berkshire from 1649 was an important early example) and Hugh May became a widely adopted model for the typical Restoration house. Its principal characteristics were a compact, double-pile main block, satisfyingly proportioned with the main floors of nearly equal importance and height, the roof adopting the fashionable hipped form, often with dormers and surmounted by a balustraded platform and cupola. Externally it

A Sheraton armchair of ca. 1785, photographed in Biddesden House in 1919.

was plain, except perhaps for a carved doorcase or pedimented frontispiece, and it was built of finely worked materials such as handmade red bricks. Pratt's contemporary, Hugh May, popularised a version that incorporated pilasters and shaped gables, drawing on Continental influences and reflecting the increasing impact of Dutch architecture at this period.

In contrast to the relatively restrained external decoration, the interiors of houses at this time often displayed new skills and techniques of craftsmanship, their surfaces embellished with finely modelled stucco work and carved wood and stone detail. Belton House is a particularly handsome late example, modelled on Pratt's famous but short-lived Clarendon House in Piccadilly of 1664–67. On a smaller scale, Honington is a more homely example—the perfect provincial Restoration house.

This strain of regional architecture continued, in parallel to the great courtier houses of the Restoration, well into Queen Anne's reign. It spawned numerous gentry residences redolent of pretty dollhouses, such as Nether

The water garden, known as "the white sea" at Sedgwick Place, Sussex. This photograph of 1901 is rare among Country Life *articles on houses and gardens in showing a living person.*

Lypiatt, with the symmetrical arrangement of double-hung sash windows that had become widely adopted by this time.

Though they incorporated certain Palladian elements and were indebted to Continental influences, these gentry houses of the later seventeenth and early eighteenth centuries were quintessentially English. However, they had no connection, as has often been misleadingly suggested, with the work of the great mathematician, astronomer, and architect Sir Christopher Wren (1632–1723), best known for designing St. Paul's Cathedral of 1675–1711. Wren was made Surveyor General of the King's Works in 1669 and was responsible for many public and royal buildings, as well as for rebuilding fifty of the city churches destroyed in the Great Fire of London in 1666. He worked on very few country house commissions, although recent research has confirmed a probable involvement at Newby Hall. Many houses attributed to Wren were in fact the work of master masons skilfully interpreting his style with the help of increasing numbers of architectural books translated into English, with illustrations that benefited from improvements in engraving techniques.

Wren's pupil and assistant was Nicholas Hawksmoor (1661–1736), whose expertise was central to the development of Sir John Vanbrugh (1664–1726), described by Sir John Soane as the "Shakespeare of architects." Vanbrugh was an extraordinary genius: soldier, herald, prisoner in the Bastille accused of spying, poet, and playwright, he turned to architecture as a gentleman amateur in 1699, when he took on Castle Howard (see page 477) with his friend and associate Hawksmoor; three years later he was made Comptroller of the [Queen's] Works. These two great masters of the English Baroque borrowed from classical sources, yet their grand, boldly massed and rhythmic buildings have a drama and originality unknown to the Palladians. The "brooding genius" that created Castle Howard culminated in triumphant

[LEFT] *The living room/library at Wardes, Kent, which was owned by the diplomat connoisseur Sir Louis Mallet when this photograph was taken in 1919. He restored the late-fourteenth-century hall house after acquiring it in 1905.*

[RIGHT] *The museum at Claydon House, Buckinghamshire, in 1901 (see page 190).*

Blenheim (see page 479), begun in 1705. These monumental piles belong to a group of Baroque palace-houses created for the Whig aristocracy, of which Chatsworth (see page 476), begun in 1687, was the first. The most conspicuous and widely adopted feature of their plan was the enfilade of rooms known as the state apartment, the function of which John Martin Robinson describes in his essay (see page 73).

In parts of provincial England a rustic version of the English Baroque, as represented here by the Ivy and Castle Godwyn, prevailed until about 1730. It was executed by masons belonging to such families as the Bastards of Blandford, master builders practising in the long-established medieval tradition of mason-architects. These men made spirited copies of architects' designs, or provided designs themselves, and adorned their buildings with lively, florid "mason's Baroque" ornament.

In 1715 Colen Campbell published *Vitruvius Britannicus*, a book of Palladian designs that heralded the return to a cooler, more intellectual strain of classicism. Campbell's Mereworth Castle of 1722–25 replicated Palladio's Villa Rotunda near Maidstone in Kent. From the Early Georgian period until the beginning of Queen Victoria's reign, almost every house built in England reflected the Palladian influence—see, for example, Kelmarsh Hall and Wrotham Park. The immensely wealthy Earl of Burlington studied Palladian architecture in Italy. There he met the painter and future architect, furniture designer, and landscapist William Kent, whom he engaged to design the decoration and garden of Chiswick House (see page 475). This villa, which Burlington built to house his collections, might have come straight from the Italian Veneto.

[LEFT TO RIGHT] *Staircases at Moulton Hall, Yorkshire; Kelvedon, Essex; and Knole, Kent.*

The return to correct classicism a century after Inigo Jones had introduced it became the blueprint for Georgian houses the length and breadth of the country. Trafalgar typifies the genre: symmetrical, oblong, and dignified in its proportions, the exterior is restrained of ornament and punctuated by regularly spaced sash windows, with a slightly projecting pedimented centrepiece on the west front.

The Georgian house and its setting were conceived as one unified composition, the surrounding parkland, designed by such men as Lancelot "Capability" Brown, suggesting a pastoral scene that Claude Lorrain might have painted. A winding drive approached the house through a landscape dotted with woods and lakes, with carefully sited incidentals to catch the eye, such as a classical "temple" on the crest of a hill or a rotunda terminating a vista.

Lord Burlington's friend and collaborator William Kent erected sham castles as adornments to his landscapes, reflecting a parallel taste for Gothic. However, this playful and essentially decorative strain of the style, dubbed "Gothick," that became fashionable in the Georgian period, together with the frivolous Rococo and chinoiserie seen in proliferation at Claydon, has eclipsed the more serious pursuit of Gothic in the eighteenth century by antiquarian-minded patrons such as Sir Roger Newdigate of Arbury. They used it for symbolic reasons and its association with the past: to emphasise (or suggest) the antiquity of their lineage, and to reaffirm the age and history of their house. For generally, as at Arbury, they were adapting or extending an existing building—Horace Walpole's influential Strawberry Hill, which contrary to his claims came rather late to the Georgian Gothic movement, was unusual in being a largely new creation.

In the second half of the eighteenth century, Robert Adam changed public taste with his refined version of neoclassicism that demonstrated a firsthand knowledge of the architecture of ancient Rome. Adam built few country houses from scratch; most of his work in this field involved redesigning and decorating existing buildings—houses such as Kedelston, and Newby Hall, where he created a sculpture gallery in the tradition of Lord Burlington's at Chiswick to display antiquities purchased by William Weddell during his Grand Tour.

Newby belongs to a group of Yorkshire houses, including Harewood and Nostell Priory, enriched by Adam's collaboration with such leading craftsmen as the furnituremaker Thomas Chippendale, who started his career as an estate carpenter and became one of the leading cabinetmakers of his age, and the plasterer Joseph Rose. The lighter, more elegant and varied style of decoration that Adam made fashionable was characterised by a fluency of rhythm and proportions, larger-paned windows with slim glazing bars, smoother surfaces, flatter plasterwork and mouldings, and the subtle use of colour. So widely imitated was it, that Adam could claim to have "brought about, in this country, a kind of revolution in the whole system of this useful and elegant art." Ironically, some of the finest examples of the style were

[OPPOSITE, CLOCKWISE FROM TOP LEFT]

The late-fifteenth-century hall at Rufford Old Hall, Lancashire, as seen through A. E. Henson's lens in 1929

The seventeenth-century great hall at Stanway House, Gloucestershire, which was altered by William Burn in 1959–60.

The hall at Lutyens' Deanery Garden in Berkshire.

Robert Adam's dining room at Syon House, Middlesex.

created by his imitators, notably his rival James Wyatt, whose Heaton Hall is an outstanding example. Henry Holland infused French elements to create a still more refined taste favoured by the Prince of Wales, represented here by the exquisite interiors of his severely neoclassical Berrington Hall.

Even more restrained and austere was Holland's remodelling of Southill, which shows the emergence of the Graeco-Roman style that would become fashionable in the early nineteenth century. Meanwhile, Sir John Soane had developed his own, highly individual abstracted version of neoclassicism, in which he emphasised space using light and shadow rather than stylistic detail (see for example Moggerhanger on page 476). C. R. Cockerell, Robert Smirke, and William Wilkins were other key architects of this period. James Stuart and Nicholas Revett's *The Antiquities of Athens* of 1762 had a strong influence on the development, several decades later, of the Greek Revival style, as represented here by Oakly Park. They advocated the architecture of ancient Greece as an even purer source than Roman buildings.

The Regency was the great age of the English country house as we know it. It coincided with the early years of the Industrial Revolution, a period of prosperity that witnessed a craze for new building. John Martin Robinson describes in his essay the changing perception of the country house as a place increasingly valued for its comfort and taste, for the entertainment of friends and the enjoyment of country sports. The naming and precise functions of the different rooms in English country houses has always been complex; he explains the changing roles of those such as the dining room and the library.

Houses associated with the fashions and society depicted in the novels of Jane Austen were characterised by a delicacy and refinement of architectural and decorative detail. Chaste, stucco-fronted buildings had tall, slender sash windows, bow fronts, and verandas with pretty ironwork that projected the internal spaces into the landscape. The gracious interiors featured exquisite plasterwork and elegant furniture and upholstery.

Under the influence of John Nash, a proliferation of Italianate villas resurrected the Horacian ideal of the rural retreat. Farmhouse villas such as Cronkhill—asymmetrical, with broad, bracketed eaves and loggias—ornamented naturalistic landscapes contrived by men such as Humphry Repton in response to the Picturesque movement theorised in the 1770s by Richard Payne Knight and Uvedale Price. In his essay on gardens and landscapes, Tim Richardson describes the settings that developed in response to the cult of the Picturesque, with their emphasis on asymmetry and irregularity (see page 377).

A new sentimentality for rural life at a time of great agricultural change culminated in the cult of the *cottage orné*, as popularised by Queen Charlotte at Kew and represented here by Angeston Grange. Architectural theorists and speculative builders such as Robert Lugar and J. C. Loudon published handbooks of designs that could be copied by local builders and masons for ornamental estate buildings in a range of fashionable styles, from rustic

[OPPOSITE] *The great hall at Welbeck Abbey, Nottinghamshire, as seen here in 1906. Recast by Elizabeth Cavendish, Countess of Oxford, after she retired here in the 1740s, this is one of the great little-known Gothic Revival rooms in England. The pendant vaults were modelled on those in Henry V's chapel at Westminster.*

to Gothick, and for the villas of a new breed of middle-class professional. A parallel taste for the exotic reached a crescendo at this period with the Prince Regent's Brighton Pavilion, which took its inspiration from Sezincote in Gloucestershire (see page 14), a Mogul-style house built for an East India Company nabob in 1805.

Inspired by the Romantic movement, enthusiasm for the Picturesque qualities of medieval architecture spawned a series of Regency castles such as Bolesworth—essentially classical buildings transformed into toy castles with the addition of turrets and towers, crenellations and other evocative detail. Eastnor Castle, with its stirring silhouette evocative of a Welsh Border fortress, demonstrates how it was now felt valid to build an entirely new family seat in a medieval idiom.

From the 1830s, a new moral and religious dynamic was injected into the style by the great Victorian Gothic revivalist A. W. N. Pugin. Under his influence, architects also began to look beyond the merely decorative to the structural possibilities of Gothic architecture; their legacy includes many of the masterpieces of the great age of Victorian church building. In a domestic context, the drawing room at Eastnor of 1849–50 preserves one of Pugin's best-surviving interiors. High Church patrons such as John Garratt of Bishops Court and William Gibbs of Tyntesfield favoured Puginian Gothic. At the Chanter's House in Devon, William Butterfield remodelled

[LEFT] *The carved parlour at Crewe Hall, Cheshire, a Jacobean house of 1615–36, which was reinstated after a fire by E. M. Barry in 1866. This room, with its alabaster copy of the original stone chimneypiece, is a re-creation of the original.*

[RIGHT] *The South Bedroom at Avebury Manor, Wiltshire, with a plaster ceiling dating from the sixteenth century.*

an existing Georgian house in the eclectic Gothic idiom that spawned a familiar genre of Victorian bourgeois domestic architecture still in widespread evidence today. The elaborate use of asymmetry, tall gables and chimneys, rich polychromy, and opulence of material and ornament that identifies the High Victorian style could not be more in contrast to the sober architecture that resulted from a parallel taste for a secular Italianate manner that flourished at this time under the influence of such architects as Sir Charles Barry, represented here by the exterior of Philip Wilkinson's Brodsworth Hall.

The master of nineteenth-century country house planning was William Burn, a Scottish architect who moved his prolific practice to London in 1844. Burn's houses such as Sandon were elaborate machines of domestic precision equipped with a complexity of attendant service spaces and facilities occupying ranges almost as extensive as the main public and family wings. Architectural nostalgia—as expressed, for example, by his popular Jacobethan style—went hand in hand with the image of the Victorian landowner as a munificent patriarchal figure. Considered unfashionable for much of the past century, Victorian country houses started appearing in the pages of *Country Life* only in the late 1950s, largely through the writings of Mark Girouard.

The last decades of the nineteenth century saw a return to preindustrial values and a nostalgia for Old England under the influence of William Morris and the Society for the Protection of Ancient Buildings. Ernest Gimson and the Barnsley brothers were typical of the idealistic young architects and designers who moved to the country to set up workshops producing furniture and other artifacts, and designing buildings that respected time-honoured traditions of craftsmanship and the use of local materials (see Daneway, page 112, and Owlpen Manor, page 100). Their aim was to revive the vernacular skills that were fast disappearing, and they did so within the framework of a socialist ideology. Many chose to migrate to the Cotswolds, a still relatively remote area of rural England that had enchanted Morris with the "quiet poetry" of its architecture when he discovered Kelmscott in 1870. For Morris and his Arts & Crafts disciples, the settled, ancient, stone manor houses and village buildings enfolded in the coombes and valleys of the Cotswolds were a symbol of the enduring values and beauty of a rural England untainted by the deadening hand of mass production.

Country Life promoted the dream with its early articles on Tudor and Stuart manor houses, and books such as *In English Homes*, illustrated with Charles Latham's bewitching black and white photographs. These, and the crisper images of A. E. Henson, who often recomposed a room's appearance by decluttering its furnishings before capturing it on film, had a strong influence on the early-twentieth-century cult of the English manor house, which saw the likes of Cothay, Parnham, and Great Dixter gently resuscitated, and others, such as Nymans and Birtsmorton, romantically re-created and furnished with old English pieces.

[OPPOSITE, CLOCKWISE FROM TOP LEFT]

The stables at Boughton House, Northamptonshire, with carving in the pediment by Duchesne, 1704.

Looking through the ca.1630 north archway to the gatehouse at Stanway House, Gloucestershire.

Roger Morris's Palladian stable block of 1733 at Althorp, Northamptonshire.

27

In 1910 Lawrence Weaver became architectural editor and, through his articles and publications such as *Small Country Houses of Today*, championed a genre of contemporary house that commuters like Hudson might build for a weekend retreat as an alternative to reviving an old vernacular building. Weaver advocated the Arts & Crafts house as most successfully synthesising the qualities of traditional buildings with a contemporary aesthetic.

With their irregularly grouped ranges, sweeping roofs, prominent gables and chimneys, tile-hanging, half-timbering, weatherboarding, and other detail derived, in particular, from the vernacular buildings of Kent, Surrey, and Sussex, these houses chimed with the idealised vision of rural England that lay at the heart of the Arts & Crafts movement and resonated so strongly with readers of *Country Life*. It was an aesthetic that arose from the same instinct for the Picturesque that had given birth to the *cottage orné* a century earlier, but it was now the preserve of artistically inclined members of the middle classes, rather than the aristocracy.

In 1890 the influential gardener Gertrude Jekyll introduced Hudson to her protégé, Edwin Lutyens, which led to Hudson commissioning a romantic new house, Deanery Garden in Berkshire (see pages 14 and 20), widely regarded as the epitome of Lutyens's Old English style. Through the magazine, Hudson played a significant role in Lutyens's rise to fame, featuring his buildings regularly and introducing him to new clients; between 1902 and 1928 Hudson commissioned Lutyens to work on three further projects. Christopher Hussey, who became the architectural editor in 1920, wrote up Lutyens's houses and published his biography. It was he who introduced modern architecture to the pages of *Country Life*, as well as developing the magazine's reputation for serious scholarly articles—notably on Georgian, and later Regency, country houses.

The Arts & Crafts movement that flowered around the turn of the nineteenth century was one of the most creative periods in English domestic architecture. Under the influence of William Morris and John Ruskin, houses such as Wightwick, Blackwell, and Voewood celebrated the interdependence of crafts and architecture and the beauty of individual materials: the house as a total work of art. Baillie Scott's design for Blackwell demonstrates how the use and planning of houses was now being reconsidered, with a breaking down of rigid rules about the specific functions of individual rooms, and a greater informality. Plans flowed more freely, with a series of interconnecting spaces centred about a central living hall, the focus of which was often a large inglenook fireplace. With their emphasis on hearth and home, domestic comfort and national identity, these houses were seen as the embodiment of Englishness.

The 1930s are represented here by the Courtaulds' creation at Eltham Palace, the sleek Art Deco interiors of which reflect the cosmopolitan glamour of an entirely different world. The emergence of modernism in the English country house is largely absent from these pages, reflecting an editorial decision that the houses built in response to the Continental avant-

[OPPOSITE ABOVE] *The stables at Houghton Hall, Norfolk, of ca. 1735, possibly by William Kent.*

[OPPOSITE BELOW] *High and Over, Buckinghamshire, built by Amayas Connell for Bernard Ashmole in 1929.*

garde of le Corbusier and Mies van der Rohe would be discordant with the general tone and appearance of the book. However, one important example—Amayas Connell's High and Over of 1929—is illustrated on page 28.

We move instead to the postwar era and the work of the leading interior designer John Fowler, co-owner of the famous decorating company Colefax & Fowler. He introduced to many National Trust and privately owned houses a style of country house decoration that combined grandeur with a new emphasis on informality and comfort. He rearranged interiors and introduced new palettes of colour with great effect, as seen at the Manor House in Hambleden, where much of his work of the 1950s still survives. In his essay on country house decoration, Tim Knox touches on this period (see page 137), which saw a growing interest in interior decoration, soon to become a subject of serious historical scholarship through bodies such as the Victoria and Albert Museum.

The twentieth century witnessed dramatic extremes in the fortunes of the country house that can only be mentioned briefly here. The First World War and the agricultural depression triggered irreversible changes to social and physical circumstances which, coupled with crippling death duties, resulted in countless sales and demolitions, and the loss or dispersal of many valuable collections; in many cases, the photographs in *Country Life* are their only record now. Never had the future looked so bleak as in the early 1950s, when virtually every week another country house was lost. It was not until 1974, when the founders of the campaigning charity SAVE Britain's Heritage mounted a sensational exhibition, "The Destruction of the Country House" at the V&A in London, that the scale of loss was publicly recognised, and the seeds of the modern conservation movement were sown.

Since then much has been done to revive the fortunes of the country house, and recent decades have witnessed a remarkable renaissance. In an article entitled "Forty Years of the Country House," published in *Country Life* in 1992, Michael Hall was able to write optimistically that "more than 1,000 country houses are still privately lived in. . . . Demolitions themselves, which ran like a scourge in the early 1950s, are now exceptional." Imaginative new uses, and diversification in the role and function of houses as well as their estates, have enabled many to earn their keep. Some have been put into charitable trusts, others rescued from dereliction with the aid of grants and returned to private use.

The Mentmore sale of 1977 was a turning point for country house collections, leading to the increasing recognition of the importance of contents as part of a unified entity and the introduction of measures to prevent sales and preserve private collections intact. Since 1983 private owners have been able to offer objects in lieu of estate duties which are then loaned back so that they remain in situ, and since 1986 important items have been granted exemption from death duties.

The National Trust, founded in 1896 to protect and promote the English landscape and later its architecture, and now with 3.5 million members, has been at the forefront of great improvements in conservation skills and pioneering approaches to restoring, displaying, and preserving country houses, sometimes, as in the case of Tyntesfield, demonstrating admirable brinkmanship in its determination to save it. The texts for Lodge Park, Tyntesfield, and English Heritage's Eltham Palace in this book touch on some of the challenging conservation dilemmas that have had to be resolved.

A new confidence in the 1980s coincided with the resurgence of classicism in country house architecture, demonstrating its continuing relevance to buildings of the modern age. Compact and understated, houses such as Ashfold and Wakeham make inventive use of the classical language, while embracing modern technology, sound ecological principles, and the requirements of an increasingly informal contemporary lifestyle.

Corfe Farm, the last house in the book, reflects a modern Arts & Crafts aesthetic, with its echo of Lutyens and sensitivity to local context and materials, continuing that particular quality of Englishness that is a unifying theme of this book. The key to it was described recently by an architectural designer as a series of "strangely contradictory Anglo-Saxon combinations" that are still of relevance today: "pride of ownership with reticence; regard for tradition with consciousness of fashion; love of land with fear of the weather; joy in hospitality with a desire for solitude, and a need for formality with a need for homeliness."

Haddon Hall, Derbyshire.

Stokesay Castle

— SHROPSHIRE —

STOKESAY Castle is an extraordinary survival. For more than seven hundred years, the late-thirteenth-century fabric of this most Picturesque of English medieval houses has remained virtually intact, a compelling source of inspiration for generations of antiquarians and artists. Its survival is partly due to the fact that it has not been occupied since 1706, and so has undergone no significant alterations since the seventeenth century. Now owned by English Heritage, Stokesay passed out of private hands for the first time only in 1992.

Situated near Ludlow in the wooded valley of the River Onny, Stokesay was built by a merchant, Lawrence of Ludlow, who bought the tenancy in 1281. Lawrence was one of the country's richest wool merchants, and his new house, highly luxurious and sophisticated for its date, was a powerful expression of his wealth and status. It has been suggested that Lawrence modelled the distinctively shaped south tower, which gives Stokesay the appearance of a castle, on one of similar character at Caernarfon Castle, begun by Edward I in 1283. Caernarfon was conceived in a consciously historicist vein as a potent symbol of imperialism. Living in the Welsh Marches, Lawrence might well have been inspired by that impressive display of the king's power as conqueror of Wales.

The house is composed of four principal parts arranged symmetrically along the west side of a moated courtyard originally protected by a curtain wall. The main block comprises the full-height hall, beautifully lit by three gabled windows on each long wall, flanked by the north tower and a two-storey cross wing. South of this, and almost freestanding, is a heavily buttressed tower. On the other side of the courtyard, a half-timbered gatehouse of ca. 1640 completes the ensemble. Old drawings confirm that other structures, including a service wing, formerly stood in the courtyard.

Lack of documentation and the loss of these structures make it difficult to assess exactly how the house functioned in the Middle Ages. The evidence is sometimes confusing; the tower at the north end, for instance, preserves on its ground floor areas of wall painting—a red scroll pattern on a white background—that do not accord with the assumed role of this room as a buttery. The jettied, half-timbered top storey is of the same late-thirteenth-century date as the tower, though its windows are seventeenth century.

The great, navelike hall with its tall, traceried windows is without doubt one of the best-preserved examples of the period. The magnificent cruck roof is innovative for its date and one of the earliest surviving in the country. It contains at least one reused timber, discovered during recent conservation work—a clue to the likelihood that there was an earlier house here. The hall was probably aisled and had a central hearth. Up the north wall runs the original staircase—a remarkable survival leading to the chambers in the north tower. The cross wing at the south end contained a series of withdrawing chambers above the ground floor, accessible only by the external (once covered-in) stair. From the principal first-floor room, or great chamber (which originally had an open ceiling), the lord could look down on the hall from a pair of windows flanking the fireplace. A bridge beyond the external stair leads to the upper floors of the south tower.

This tower is one of Stokesay's most interesting features. Assumed to date from around 1291, when Lawrence obtained a licence to crenellate, it has a sophisticated and unusual form that fuses a semioctagon with two polygonal towerlike projections (visible respectively from the courtyard and from the west). But the complicated plan and battlemented outline were more symbolic than genuinely defensive, conceived to display the owner's status. The tower's unusually shaped rooms were well lit and would probably have been

[LEFT] *The north tower, with its deep, battered base, is now believed to be contemporary with the rest of the house—late thirteenth century—although the windows of the jettied upper storey date from the seventeenth century.*

[RIGHT] *One of the carvings on the seventeenth-century gatehouse.*

used for guest accommodation (it was gutted by fire in the early nineteenth century, so they no longer survive).

From 1620 to 1706, the Baldwyn family were tenants at Stokesay, and thus oversaw its evolution into a seventeenth-century country house. The elaborate timbered gatehouse is an addition probably of the 1640s for Samuel Baldwyn, a successful lawyer who carried out repairs to the curtain wall following its destruction in a Civil War skirmish of 1647, and was also responsible for fitting out the principal chamber in the cross wing with panelling and a ceiling. Like many of the gentry at this period, he was a keen antiquarian; contemporary accounts describe this room as being displayed with shields and heraldic glass, and a diary entry by William Dugdale records "a booke of armes of the gentlemen of Shropshire finely tricked out." Baldwyn may have reused existing woodwork—certainly the elaborate overmantle looks early seventeenth century—and he also inserted medieval-looking ogee-headed lancets and other Gothic detail.

The Craven family, who owned Stokesay from 1620 to 1869, never lived here. But in the 1840s Lord Craven was encouraged by a local antiquary to initiate the first of several restoration campaigns (some of the buildings at this time were in agricultural use). More recently, English Heritage's detailed programme of conservation has confirmed that the surviving fabric is largely of the late thirteenth century. It has also revealed fragments of original wall painting that show how vibrantly coloured the interior once was.

Birtsmorton Court

— WORCESTERSHIRE —

ENOUGH survives of Birtsmorton's late medieval fabric to justify its inclusion among the earlier pages of this book. However, the ancient-looking range seen on the left dates entirely from 1929, and the dreamy appearance of the house today owes much to the cult of the manor house revival. Birtsmorton is one of the many old English houses that were rediscovered in the early twentieth century and atmospherically resuscitated and "restored" by nostalgic-minded owners.

The house is situated between the hills of Malvern Chase and the River Severn on the site of an earlier building documented in 1241. Noted for its wonderful moated setting, Birtsmorton possesses the rarity of having not just one intact moat, but an outer moat too, the channels of which are fed by stream waters from the Malverns, which collect in a large pool said to have been dug in 1269. Encircled by the moat's reflecting waters, the whole composition, with its tall, moulded brick chimney stacks and gabled, tile-roofed ranges of pale stone, weathered timbers, and soft red brick, is irresistibly romantic and ancient-looking.

From the fifteenth until the eighteenth century, Birtsmorton was the seat of the Nanfans, a distinguished Cornish family with properties in several English counties and Wales. John Nanfan, who bought Birtsmorton in 1424–25, was a loyal supporter of Henry V; he fought in the French wars and held various official titles, including governor of the Channel Islands. It was he who pulled down most of the medieval house and built a semi-fortified grange around a courtyard entered from the north. Opposite the surviving battlemented gatehouse, the great hall still forms the south wing. It is entered, as one would expect, by a door at one end leading into a screens passage, which was probably installed around 1500. The cross wing, entered from the hall's west end, is also thought to date from this time. The ground floor parlour in this wing (now known as the Council Chamber) has an elaborately carved heraldic overmantel dating from between 1572 and 1580, around the time that Giles Nanfan carried out a major reorganisation of Birtsmorton. This included the creation of what is known as the Banqueting Hall, a range running out at right angles to the entrance gateway, possibly a remodelling of the original service wing. This double-height room, with half-timbered walls and a plastered ceiling decorated with Tudor roses and

[OPPOSITE] *Francis Bradley-Birt's "medieval" range of ca. 1929, seen from the south. The tower of ca. 1400 belongs to the church of St. Peter and St, Paul, which stands close by.*

fleurs-de-lys, continues to be used for banquets today. Also datable to the 1570s are fragments of an important scheme of wall paintings found in an upstairs chamber in 1964.

Between the sixteenth and twentieth centuries few changes were made, and most of those were of a minor or cosmetic nature. A dining room was added at the east end of the great hall, probably in the seventeenth century. The cross wing was encased in brick in the late eighteenth century, and an elegant Georgian staircase added at its north end; in the nineteenth century, the drawbridge was substituted for a permanent stone bridge. But by 1900 Birtsmorton had been reduced to the status of a tenant farmhouse. It owed its run-down but little-altered state largely to the fact that it had become a secondary seat, and that, following the death in 1766 of Richard Coote, Earl of Bellamont (see p. 427), who had inherited Birtsmorton through his mother, it had always been let out.

The original east wing was destroyed by fire in the eighteenth century, so that when *Country Life* featured Birtsmorton in 1902, the east side of the house consisted of just the gable end of the Banqueting Hall and a series

of low outbuildings. Today, the same view across the moat is dramatically different, with the quadrangle once again fully enclosed by a large, gabled range seamlessly integrated with walls panelled in weathered brick and timber, moulded chimneys, and cross wings. This addition changed the balance of the house both inside and out, but its air of antiquity is convincing. It was part of an ambitious remodelling carried out, with the help of the architects A. Hill Parker & Son, by the antiquarian-minded Francis Bradley-Birt after he retired from the Indian Civil Service in 1929. His grandfather had acquired Birtsmorton in 1911, and his father, John, had done some work to the house in the 1920s.

Bradley-Birt died without heirs in 1963, leaving instructions in his will that Birtsmorton be given to the nation, preserved "substantially as it is at my death so that it may be seen by future generations as it was lived in during the first half of the twentieth century." But the income of the estate was insufficient to uphold this unusual clause, and in 1964 the house, its contents, and 295 acres were auctioned off by the trustees. The present owner's parents, George and Kay Dawes, a Birmingham businessman and his wife, bought the property for £63,500.

Bradley-Birt's enthusiasms had been largely directed on the new wing, so that when George Dawes died a year after buying Birtsmorton, his widow found herself in charge of a badly deteriorating house. Valiantly, she embarked on an extensive programme of repairs, employing as her architects S. T. Walker and Partners of Birmingham. She brought in experts to clean and conserve or renew elements such as panelling and plasterwork. The heraldic decorations in the great hall were removed, cleaned, and replaced, as was the fine panelling in the former parlour, where the remarkable overmantel, blackened with smoke, dirt, and varnish, was also cleaned. This campaign of works included remodelling the interior of the 1920s east range and various other alterations.

Following Kay's death, her son Nigel and his wife, Rosalie, came to live at Birtsmorton in 1975, and it continues to be their family home. Their principal contribution has been the creation of the wonderful flower gardens, for which Rosalie has been responsible, with the help of garden designer Veronica Adams. Notable features include the White Garden, courtyard garden and potager, and a new gate by Mike Roberts.

[OPPOSITE] *The Elizabethan Banqueting Hall (right-hand gable) and, beyond it, the addition of 1929 with its own bridge across the moat, as seen from the church tower.*

Cothay Manor

— SOMERSET —

HIDDEN away, down steep-banked lanes in the depths of rural Somerset, this ravishing ensemble of weathered stone and tiled ranges is the perfect example of a small, late-medieval manor house. It was built on the site of an earlier house for Richard Bluett, whose family had been landowners in the area since the fourteenth century. A document suggests that the present house, which incorporates earlier fragments, was complete by 1488, and that it had a surrounding "ditch," pools, an orchard, and a garden.

The beautiful, tawny-coloured walls were built of rubble finished with a traditional roughcast render, but interestingly, this stone is just a skin—Cothay is, in fact, a timber-framed building. This attempt to disguise the vernacular construction and make it look grander than it actually was did not extend to the door and window surrounds, which are generally quite crude. Very little dressed stone was used; indeed some of the detail is of wood, cut to resemble stone.

The arrangement of buildings around a courtyard conforms to the standard medieval formula, whereby houses were entered in a sequence of stages. First there is the gatehouse, with an arched entranceway through the base of its tower (the gatehouse was restored and the tower rebuilt from ruin in the 1920s). This was flanked by two lower ranges, only one of which survives. Crossing the courtyard, one enters the house through a two-storey porch, the arch of which is thought to have been reused from an earlier building. The porch shelters the original front door, which has fine wrought-iron fittings of about 1500. As one would expect, it leads into the screens passage—a lobby at the "low" end of the great hall with a draught-excluding partition, here of a fairly rustic type.

The hall is the climax of this progression into the interior, with a shallow step at its "high" end marking the line of the dais on which the owner's table would have stood. Though relatively intimate in scale, the room has a magnificent arch-braced roof with an unusual and complex design that seems to have been devised more as a reflection of the owner's status than for any structural advantage; angel-carved corbels support its timbers. The room's other great feature, of particular rarity for its secular theme, is what survives of a cycle of medieval wall paintings of episodes from Reynard the Fox.

[OPPOSITE] *The great chamber in the north range. The fine open-timber roof, with its tiers of wind braces, is typical of late-medieval Somerset craftsmanship. The walls are decorated with carrots, sweet peas, cornflowers, tulips, pears, and quinces painted by Arabella Arkwright, daughter of the present owners.*

[ABOVE] The eighteenth-century staircase, salvaged from a nearby demolished house and introduced to Cothay in 1932 to replace the original spiral stair, the treads of which survive.

[RIGHT] The dining room, added to the west of the screens passage by William Every in 1609. The plaster ceiling was modelled by local craftsmen. Above the oak panelling is a frieze with linenfold carving. The timber overmantel is carved with strapwork and arabesques, figures of Plato's Cardinal Virtues, and coats of arms. The Robbs have furnished the room mostly with eighteenth-century pieces.

[ABOVE] The Gold Room, so called because of the particles of gold paint found on the walls, with its remarkable fresco of the Virgin and Child, heavily "restored" in the 1930s. The table was made in Exeter in 1600.

[OPPOSITE] The view from the east showing the gatehouse and its tower, which was originally crenellated and used for servants' accommodation. On the right is the old cider house, which was joined to the main house with a new wing (just visible behind) in the 1930s.

[LEFT] *The Book Room window on the west side of the house, with a profusion of geraniums and a stone garden bench.*

[OPPOSITE LEFT] *The entrance front, reached from the gatehouse across a courtyard garden planted to reflect the apricot hue of old render still clinging to areas of the masonry. Behind the buttressed wall to the right of the two-storey porch is the great hall.*

[OPPOSITE RIGHT] *A view of the Bishop's Room, a garden off the yew walk planted in memory of Mary-Anne Robb's uncle, Bishop Henderson of Bath and Wells, with purple and scarlet flowers representing the Episcopal colours.*

The hall is flanked by cross ranges, creating an H-plan building under a continuous roof. In the two-storey north wing, a parlour with Jacobean oak panelling painted to resemble walnut veneer opens off the hall. A mural staircase leads from here to the former great chamber above, now amalgamated with an adjacent room to create a drawing room running the full length of the cross-wing under a robust open timber roof. The west gable is pierced by a beautiful little traceried roundel, again possibly salvaged from an older building.

At the opposite end of the hall runs the three-storey south range, the ground floor of which housed the medieval buttery, pantry, and kitchen. This

rescue from a state of neglect in the early years of the twentieth century added a significant Arts & Crafts layer. Having passed into absentee ownership and been relegated to the status of a tenant farmhouse, it was bought in 1925 by Lt. Col. Reginald Cooper, whose restoration of Cold Ashton in Gloucestershire Christopher Hussey had praised in *Country Life* earlier that year: "everything has that natural and untouched appearance that only the most sympathetic restoration can give." With the help of the architect/archaeologist Harold Brakespear, Cooper resurrected Cothay in a similar vein, and it was he who uncovered the fifteenth-century wall paintings. Input by subsequent owners included a new north wing and the insertion of a

wing contains another rarity: fragments of a series of Tudor domestic wall paintings in what was probably a pair of family withdrawing apartments on the first floor. The so-called Gold Room (now an anteroom) was painted with stripes to imitate wall hangings. Here, preserved on one wall, is a magnificent frescoed roundel of the Virgin and Child. The other room, known as the Guest Chamber, has a scroll-patterned frieze, originally with English inscriptions, and three paintings, one depicting the Annunciation. Beside this painting is a squint into a tiny room over the porch that is still used as an oratory. It opens onto the gallery above the screens passage, which was one of William Every's significant additions to the house. He bought Cothay in 1605 and a few years later added a west wing containing a panelled dining room with an ornately carved timber overmantel.

Cothay belongs to a group of medieval and Tudor houses whose gentle

salvaged Georgian staircase in the hall that connects this wing with the old house, both dating from the 1930s for Sir Francis Cook.

The present owners, Alastair and Mary-Anne Robb, who bought Cothay in 1993, have carried out further works in the same sensitive spirit as Cooper. Mrs. Robb collects early medieval artefacts, and the house is full of the objects of her collecting and creation, including curtains made from cloth woven specially by Christopher Elvy to medieval designs. But the Robbs' principal triumph is the gardens they have created at Cothay, enlarging and replanting within the framework laid out by Cooper in the 1920s. Among their additions to this celebrated romantic setting are the many garden "rooms" opening off the long yew walk; the Courtyard Garden, planted to reflect the apricot hue of old render still clinging to walls; and the delightful Walk of the Unicorn.

East Barsham Manor

— NORFOLK —

URING a late tour of Norfolk, I saw the remains of an old Manor-House, which I believe in richness of moulded brickwork, exceeds anything of the kind in England." It is difficult to believe that East Barsham Manor had been ruinous for nearly a century when John Adey Repton surveyed it in 1807. Today it appears the perfect early Tudor manor house, its complex of red brick ranges intact and well maintained.

The house is an arresting vision in the North Norfolk landscape. Towered and turreted, its exuberant skyline bursts with crenellations, finialled pepperpots, and highly decorated chimney shafts. Then there is the profusion of dazzling brick and terra-cotta ornament that enlivens the principal elements of the building. These structures—the Tudor gatehouse, porch, main tower, and chimneystack—withstood collapse and survive today, along with most of the principal façade, largely intact. Much of the rest of the building belongs to the restoration carried out for two different owners in the 1920s and 1930s by the architect John Page. Although somewhat conjectural, this rebuilding was sufficiently careful to protect the beautifully seasoned brickwork and terra-cotta decoration, and to incorporate the new fabric convincingly with the old.

The house, which was known as Wolterton Manor until the early 1900s, was built in the early sixteenth century for an ascendant local family with good connections at court. Sir Henry Fermor had come into the estate through his wife, for it had been the property of her first husband, John Wode (d. 1496), whose children he eventually bought out. Assessed to be the richest man in Norfolk in 1523, Fermor became High Sheriff of the county a decade later and received a knighthood. Self-confident and pushy, he vaunted his status and political allegiances through bold use of architectural detail and ostentatious heraldry on his fashionable new house at East Barsham. Emblazoned on the gatehouse and main porch, and repeated along the stringcourse friezes, are coats of arms in carved brick and moulded terra-cotta, including two sets of royal arms. One, over the gatehouse arch, bears griffin and lion supporters; the other must be slightly earlier, for it features a greyhound, which in 1527 was replaced by a lion. All this florid ornament belongs to a relatively short-lived fashion, particularly evident in East Anglia, where it occurs on several other local gentry houses such as Great Snoring.

[OPPOSITE] *The gatehouse from the south, its crenellations, polygonal buttresses rising into pepper-pot turrets, and dazzling red brick and terra-cotta decoration designed to leave visitors in no doubt about the owner's status. The dominant feature is the royal arms of Henry VIII, flanked by arms of the family of Sir Henry Fermor, who built the house.*

The gatehouse leads into a courtyard, from where the house is entered through a porch chequered with stone and flint. The extended length of this principal façade, and its proximity to the gatehouse, is characteristic of a number of Norfolk houses of the period.

Although we cannot be certain of the original plan, the location of the principal rooms is clear. The great hall occupied the western half of the main range, with the family apartments beyond the massive chimneystack to its west. These comprised the parlour, with a chamber above connected by a private stair. The hall was always single storey, as its relatively small windows suggest—a relatively unusual feature more often associated with houses of a lower social standing. It became a semi-ruinous shell, but the huge fireplace and ten-shafted chimneystack, each shaft individually patterned in terracotta, survived, and the room was rebuilt as a hall.

The great chamber (the principal entertaining room) occupied the floor above. Now two bedrooms, it was rebuilt in the 1930s with a flat roof instead of the original pitched one. To the right of the porch stands a three-storey tower with elaborate brick groin vaults to the ground and first-floor rooms. This almost certainly housed the owner's private withdrawing and lodging

[OPPOSITE] *The drawing room, originally the parlour, at the west end of the great hall. Part of the original family apartments, it was rebuilt from total ruin in the 1930s in a Tudor style.*

[BELOW] *The north front, restored to its present appearance in the 1930s. The left-hand part was occupied as a farmhouse after the main part of the house became ruinous.*

55

chambers, an arrangement dating back to the early fifteenth century. In his *History of Norfolk* (1769), the Rev. Francis Blomefield gives an idea of the richness of East Barsham's Tudor interiors, observing that the great chamber had "several antique heads of men and women in antique dresses, on the wainscot; under the heads of one man and woman, the arms of Farmor." These carvings had disappeared by the end of the century.

The male line of the Fermors died out in 1628, and East Barsham subsequently passed by female descent through various Norfolk families, including the L'Estranges and Astleys, becoming a secondary property to their larger estates. Inevitably the old house suffered neglect and by the early eighteenth century had sunk into ruin, although the northeast part was adapted as a tenant farmhouse. It became a source of romantic inspiration for artists and antiquaries such as Cotman and J. C. Buckler, and for architects such as A. C. Pugin, whose conjectural restoration was published in 1830 as part of *Specimens of Gothic Architecture*. Illustrations appeared in other surveys and books about old English houses, and its architectural detail influenced the work of a number of nineteenth-century architects, notably William Wilkins.

In 1922 Douglas Coleman, who bought East Barsham in 1914, carried out a partial restoration, making the east end habitable. This was followed in 1936–38 by the reinstatement of the hall, the repair of the gatehouse, and other works for Count Jeremie Habsburg-Lothringen, a colourful figure born Jeremy Willoughby, who claimed illegitimate descent from an Austrian archduke. He salvaged many old materials and historic fittings for East Barsham and was clearly sympathetic to its historic fabric, but in 1938 he disappeared, leaving a trail of debts, and the house was sold. After passing through several more owners, it has been the home since 1997 of Sir John and Lady Guinness.

[BELOW] *A detail of the Gothic ribbed groin vault to the ground-floor room of the tower, a jeu d'esprit rather than a structural necessity.*

[OPPOSITE] *A view from the south of part of the main front, with the three-storey lodging tower on the right. This asymmetrical façade is punctuated by eight polygonal buttresses that rise up into finialled turrets, and was enriched by friezes of moulded brick and terra-cotta panels decorated with arms, tracery, and heads. In the foreground is the gatehouse, now freestanding but originally linked to enclosing courtyard walls.*

Sutton Place

— SURREY —

SECRETIVE and sequestered, Sutton Place is one of the most important private houses to have been created in the years following the building of Hampton Court, although little of its original interior survives. Built by an intimate of the Tudor court, and more recently owned by a succession of American plutocrats, it has long presented something of an enigma to outsiders. Though situated close to London, between the urban sprawl of Guildford and Woking, the parkland setting and its owners' almost obsessive desire for privacy have isolated Sutton Place. Architecturally, too, it is a house that has long teased historians with its mysteries.

Often celebrated as a pioneer of the English Renaissance—"the single extant production of a peculiar and suggestive type of Renascence Gothic," wrote Frederic Harrison in *Annals of an Old Manor House* in 1893—the house was built, probably between 1525 and 1532, for Sir Richard Weston, who acquired the estate in 1521. A protégé of Henry VIII, Weston somehow managed to remain on intimate terms with the king even after his only son was executed in 1536 for an alleged liaison with Anne Boleyn. Weston's new house formed a quadrangle enclosing a courtyard, the north range of which we know from surviving illustrations had a turreted gate tower similar to that at Knole in Kent. This entrance range was demolished in 1782, leaving a U-plan complex with the main entrance in the principal block containing the hall, and the owner's lodgings in the east wing.

The exterior is distinguished by the lavish use of terra-cotta decoration, a short-lived fashion for which occurred in the 1520s (see also East Barsham, page 53). At Sutton, it takes the form of small, ornamental panels bearing Renaissance motifs, and is also used for architectural detail, such as quoins, window frames, and mullions. The contrast of creamy terra-cotta against the dusky red of the diapered brickwork is one of the most striking features of the house.

But all is not quite what it seems, as the architectural historian Nicholas Cooper confirmed when he carried out a survey in the 1980s. The courtyard façades, with their mirrorlike symmetry and identical-sized large and perfectly spaced windows, had seemed so puzzling for such an early date. Now we can be almost certain that they are the result of an eighteenth-century remodelling that reused much of the early-sixteenth-century brick and terra-

[OPPOSITE] *The chimneypiece in the great hall was carved in Bristol in the mid-seventeenth century and bought for the house by Frederick Koch in the 1980s.*

[OVERLEAF] *Sutton Place from the north, showing the ranges that were made symmetrical and remodelled with a Tudor-style centrepiece in the eighteenth century. A striking feature of the exterior is the lavish use of creamy terra-cotta decoration. Groups of panels embellished with amorini and rows of quatrefoil, lozenge, and cusped arch patterns create an effect that has been likened to embroidery.*

cotta, and introduced the turreted, Tudor-style centrepiece. Whether this antiquarian-minded scheme was carried out by John Weston in the 1720s, or for John Webbe Weston when he demolished the gate tower range in the 1780s, is uncertain.

Extensive alterations and the absence of historical documentation have made it impossible to piece together the entire original plan. However, there is evidence to confirm that, unusually for a house of this status, the great hall was originally single-storeyed, probably with the great chamber above, and that it was entered via a screens passage at one end, as was the standard arrangement until the seventeenth century. The hall seems to have been rebuilt to its present double height, with the entrance at its centre, following the devastating fire of 1561 that gutted much of the house.

The direct male line died out with John Weston in 1730. In 1857 Francis Salvin inherited Sutton, and he introduced heraldic stained glass by C. A. Buckler and also filled the hall with comfortable Victorian furnishings, as illustrated in a series of surviving watercolours. The house was let out from 1878, rented or owned by various aristocrats from 1900, and then in 1959 bought by the reclusive J. P. Getty. He and his successor, Stanley J. Seeger, made numerous alterations that left the house bereft of interesting and authentic-looking rooms, although it did acquire magnificent new gardens by Geoffrey Jellicoe.

Then, after purchasing Sutton Place in 1986, the American collector Frederick Koch commissioned a major programme of conservation and internal remodelling. Julian Harrap supervised sensitive repairs to the fabric, and Rodney Melville removed much of the muddle of the previous decades, creating a series of finely crafted new interiors that would enable the house to function in its intended role as a scholarly foundation and a home for Mr. Koch's collection of late-nineteenth-century British and European paintings and sculpture. These photographs were taken in 1996, when *Country Life* celebrated the fact that "for the first time this century [Sutton] has interiors worthy of its architectural importance." But the hopes that it would become "a house of mystery no longer . . . regularly opened to visitors . . . who are made welcome as never before" have since faded, and today the doors remain firmly closed to the public.

[TOP] *Crudely modelled but wonderfully robust terra-cotta amorini over the front door—sixteenth century Renaissance detail reused in the eighteenth century remodelling.*

[LEFT] *A detail of the south front, where much of the irregularity typical of English medieval houses can still be felt.*

[OPPOSITE] *The great hall facing west, with the great chamber beyond the opening on the first floor. The plaster ceiling was made by Clark & Fenn in the 1980s to designs by Rodney Melville; the floor, to a chequerboard design of Purbeck and Salterwath marbles, is the most elaborate in the house.*

Parnham

— DORSET —

IT is difficult to believe that Parnham House has been remodelled four times over the past two centuries. Situated in a deerpark encircled by the Beaminster downs, this mellow complex of golden-brown Ham stone mottled with age has a timeless quality that belies its recent history.

From the mid-fifteenth century to 1764, Parnham was the seat of the Strode family. In 1522 Robert Strode married the granddaughter of Henry VII's Chief Baron of the Exchequer, and it long been held that, sometime between then and his death in 1558, he remodelled the old house to its present form, best preserved today on the entrance front. But such a tall, compact, and regularized composition would be highly unusual for this early date, and on stylistic grounds Parnham is much more likely to date from the later 1500s. We know that before his death in 1581 Robert Strode's son, John, added a gatehouse, schoolhouse, and other structures that no longer survive; could he have carried out the remodelling? (A windowpane in the hall engraved with his name and the date 1559 could have been moved from an earlier building).

Following various alterations in the seventeenth century, Parnham was modernised by George Strode in about 1730. He installed sash windows and fielded panelling, as well as a staircase with turned balusters in a bay projecting beside the porch. He also swept away the Elizabethan forecourt and gatehouse and landscaped the park. But then in 1764 the male line was broken; the heiress married and moved to the Isle of Wight, and the house was abandoned. For fifty years it stood empty, until in the early nineteenth century her son, Sir William Oglander and his wife, Lady Maria Anna Fitzroy, returned to make Parnham their home.

The couple engaged John Nash, who, between 1807 and 1811, romanticised the exterior with picturesque Gothic Revival detail. He replaced much of the early Georgian work and introduced the battlemented parapets, moulded gable copings, and buttresses rising into hatted pinnacles that give the house its distinctive profile today. The south and west fronts are to Nash's design, and he also added a service wing.

The interiors acquired plasterwork and chimneypieces in the Regency Gothic style and a fashionable suite of entertaining rooms: an interconnecting library and drawing room in the south wing and a large, new dining

[OPPOSITE] *The view from the west. The formal terrace and gardens were laid out by Hans Sauer and Harry Lindsay around 1910 on the model of those at Montacute.*

[OPPOSITE] *The dining room, with a table from Seeburg, the Treichl family home in South Tyrol, and chairs designed by Robert Kime, who decorated the house for the present owners. The Jacobean-style stone mullion-and-transom windows were introduced in the early 1900s by Vincent Robinson, who brought them here from Wroxton Abbey, Oxfordshire, to replace Nash's timber mullions.*

[ABOVE] *The drawing room, where the Treichls have repainted the Georgian-style plaster ceiling, mouldings and architraves, and reintroduced a period chimneypiece.*

[BELOW] *The master bedroom, with a Jacobean-style plaster ceiling restored by the Treichls, and original stone mullioned windows.*

[OVERLEAF] *The east-facing entrance front, its prominent three-storey porch leading into the screens passage at the north end of the two-storey hall. The south cross wing contained the family parlours. The north wing, incorporating earlier fabric, accommodated the kitchen offices; it was altered to its present three storeys with regularly spaced mullioned windows in the seventeenth century and internally remodelled by William Bertram in 2002. The pinnacles on the gables belong to Nash's Regency Gothic remodelling of 1807–11.*

room behind the hall, doubling the depth of the central range. Evidence for Nash's decoration of these rooms is provided by a set of photographs dated 1875, but none of it survives.

Parnham was sold for the first time in 1896 to Vincent Robinson, an eccentric antiquarian collector who reversed much of Nash's work and turned the house into a "museum of the decorative arts of 16th- and 17th-century Europe," cramming the rooms with his hoard of armour, metalwork, carved wood, and other decorative arts. Fourteen years later he sold it to Hans Sauer, a colleague of Cecil Rhodes, who embarked on one of the most sensitive manor house restorations of the period.

The collaboration between this antiquarian-minded owner with South African diamond money and the amateur gentleman architect Col. Harry Lindsay, owner of Sutton Courtney Manor and husband of garden designer Norah Lindsay, transformed Parnham. Sensitive to the tonal and textural qualities of its early fabric, they revived the house's Elizabethan character with fittings salvaged from contemporary buildings. In the hall, they revealed the original ceiling beams and reintroduced a screen and minstrels' gallery using salvage from a Surrey church; the chimneypiece they assembled from parts of a fifteenth-century screen. Other rooms were fitted with appropriate panelling, chimneypieces, and plasterwork, some of it genuine, some of it reproduction.

Following various institutional uses during and after the war, Parnham again stood empty and at risk. But in 1976 John Makepeace bought and repaired it and established his famous School for Craftsmen in Wood here. His departure in 2001 heralded the brief threat of a flat development, but mercifully this was shelved when Michael and Emma Treichl bought Parnham later that year.

The Treichls engaged two experts: Robert Kime to redecorate the main rooms in harmony with the spirit of Lindsay's restoration, and the Bath architect William Bertram to replan the service wing for modern family living. Bertram's grand oak staircase, rising beneath a ceiling modelled by the leading stuccoist Clare Venables, has become the new heart of the house, linking the different areas and levels on the site of a former internal courtyard.

Mr Treichl's Austrian heritage is reflected in the armour, paintings, and game trophies that have found a new home at Parnham, alongside portraits of his Scottish maternal forebears. He has added to these ancestral collections a number of significant acquisitions of his own, notably Thomas Lawrence's full-length portrait of Maria Anna Oglander, bought from the Kimbell Art Museum in Fort Worth and now back in the room where it originally hung. And beyond the gardens, which the Treichls have replanted, deer can be seen grazing in the park once again.

[OPPOSITE] *The view from the re-created screens passage to the new stair hall. The oak staircase, with finials modelled on Nash's exterior ones, was created for the present owners by William Bertram. Rugs and textiles found by the decorator Robert Kime complement the owners' collection of pictures and furniture.*

[LEFT] *The great hall, looking west from the screen. The fittings and decoration are largely twentieth century, although the fine armorial glass is one of the few original fittings to survive at Parnham. Vincent Robinson brought back to this room the door and a carved oak beam (now over the fireplace) from a house near Taunton, where they were taken when Nash removed them in the early 1800s.*

I T is often said that the English country house in its established form emerged under the Tudors in the sixteenth century, but in fact its origins and many of its characteristics can be traced back to the early Middle Ages. Thanks to the strong government of the Norman and Plantagenet kings and the happily secluded island geography, England enjoyed comparatively stable social conditions from the twelfth century onwards, except in the far north, Scottish Borders, or Welsh Marches, which remained troublesome into the sixteenth century. Conditions in the Midlands and south, however, early encouraged the construction of non-fortified houses, usually called "manor houses"—the houses of the squirearchy—as well as the great castles of the barons, within a hundred years of the Norman Conquest and settlement. The perfect manor house at Boothby Pagnell in Lincolnshire was built as early as 1200, and its plan and general form are characteristic of the houses built across England over the following three centuries. Its only defence is a moat, more a system of drainage and a deterrent to burglars than a military outwork. Inside, it has a large great hall, with the kitchen at the lower end, and the solar—or family chamber—at the high table end. This was the standard nucleus of the English country house plan.

℃ The great hall was the most important room in all country houses well into the sixteenth and seventeenth centuries, and is one of the features of English house planning that differs from the *châteaux* of France and the great houses of the Continent. There, the owner, whether lord or squire, dined ceremonially surrounded by his family, household, and dependents, and it was there that his estates were administered, rents collected, manorial courts held, justice dispensed, and entertainment provided on the great feasts and occasions of the rural year.

℃ The distinguishing feature of the English country house is that it was the capital of a landed estate, the centre of a social and economic entity with farmland, tenants, woods, pleasure grounds, sporting, and subsidiary buildings. Ownership of a landed estate gave its proprietors power and influence, economic security, independence, and an established position in society, as well as retirement, recreation, and sport. For many centuries, from the Middle Ages onwards, the ownership of land was the only sure base of power and influence in England, and the only solid long-term investment. Therefore, anybody who made money by whatever means—from the law, from trade and commerce, or from royal service and warfare— automatically invested the proceeds in a country estate and country house and set themselves up as a landed dynasty, and this continued long after the development of a pluralist, capitalist economy.

℃ As Mark Girouard explained in his pioneering *Life in the English Country House* (1978), the country house was the headquarters from which land and tenants were administered, and local power organized.

"It was a showcase in which to exhibit and entertain supporters and connections." Hence the key position of the great hall in medieval and Tudor country house plans. It was the place where the whole hierarchical community gathered under one roof and ate together, the squire or lord and his guests on the high table, and the household below, as is still the case with dons and students in the colleges at Oxford or Cambridge—the principal still-working survivals of communal medieval households in the modern world.

℄ Gradually, as society became more complex, richer, and mobile, and the single household gave way to a disparate, more class-bound form of society, so the nobility and gentry came to value their privacy, and retreated from the great hall to separate rooms of their own, where they lived more isolated from those beneath them. Thus, by the end of the Middle Ages, most houses had a two-storey wing beside the hall, with a parlour for informal family use and a grander chamber above (often termed a solar), which in earlier times had served as the lord's grand bed-sitting room, but now became the great chamber for eating in. These gradual developments in planning can be traced visually in conglomerate houses like Haddon (see page 13), Penshurst, or Knole (see page 19), where additional rooms, ranges, and courtyards have been grafted onto the original nucleus of hall, kitchen, and solar, in response to the need for privacy and a more sophisticated way of life.

℄ Even as early as the mid-fourteenth century, the lord and his family had begun to eat and entertain in private rooms of their own, except on special occasions and traditional feasts. This gradual withdrawal of the family from the hall altered the plan of the country house, and in the process the hall became just a large entrance space. The high table, where the family and their guests ate, moved to the great chamber, usually situated on the first floor at the dais end of the hall. This in turn led to the development of other features in the planning of houses, such as ornamental staircases leading to the chamber, and separate private lodgings for personal accommodation. These in due course were to become major architectural features of later houses.

℄ By the sixteenth century, a great person could expect to have a private apartment composed of a bedroom, a closet, and a dressing/sitting room, often approached by galleries, as at Knole in Kent. The grandest version of this became the state apartment, which began to emerge in sixteenth-century royal palaces, and then in the Prodigy Houses such as Burghley, Holdenby, and Audley End, built by prominent courtiers for the reception of the monarch. The state apartment became the most conspicuous feature of the internal planning of the great houses of seventeenth- and early-eighteenth-century England, from Wilton (see page 477) to Blenheim (see page 479)—though after Charles I few English monarchs paid ceremonial visits around the country to be entertained by their great subjects. Nevertheless, a state bedroom, with an elaborate upholstered bed for the reception of the monarch, situated at the end of a richly decorated enfilade of rooms, was the major showpiece of Baroque house plans.

℃ From the Middle Ages until well into the eighteenth century, life in the country house was formal and ceremonial, meals being served in a ritualistic way, conversation and other activities undertaken according to the strict rules of etiquette, especially the reception and entertainment of guests. The formal house reached its apogee in the great houses of the Whig aristocracy, such as Chatsworth (see page 474), Boughton (see page 27), Castle Howard (see page 477), and Blenheim, when the layout and decoration of the rooms were the expression of etiquette and ritual rather than practical need. But gradually, as the eighteenth century progressed, privacy, comfort, and informality came to be preferred, and the country house entered the modern world.

℃ This was partly the result of a radical change in the social makeup of households. In medieval and Tudor times, great households had been composed of all ranks, with gentlemen and yeomen retainers as well as serving men, all mixing hugger-mugger with the family. The increasing stratification and diversity of society led to gentry ceasing to work or live in other people's houses, so that the staff became entirely a service class of "lower orders," segregated by the "green baize door" from the family itself. This led in turn to the development of separate and increasingly elaborate servants' quarters, often in the basement and attics or screened rear wings, with back stairs, specialist cleaning and work rooms, segregated bedrooms or dormitories for male and female staff—a whole separate invisible world alongside or underneath the main rooms. The provision of separate servants'

accommodation reached its greater complexity in the Victorian and Edwardian country house, and then with astonishing speed disappeared as the twentieth century progressed; in most houses the kitchen itself had become a family living room by the beginning of the twenty-first century.

℃ On the other hand, the principal rooms of a country house and their functions have changed very little in the last two hundred years, and most continue to function as they were planned to do in the opening years of the nineteenth century. For the country house as we know it—the centre of a self-contained estate, valued more for its amenity, aspects, and as the setting for house parties and private family life than for economics or power and patronage—is essentially a product of the Regency era. Many of its distinctive characteristics were established in the thirty or forty years between the 1790s and 1830s. Thanks to the flowering of the Picturesque as the defining English aesthetic, the countryside and country houses came to be admired and enjoyed for their own sake, as they are today. The role of the country house as a political power base began to change with the Industrial Revolution, as acknowledged by the Great Reform Bill in 1832, which tipped the balance of political representation from the country to the town, and all subsequent social and political movements have further acknowledged urban economic realities, though the country house has continued to play a ceremonial, social, cultural, and figurehead role in its area.

℃ The Regency period saw the country estate, of which the house is the focus and centrepiece, reach its present attractive form. Prior to the eighteenth century, great estates had been sprawling agglomerations of mixed lands, feudal dues, and customary rights and tenures, being as much legal concepts as physical entities. By the early nineteenth century, most English estates had been transformed into compact, ring-fenced units with self-contained tenant farms, villages of model cottages, and centralized management by professional land agents. Outlying properties had been sold, customary tenancies and manorial rights bought out or enfranchised, the farms reorganized, and woods planted to create the recognisable modern rural landscape.

❡ Houses were built or remodelled in the Regency period to accommodate a more developed social life quite different from the old ceremonial formality. Rooms were provided for specific functions and activities: breakfast rooms, billiard rooms, sculpture galleries, ballrooms, and guest bedrooms. The use of country houses became more like that of London houses, geared up for entertaining smart new guests (not dependents) in a metropolitan way, with rooms for cards, music, and dancing. Houses were adapted for entertaining as well as private family life. Field sports, especially hunting and shooting, became the social bedrock in the country. As transport links improved, first with tarmacadamed toll roads, then railways in the 1830s and '40s, and finally motor cars in the opening years of the twentieth century, making homes more accessible, speedy mobility boosted the popularity of the house party, especially the "weekend," that most civilized of English inventions.

❡ This new type of entertaining explains the scale and purpose of the Regency and Victorian, and to some extent the twentieth-century country house. There were cosy private family sitting rooms, as well as a big living room for gathering during the day. This was often the library, which became the largest and most comfortable room in the house. The dining room was the other distinctly English feature of house plans. It emerged in the eighteenth century as a particular response to English social conditions as a room where the men liked to congregate and discuss politics, news, and other matters. As Robert Adam pointed out, in English homes "eating rooms are considered as the apartment of conversation," and thus were treated as principal reception rooms, unlike in France. The ample provision of comfortable, informal, guest bedrooms, often prettily decorated with chintz, was also an innovation of the Regency years and has continued to be a distinctive feature of the country house.

❡ Thus the English country house, which first emerged as a recognizable architectural type about eight hundred years ago, has gradually adapted, socially and architecturally, over the intervening years. Starting out as the feudal capital of a manorial landowning, with an hierarchical household centred on the great hall, it has passed through many transformations, veering alternately between family privacy and ceremonial formality in its planning, until it was finally polished into its current civilized and comfortable form in the Regency period. Throughout history, however, it has remained the architectural centre and focus of a landed estate.

Pages 72 and 77: Charlecote Strapwork, ca. 1820, Hamilton Weston Wallpapers

Trerice

— CORNWALL —

THIS beautiful, silvery ochre Elizabethan manor house represents an intriguing chapter in the story of the Arundell family, who were dominant in Cornwall from the thirteenth to eighteenth centuries. Hunkered down on the side of the Gannel Valley near Newquay, it possesses certain features, such as the delightful run of curvacious Dutch gables, that are surprisingly advanced for their date, and unexpected in a house so relatively remote.

They suggest that Sir John Arundell, who remodelled Trerice in 1572–73, was more sophisticated and well connected than might be expected of a fairly minor landowner in sixteenth-century North Cornwall (the estate probably never extended to more than about eight hundred acres). His father, Esquire of the Body of Henry VIII and a favourite of the king, became Vice-Admiral of the Western Seas under Edward VI. His son, also Sir John, was a staunch Royalist who defended Pendennis Castle for Charles I. This branch of the Arundell family had acquired Trerice by marriage in the fourteenth century and remained its owners until the death of the 4th and last Baron Arundell of Trerice in 1768.

Sir John Arundell's house, which incorporated an earlier hall house with a tower, adopted an Elizabethan E plan. Although no architect is recorded, it has been suggested that his remodelling may have had links with Matthew Arundell's progressive alterations at Wardour Castle, which were carried out in the same decade with the involvement of Robert Smythson.

The most delightful feature of Trerice is the east-facing entrance front, with its flourish of gables: scrolled and sprouting from masked corbels over the projecting wings and central porch; trefoil-shaped in between. The interplay of curves on different planes and the balanced relationship of glass to locally quarried Pentewan limestone are highly accomplished. As John Cornforth noted in an article in *Country Life* (October 29, 1992), Trerice's Dutch-style gables are the earliest of their kind surviving in England, built less than a decade after the form was first engraved in Jan Vrideman de Fries's *Architecture* of 1563.

As one would expect, the front door leads into a screens passage, from which the double-height great hall opens to the left, its great mullioned and transomed window almost filling the space between the porch and south

[OPPOSITE] *The great hall, which is lit by 576 glittering panes of glass, many of them original. The elaborate geometrical ceiling of interlocking oak leaves and scrolled designs (extensively restored in ca. 1840) is a fine example of West Country plasterwork.*

[OVERLEAF] *The entrance front of the Elizabethan house, dating from the early 1570s. The Dutch gables are the earliest surviving examples of their type in England. The wing to the right of the porch was ruinous when the National Trust took the house on in 1953; it was restored by a tenant, J. F. Elton.*

wing. The window, divided into twenty-four lights, glitters with 576 panes of glass, much of it original. High up at one end, set into the frieze, is a little arcade opening into a gallery hidden behind, above the screens passage.

The plasterwork at Trerice is a fine example of West Country craftsmanship of the period. The great hall has an overmantel supported by terms, dated 1572, and an elaborate geometrical ceiling of interlocking ribs and pendants ornamented with oak leaves and scrolled designs.

The great chamber on the first floor, the principal reception room, faces south through a bow window to an orchard planted on the site of the formal Tudor garden. This room has more fine plasterwork, presumably by the same craftsmen, its overmantel dated 1573 and bearing the family's arms. The plaster ceiling is a wonderful barrel-vaulted structure, ornamented with pendants and a Tudor rose motif. Below, where the early sixteenth-century hall was, a low-ceilinged drawing room has been re-created, its sash windows and chimneypiece dating from the nineteenth century.

In 1802 Trerice passed to cousins, the Aclands of Killerton, who owned it until 1915. Sir Thomas Dyke Acland's repairs to the house in the 1840s

[LEFT] *The great chamber on the first floor, the main reception room of the Elizabethan house, facing south through its bow window. The elaborately ornamented barrel-vaulted plaster ceiling dates from the 1570s; in the lunette above the frieze are the arms of Henry FitzAlan, 12th and last FitzAlan Earl of Arundell and Knight of the Garter.*

included the extensive restoration of the plasterwork, but he did not live here, and for most of the nineteenth century it was rented out to farming tenants. In the 1860s the north wing, which had become derelict, collapsed during a gale.

The house was very down at heel when the National Trust bought it in 1953 and let it out on a repairing lease. It was a tenant, J. F. Elton, who rebuilt the north range (where now the shop is), and thereby restored the front to its original symmetry. In 1969 the trust carried out further improvements, including restoring the long gallery, with a view to opening the house properly to the public. Among the furnishings, paintings, and other contents assembled, some through generous bequests, were a notable collection of clocks, seventeenth-century embroideries, and a library table made by Peter Mackenzie of Truro—the only documented Georgian piece of Cornish furniture.

Trerice survives as a fascinating monument to Tudor Cornwall and the Arundells. Its setting among fields and agricultural buildings (notably the Great Barn, now a tea room) reflects the estate's reputation as one of the best farms in the county. It reminds us that it was land that lay at the source of the Arundells' power, making them Cornwall's wealthiest dynasty.

Chavenage

— GLOUCESTERSHIRE —

CHAVENAGE is one of the iconic manor houses of the Cotswolds celebrated by *Country Life* in its influential early articles. Writing in 1911, H. Avray Tipping described it as "a fine example of the ample and skilled use of the excellent building materials of the district, of ashlar and rubble for its walls and windows, of stone tiles for its roof-covering and of oak for its interior fitment." These are the enduring qualities of the countless finely worked stone buildings that give this "tumbled region of hill and dale" its highly individual character.

Built around a medieval core, Chavenage is more complicated than it first appears, for much of its late medieval, Tudor, and Jacobean detail was introduced in the nineteenth century, although no documentation exists to confirm exactly when. This antiquarian layer contributes greatly to its atmosphere, which is further enriched by the stirring stories of ghostly apparitions and curious events relating to its vivid Cromwellian history.

The lands of Chavenage belonged to the manor of Horsley, which was owned from the thirteenth century by a small, dependent Augustinian priory. At the dissolution these lands were granted, along with many other Cotswolds manors, to Sir Thomas Seymour, later Lord Seymour of Sudeley, who later fell from favour and was beheaded. Chavenage then passed to Sir Walter Denys of Dyrham, whose son sold it in 1564 to Edward Stephens, son of a wealthy wool merchant. Although Eastington was his main seat, Stephens reconstructed Chavenage probably as a dower house or a home for his heir; by 1654 it was described as "the great farm house." But then in the eighteenth century the family abandoned their grander house and made Chavenage their main home.

The house is first viewed through urn-topped gate piers, from where a short drive shaded by cedars approaches the east-facing entrance front. This forms a standard E plan, with the porch as the central projection and asymmetrical cross wings enclosing the forecourt on each side. Carved into the diamond-shaped label stops of the hoodmould over the front door is the date 1576 and the initials ES and IS (for Edward Stephens and his wife, Joan). But the dominating feature of the porch is the Gothic window lighting its upper storey, which has genuine fourteenth-century Decorated tracery and seventeenth-century glass. This, along with many other reused fragments,

[OPPOSITE] *The Mortlake tapestry in the Cromwell Room, one of a complete series dating from ca. 1640. The room is one of a pair of bedchambers in the southeast wing whose names reflect Chavenage's strong Cromwellian associations (the other being the Ireton Room).*

[OVERLEAF] *The east-facing entrance front, with its odd assortment of windows inserted at different dates. The left-hand wing, probably rebuilt in the midseventeenth century, contains the library, with the tapestry-lined Cromwellian bedrooms above, and the billiard room (obscured by branches). The right-hand wing (behind the tree trunk) contains the service quarters.*

[ABOVE] *The Ireton Room, lined with Flemish tapestries of ca. 1640 on the theme of Don Quixote. The room is named after Oliver Cromwell's son-in-law, General Henry Ireton, who is said to have visited Chavenage in 1648 to persuade the Parliamentarian Colonel Nathaniel Stephens (the owner from 1608 to 1660) to support the Bill of Impeachment against Charles I. The story tells of a reluctant Stephens being persuaded to vote for the king's execution, as a result of which he was cursed with weird happenings and*

probably came from the dissolved priory nearby, or perhaps from the earlier manor house here; it must have been inserted in the nineteenth century, for it does not appear in an engraving of 1807.

The position of the great hall is indicated by the pair of tall windows divided by a buttress seen on the left of the porch. These windows also contain reused stained glass, including some seventeenth-century heraldic pieces. The differing shapes, sizes, and styles of the windows at Chavenage, their often eccentric positioning and assortment of heraldic and other glass from different sources, are among the delights of this enigmatic house.

The hall is entered from the screens passage, which leads from the porch to a stone spiral staircase possibly of late medieval origin. Above the oak screen is a minstrels' gallery with an eighteenth-century chamber organ and

a long and ultimately fatal illness. It is said that at the funeral, a ghostly carriage driven by a headless driver in royal robes suddenly appeared and bore the spectre of the dead man away.

the studwork of a shallow plaster vault that probably originally extended over the entire room (the hall's present flat ceiling is a later addition). The Renaissance-style chimneypiece, inset with a black marble medallion framed by a wreath of bay leaves, and with swags, cartouches, and escutcheons, looks as if it might have been carved in a local workshop around 1600. Nikolaus Pevsner, however, suggests that it is early nineteenth century, and certainly it resembles the one in the billiard room of that date.

An impressive doorway leads south from the hall into the Oak Room, formerly the parlour. Here, again, things are not what they seem, for closer inspection suggests that the door surround is made up of various elements, some probably continental, and that the Oak Room's ensemble of Jacobean wainscoting, carved panels dated 1627, and sixteenth-century chimneypiece

[ABOVE] *The Oak Room has fine Jacobean panelling divided into sections by pairs of fluted and gilded pilasters with Corinthian capitals. The mid-sixteenth-century gothic-survival chimneypiece is probably contemporary, with the panelled overmantel inset with Flemish-style portrait roundels. In the sideboard recess (not seen in this view) are four carved panels depicting the Muses below, a depiction of the Tree of Life, and a reset panel dated 1627.*

and overmantel was in fact pieced together at an unknown date (some of it perhaps from Eastington) and inserted in the nineteenth century.

The main period of antiquarianism at Chavenage dates from around 1800, when Henry Willis Stephens was the occupant. He was a schizophrenic but also a remarkably early subscriber to Neo-Jacobean taste. The billiard room opening off the library in the southeast wing and the battlemented bay windows on the south front were among his additions, as were various pieces of architectural salvage incorporated into the fabric. The chapel, which was built onto an eighteenth-century folly tower and embellished with an array of reused architectural fragments, was first recorded in 1803 and so was probably also Stephens's work. He died in 1821, and it is believed that his heir, Maurice Townshend-Stephens, carried out some further alterations in an antiquarian spirit, although nothing is documented. But Townshend-Stephens preferred to live on his Irish estates, and for most of the century Chavenage was let or heavily mortgaged, its contents sold.

Then in 1891 it was bought by George Hoole-Lowsley-Williams, who had inherited land nearby. He added the Neo-Tudor south wing in 1904–05, designed by J. T. Micklethwaite to provide a ballroom and further domestic offices. His grandson, David Lowsley-Williams, is the present owner of Chavenage, which his uncle gave to him when he married.

[LEFT] *The chapel's Norman font, which was found on the estate.*

[OPPOSITE] *The hall, facing north to the screens passage and the door into the service quarters. The oak screen has been much altered and ornamented with a variety of decorative details from different sources.*

Chastleton House

— OXFORDSHIRE —

A BITTERSWEET history, combined with its owners' deeply romantic attachment to the place, has left Chastleton one of England's most complete and hauntingly atmospheric Jacobean houses. The sense of time arrested owes much to the prolonged impoverishment of the family that owned it for nearly four centuries, a consequence of their Royalist and Jacobite allegiances. Lack of money might also explain why, instead of a stately avenue through a landscaped park, Chastleton's approach is the village street, at the top of which it stands flanked by stables and the church.

The house was built for Sir Walter Jones, who in 1602 bought the estate from Robert Catesby, one of the ringleaders of the Gunpowder Plot. The son of a Witney wool merchant, Jones had trained as a lawyer and was three times an MP; becoming the squire of Chastleton consolidated his ascent from trade to gentry. The house he built in 1607–12 to replace the medieval manor conformed to contemporary taste in being tall and compact, with four outward-looking wings arranged squarely around an inner courtyard. The south front is dramatically massed, with a tight rhythm of five narrow bays advancing and receding between matching stair towers. In counterpoint to these alternating planes, spikey gables and the horizontal lines of string-courses and transoms step up and down with the changing levels and window sizes. It is undoubtedly a sophisticated composition, although there is a brooding austerity about the towerlike gabled and battlemented bays, and much of the detail was wrought by skilled local masons and joiners working in the Cotswolds vernacular. This tension between the stylish and the provincial recurs throughout the house.

Who designed Chastleton remains unknown, but it is accomplished enough to suggest the involvement of a leading architectural talent—somebody of the status of Robert Smythson, whose Burton Agnes Manor in Yorkshire bears many similarities. The plan retains the traditional arrangement of a great hall at the centre, as signified on the principal front by the increased concentration of glass in the central bays. A pair of formal family rooms—the White Parlour (or high parlour) and the great parlour—lead off the hall's high end, both decorated with rich plasterwork and chunky Jacobean friezes. The principal entertaining rooms are on the first floor, reached by the east staircase. The grandest in this enfilade is the great

[OPPOSITE] *The east front of Chastleton, with one of the twin battlemented stair towers that contribute to its picturesque grouping. The stair towers derive from houses being built in the outer suburbs of London at this time, the earliest known example dating from 1596. The topiary garden was laid out in the seventeenth century and has been replanted on at least one subsequent occasion, in 1833. Enclosed by a circular yew hedge, it features twenty-four box figures, including a galleon, a cat, and a horse.*

[OPPOSITE] *The view into the Fettiplace Room from its closet, which is lined with rare early-seventeenth-century flame-stitch or "Irish stitch" hangings. Mentioned in the 1738 inventory, these textiles are probably reused bed hangings. The bedchamber itself has arcaded panelling and a wooden overmantel carved with arms signifying the marriage of Anne Fettiplace to Henry Jones in 1609.*

chamber, lavishly decorated to signify its status as a room for receiving distinguished guests, and for formal dining and dancing. With its ebullient plasterwork, carved wainscoting, and bogus armorial chimneypiece, this florid room is a tour de force of nouveau riche aspiration.

One of the glories of Chastleton is the survival of its textiles and tapestries. The superior bedchamber, the Fettiplace Room, is hung with three panels depicting *The Story of Jacob* from a set of Flanders tapestries mentioned here in 1633; rare flame-stitch hangings line its closet. But the climax of the house is reserved for the top floor: one spectacular space running the full length of the north range with views on three sides through myriad

[OVERLEAF] *The south front, a perfect Jacobean composition of tawny, lichen-mottled limestone that changes from pinkish-red to ochre in different lights. The façade reflects the traditional internal arrangement of a central great hall with a large window at the dais end (see the right-hand projecting bay) and the entrance at the low end (the porch is in the corresponding left-hand bay). The placing of the entrance in the returning flank of the porch conceals its off-centre position, thus preserving the symmetry of the facade.*

[ABOVE] *The great parlour, originally used by the family as a dining room, with an unmatched set of oak dining chairs dating from about 1660. The Jacobean-style ceiling and frieze were installed by John Henry Whitmore-Jones in 1829, and until the 1890s the room was panelled. The tapestry of ca. 1730 was probably made in Lille and moved here from the library.*

glittering diamond panes. Sparsely furnished and lined with a jigsaw of oak panelling and undulating boards, the long gallery at Chastleton has been described as "one of the most glorious rooms in England." The sweeping barrel vault, with its interlace of ribbons and roses hand-modelled in stucco, is one of the least altered ceilings of its type, closely resembling contemporary work at various Oxford colleges.

Chastleton's history is remarkably uneventful, with long periods when the house was simply abandoned to benign neglect. Successive generations left their mark, but mostly with the intention of preserving and enhancing the air of antiquity rather than introducing drastic change. The first major repairs were carried out by John Jones and his brother, Arthur, around 1800. They both died childless, and in 1828 their cousin, John Henry Whitmore-

[ABOVE] *Rustic virtuosity meets metropolitan panache in the great chamber, the grandest room in the house, with its elaborately modelled plaster ceiling, carved wainscoting decoratively set out and ornamented with strapwork cartouches and pierced arabesques, frieze inset with painted roundels of prophets and sibyls, and spectacular carved stone chimneypiece surmounted by a coat of arms contrived by Walter Jones. The latter still bears traces of its original rich red, blue, and gold paint.*

Jones, became the squire. He modernised the domestic arrangements and carried out further antiquarian embellishments. But the family was increasingly beset with financial difficulties, and by the 1950s almost the entire estate had been sold off and the house was "held together by cobwebs." Threatened with collapse, it was sold in 1991 and transferred to the National Trust.

The trust's approach has been "to lay as light a hand as possible on Chastleton, to arrest 150 years of progressive decay with an almost imperceptible tightening of the reins." The fragile interiors have been taken apart and put back together again, their contents cleaned, repaired, and stabilised but not restored, so that the illusion prevails that nothing has been touched. Areas of missing panelling still gape, green emulsion peels from walls, woodwork is gnawed and pitted, and the kitchen's smoke-blackened ceiling remains unpainted. No other house open to the public manages to beguile its visitors so successfully into thinking that they have stumbled across a sleeping beauty, and one that has somehow been forgotten not just by the twentieth century, but by the nineteenth and eighteenth centuries too.

Owlpen Manor

— GLOUCESTERSHIRE —

THE view of Owlpen Manor from the field in front of the house has become an iconic image of the Cotswolds. With its attendant church, courthouse, and barn, this is the very essence of the English domestic ideal: a group of silvery-grey stone buildings spanning seven centuries, seen in one harmonious composition with an ancient topiary garden and meadows backed by beech-hung hills.

By the end of the nineteenth century, Owlpen had sunk into obscurity, enveloped by "gigantic black pylons of yew," ivy-choked, and on the verge of collapse. But in the early 1900s it was rediscovered by a group of like-minded romantics, and *Country Life* featured it in 1906. Architects and artists such as Ernest and Sidney Barnsley and Alfred Powell; the garden designer Gertrude Jekyll; and Thackeray Turner, W. Troup, and A. R. Powys of the Society for the Protection of Ancient Buildings all visited and took an interest, and there was a move to encourage urgent repairs. Then in 1924 the octogenarian owner, Rose Trent-Stoughton, died, and the following year Owlpen was sold for the first time in eight hundred years.

It was bought by the young Arts & Crafts architect Norman Jewson, son-in-law of Ernest Barnsley and a former student at Sapperton of Ernest Gimson and the Barnsleys, with whom he had worked on a number of Cotswold houses. Jewson found Owlpen full of "symbols of the accumulated experience of the past" and resolved that "this exceptionally beautiful and interesting old house might still be saved." He paid £3,200, acquiring the house and gardens, orchards, gardener's cottage, mill, barn, and outbuildings.

The house conforms to a standard H plan, of which only the east wing survives from the medieval manor house of the de Olepennes. In 1464 it passed through marriage to a clothier called Daunt, and it was his descendants who, between then and the early 1700s, rebuilt the rest of the house in stages. This piecemeal evolution is reflected in the disparity between the three dominating wide gables on the south front, which contributes to Owlpen's enjoyable architectural idiosyncracies.

The central block comprised the hall with, above it, the great chamber (now Queen Margaret's Room), which is connected to the wings by a passage on the north side linking a pair of staircases. This range is believed to

{OPPOSITE} *Grouped with its attendant buildings among terraced yew gardens on the south-facing slopes of a wooded coombe, Owlpen is the essence of the picturesque Cotswolds manor house. The west wing is seen here below the Victorian church, with the Jacobean courthouse on the far left beyond the topiary "yew parlour," one of the "dark, secret rooms of yew hiding in the slope of the valley" admired by Vita Sackville West. To the bottom right is the "exquisite gateway surmounting a cone of grey steps" dating from the early eighteenth century.*

have been rebuilt by Christopher Daunt, who inherited Owlpen in 1542. The main entrance at the low end of the hall has been replaced by an every-day entrance in the east wing, and the screens passage has disappeared, but much else survives, including fragments of heraldic wall paintings.

The west wing, with its lofty, battlemented bay window inscribed "TD 1616," provided Thomas Daunt II with a parlour/solar block at the upper end of the hall, an interesting example of the survival of medieval planning in a Jacobean construction. The Oak Parlour now runs the full length of this wing, having been amalgamated with a small room to the north by Jewson, who was also responsible for the elm floor and rearranging the panelling.

The final phase of alterations dates from about 1720, when Thomas and Elizabeth Daunt created a panelled drawing room and a bedroom above lined with painted canvas hangings in the east wing, which they equipped with fashionable Georgian sash windows. The panelled drawing room opens off the hall through a handsome Georgian doorcase typical of the fine wood-work being executed around Bristol at this time. Thomas Daunt also laid out the terraces in 1723, probably planting the topiary that has become such a feature of the gardens. He died in 1749, and thereafter Owlpen became a secondary seat of his descendants, declining into obscurity after a grander house was built in 1848. By 1906 it was "practically uninhabitable . . . a garden house more than anything else, because of its crumbling age."

Jewson's gentle resuscitation is admired today as a model of Arts & Crafts sensitivity. He employed local craftsmen to carry out repairs using tradi-tional materials and techniques, and introduced restrained Arts & Crafts detail that is difficult to distinguish from the old. He was determined to make the house viable for continued domestic use, and so he simplified the circulation, altered floor levels and relocated staircases, reordered the kitchen and service quarters, and introduced heating. But he knew he could never afford to live here and in 1926 was obliged to sell Owlpen at a loss.

Jewson was in his nineties when the present owners, Nicholas and Karin Mander, befriended him, having bought Owlpen in 1974, a year before his death. He left them old papers relating to the house, his sketchbooks, an oak settle made by Sidney Barnsley, plaster moulds, and a worktable, a collection to which the Manders have added many further Arts & Crafts pieces. They have restored outbuildings and cottages, made a restaurant in the barn, and replanted yews cut down in the 1950s. The beautiful Arts & Crafts garden they have created at Owlpen often deceives visitors into thinking it is the work of their hero Norman Jewson.

The great hall facing west. Norman Jewson repaved the floor with flagstones, repaired the ceiling timbers, and reinstated the Tudor form of the chimneypiece. On the right is his settle, made by Sidney Barnsley and formerly owned by Ernest Gimson, which Jewson bequeathed to the present owners of Owlpen.

[ABOVE] *The Little Parlour created in ca. 1720 by Thomas and Elizabeth Daunt within the shell of the medieval service wing, with Georgian panelling and a shell-headed alcove. Jewson raised the floor and relaid it with locally sawn elm boards.*

[BELOW] *Queen Margaret's Room above the hall, originally the great chamber. It is named after Margaret of Anjou, who is said to have slept here in 1471. The walnut and ebony cabinet was made around 1914 by Sidney Barnsley.*

[OPPOSITE, CLOCKWISE FROM TOP LEFT] *A detail of the cloth hangings now in Queen Margaret's Room, which were painted in water-based tempera on canvas and depict scenes from the story of Joseph and his brothers. A rare survival, they were originally introduced as a cheap substitute for tapestries, bought ready-painted and then cut to fit. They were moved to this room in 1964, having formerly decorated the bedroom in the east wing.*

The newel staircase leading from Queen Margaret's Room to the attic, with an original oak door still with its fine hinges and lock plate.

An Owlpen owl in the great hall, a piece of hand-modelled plasterwork introduced by the present owners from a mould by Norman Jewson.

The east wing viewed from the kitchen garden. The oldest part of the house, this was originally the service wing, opening off the low end of the hall.

Newe House

— SUFFOLK —

THIS delightful Jacobean house of beautifully mellowed Suffolk brick was built in the early seventeenth century as a secondary residence of the Bright family. It has many features of interest, but it is also significant in a social context as an example of how wealthy gentry families provided for themselves and their descendants once primogeniture had become universal among their class. Robert Bright, whose forbears had made their money as merchants in Bury St. Edmunds and London, bought Nether Hall, one of the two manors of Pakenham, in 1601. He built Newe House shortly before 1622 (the date on the porch) as a place to retire, so that he could hand over the responsibility of the main house and estate to his eldest son. But it was also intended as a property that he could give to his second son, Henry, who became the owner of the "new built house and grounds" in 1621, nine years before Robert's death. This was not an uncommon pattern of ownership, and it explains why such houses appear architecturally grander than might normally be expected of a relatively modest-sized building. Newe House did not have its own large estate, but it was designed as a handsome gentleman's residence with some architectural presence to reflect the social status of its owner.

The house stands prominently on top of a hill, with the church of Pakenham a field away to the south. It is reached today by a short winding drive, though evidence suggests that it was originally approached across a formal forecourt. The house's height is stressed by the polygonal two-storey porch, and by the parade of three matching gables topped with ball finials, which emphasise the symmetricality of the entrance front, unusual for a house of this date and size. The "Dutch" gables are of a type found in London from the 1590s, derived from more elaborate versions fashionable in Holland since the 1570s.

Robert Bright's will of 1630 survives, providing important information as to the original plan and a fascinating insight into the furnishings of a house of this status. They included hangings in the chambers, painted cloth "over the kitchen chamber," and three painted bedsteads "in three several rooms."

The plan, which comprised three rooms on each of two main floors, included the fashionable arrangement of a first-floor "dining chamber." Bright's will does not mention the hall, but it is clear that this was the room

[OPPOSITE] *A view into the dining room, originally the kitchen, through a doorway with a surround that originally belonged to an outside door. The carved Jacobean overmantel was introduced in the early twentieth century.*

[OVERLEAF] *The entrance front from the northwest, shaded by an early-nineteenth-century cedar. The house was originally approached through a formal symmetrical forecourt.*

which still exists in the middle of the ground floor, flanked by the kitchen on the left (which still has its great chimney stack and is now the dining room) and the parlour on the right. In an article published in *Country Life* (February 13, 2003), Nicholas Cooper pointed out that where one would expect to find a screens passage at one end of the hall in an early seventeenth-century house of this type, here, most unusually, there is none, and instead it is entered from the centre. He suggests that this was because Newe House was the family's secondary residence, and it could therefore dispense with the more formal layout associated with the traditional ceremonial function of the hall.

The first floor had rooms above the kitchen and parlour, with the dining chamber extending the full width of the house in the centre, lit by the bay window over the porch. This great chamber survived into the late nineteenth century—in 1881 it was described as the "bow drawing room"—but has since disappeared, the first floor reconfigured as three bedrooms and bathrooms with just a passage lit by the central bay window.

When Henry Bright died in 1652, Newe House was sold. It came later into the ownership of Sir William Spring, whose family had made its fortune in the cloth and wool trade. Sir William was the great-nephew of the "great clothier" Thomas Spring, who left his widow the richest commoner in the county when he died in 1523, and whose second son, Robert, bought Pakenham Manor in 1545. Sir William's grandfather, also called William, was the high sheriff who in 1578 had entertained Elizabeth I here, along with "200 young gentlemen clad all in white velvet, and 300 of the graver sort, apparelled in black velvet coats and fair chains . . . with 1,500 serving men more on horseback, well and bravely mounted in good order."

In adding Newe House to his Pakenham estate, Sir William was able to further consolidate his family's property and status in the area, as well as acquire a dower house. But the 4th baronet died in 1736 with no male heir and, after passing through the female line, Pakenham Manor was sold and by 1800 had been demolished. Newe House, meanwhile, was let out on a repairing lease to a local farming family for much of the eighteenth century, and as a result the house has been preserved in a remarkably good state. Though some alterations took place in the nineteenth and twentieth centuries, including the possible relocation of the stair, they were generally modest and in keeping with the house's character: sash windows on the rear elevations and some Georgian panelled doors, for example, introduced by a descendant of Sir William Spring's when she and her husband, the vicar of Pakenham, came to live here around 1800. Since then, most of the original chimneypieces have been replaced, but the servants' garrets survive virtually untouched. Newe House is a telling example of how benign the effects of a long-term tenancy can be, with no incentive from either party to initiate a dramatic change. Since 1947 the house has been owned by three generations of the same family, whose improvements have been similarly respectful.

The present drawing room. The ceiling plasterwork dates from the nineteenth century; the chimney-piece is Jacobean, though not original to the house.

Daneway

— GLOUCESTERSHIRE —

WHEN Ernest Gimson and the Barnsley brothers settled in Sapperton and established their village industry of traditional handicrafts, Daneway acquired a new and lasting identity as the focus of their Arts & Crafts ideology. These men belonged to a group of artisan visionaries who migrated to the Cotswolds around 1900 in search of a simple, honest way of life and the survival of unindustrialised workmanship. Sequestered in one of the deep wooded valleys carved into the western escarpment, Daneway epitomised the romance of the smaller manor houses of the Cotswolds, several of which, after years of obscurity, took on a new lease of life in the hands of these architects and craftsmen (see Owlpen, p. 101, and William Morris's beloved Kelmscott, p. 355). Daneway had been the centre of its own small, solitary domain for centuries, but by 1899 it had become a semi-ruin. The 7th Earl Bathurst bought the house to save it from demolition and employed Ernest Barnsley to carry out sensitive repairs. Then from 1908 until 1919 he leased it to Gimson and the Barnsleys, who used the outbuildings as workshops and the house as a place to exhibit their furniture. Their simple, solid dressers and tables, and smaller, more decorative Georgian-style pieces can be seen in *Country Life's* photographs of 1909.

Daneway has evolved quietly and organically into a picturesque complex of gabled ranges that possess an instinctive harmony despite the lack of an integrated plan. Architectural ornament is discreet and defies stylistic analysis, for parts of the house look earlier than they are, yet the hall range has now been dated using dendrochronology to 1315—a good century earlier than had always been assumed. Its original soot-blackened roof timbers can still be seen above the later ceiling; the central hearth was replaced by a massive stone chimney breast in the later fifteenth century.

The twin gabled unit of porch/entrance hall and southwest wing acquired its present appearance in the late seventeenth century, showing how late the old traditions of medieval masonry could survive in these remote valleys. The trefoil-arched doorway in the entrance hall originally opened onto a staircase that led to the porch's upper room. This may have been the oratory described as "newly built" when Henry and Matilda Clifford obtained a licence to celebrate mass here in 1340.

But Daneway's most distinctive feature is the "high building," which

[OPPOSITE] *The picturesque complex of gabled ranges viewed in their wooded coombe from the west. Daneway was described by H. J. Massingham in* Shepherd's Country *(1938) as "a modest little manor that expresses an affectionate reconcilement between the fourteenth and the seventeenth centuries by means of the effortless mastery of the Cotswold style which has subdued all opposition between Gothic and quasi-classical to its own local preference."*

stands slightly aslant on the southeast corner. This curiosity, with its cross-gabled roof and old-fashioned detailing, suggests a medieval solar tower or Jacobean prospect tower but is now known to date from about 1674. Five rooms, one on each floor, comprise a wine cellar; withdrawing room, known as the Trout Room and connected to the hall by a corner opening; principal chamber, with an internal timber porch; summer sitting room (unheated); and attic prospect room with views on three sides. The three main rooms, connected by a spiral staircase, have decorative ribbed plaster ceilings and friezes, which inspired Gimson and Barnsley's later work.

The tiny courtyard between the high building and the porch is treated as a formal entry to the tower, with a pair of archways combining Renaissance and Gothic detail in a charmingly naïve manner. The high building reflects the conservative building practices of Cotswolds masons, but it was a conscious anachronism on the part of William Hancox, who inherited Daneway in ca. 1672. His yeoman forbears had been tenants here from 1532, but in 1647 his father, a captain in the Parliamentary army, bought the manor.

[LEFT] *The view from the southeast, showing the anachronistic "high building" that was added in ca. 1674 but looks much earlier. Built as a self-contained bachelor wing, it occupies the site of a medieval range. Seen to the left are the twin gables of the southwest wing and porch. The archway to their right includes a tentative flirtation with Renaissance detail in its rusticated voussoirs.*

[OPPOSITE] *The entrance hall, looking through the simply chamfered doorway that was originally the main entrance, along the screens passage to the enclosed garden beyond. The trefoil-arched doorway on the left probably provided access to a staircase leading to the upper room in the porch, which may have been the oratory that is documented as being newly built in 1340.*

It seems that successive generations shared Hancox's antiquarian tastes, and Daneway survives today largely in its seventeenth-century form. It was owned by the same family until the 1860s, after which it became derelict.

The Arts & Crafts tradition established here by Gimson and the Barnsleys has continued to the present day. From 1919 to 1932, Daneway was the home of William Morris's friend and mentor, Sir Emery Walker. Then, from 1948 to 1968, the architect Oliver Hill and his weaver wife, Titania, lived here, a period reflected by a more colourful "European and Catholic aesthetic." They were responsible for laying out the gardens, and for such jeus d'esprits as the marble/terrazzo table in the barn and the blessing carved onto a buttress

[ABOVE] *The present dining room in the southwest wing, the appearance of which dates from the early seventeenth century. The portrait of Edward VI's chamberlain, Sir Anthony Wakefield, is by William Scrots.*

by their great-nephew, the sculptor Simon Verity. Their brother-in-law, the painter Sir Anthony Denny, lived here from 1974 until 1993, when the present owners bought Daneway from Lord Bathurst.

Nicholas and Kai Spencer have undertaken a painstaking restoration with the help of architects Nicholas Johnston and Peter Cave Associates. With great feeling for what H. J. Massingham described as Daneway's "benedictive quietude" and "soft radiance," they have furnished it with an eclectic mix of old English furniture and portraits, modern paintings and prints, Tibetan rugs, and Oriental ceramics. They have revived and further developed the gardens, planted formal yews and many other trees, built drystone walls, and created a new approach. And, in the spirit of their predecessors, they have introduced new works by outstanding contemporary craftsmen and stone carvers, such as Rory Young and Emily Young.

[ABOVE] *The breakfast room, originally the undercroft beneath the private chamber. It was later used for storage and converted into a stair hall in the sixteenth century; subsequently it became the kitchen (the medieval kitchen having been outside the main building). The present kitchen is in the north range.*

[OPPOSITE] *The study, originally the parlour, which was built into the slope of the hill to the east of the hall (now the drawing room) in the earlier fifteenth century.*

Lodge Park

— GLOUCESTERSHIRE —

Lodge Park is something of an exception in this book: although later converted to a house, this richly ornamented classical pavilion was built as a deer-coursing grandstand. Its date of about 1634 is confirmed by a recently discovered account written by a Lieut Hammond, who described "one stately, rich, compacted building all of Freestone, flat and cover'd with Lead . . . [with] rich furnish'd rooms." The owner was John Dutton, a wily hunchback known as "Crump," who created a deer park here on his Sherborne estate from the 1620s. He built Lodge Park not as a hunting lodge to accommodate guests overnight, but rather as a place to entertain large numbers of spectators as they enjoyed the popular sport of chasing stags with dogs.

Who designed this glorious pavilion for feasting and gambling? Certainly it displays a good knowledge of Renaissance detail and for a long time was thought to be the work of Inigo Jones. However, the awkward manner in which the different elements are crowded together on the square, compact facade suggests a provincial hand, although surely one familiar with Jones's Banqueting House in Whitehall of 1622. The finely wrought stone ornament has the artisan character of work by skilled country craftsmen.

The National Trust acquired the estate in 1982, and in 1991 began an extensive restoration of Lodge Park, which raised some important questions about approaches to conservation. Although the façade had survived intact, the interior had become so altered that it was virtually devoid of visual interest and the structure stood on the verge of collapse. So the trust made the controversial decision to depart from the widely accepted "conserve as found" philosophy, and to opt for a more radical intervention.

The building archaeologist Warwick Rodwell carried out a detailed analysis, and successive layers of alteration were stripped out in order to return the building as much as possible to its seventeenth-century plan. Inevitably, this project involved some conjecture, but only so much as was necessary to hint at the original appearance and detail of the rooms, and to engage the visitor's imagination—the trust did not go so far as to speculate on the whole decorative scheme. In repairing the existing fabric, care was taken to capture the spirit of the original craftsmanship: where stone balusters on the parapet were heavily eroded, replicas carved with the same robustness and

[OPPOSITE] *Lodge Park stands out in the landscape like a stage set from a Jacobean masque. An elaborate grandstand designed for spectating, feasting, and gambling, it is seen here from its former deer course. The first-floor banqueting room has convincing dummy windows at either end.*

The banqueting room, or great room, is a perfect double cube on plan. Originally it was probably much richer, with lavish gilding, walls hung with tapestries, and a chimneypiece inset with coloured stones. This photograph shows the room with William Kent's pair of "Mahogany settees for ye Dining Room at ye Lodge carved £30" returned on temporary loan (they were sold in 1940). Kent also provided two carved, painted, and gilded tables, almost certainly those now flanking the great chimneypiece, which are missing their original marble tops.

slight imperfections of the originals were made to replace them.

Lodge Park has now regained its progression of grand internal spaces. One of the few original features to have survived intact was a limestone arch of impressive scale. This directed the flow of visitors from the hall to a monumental staircase, up which the excited company would pour to the banqueting room, which opened onto a balcony above the loggia-portico. Above this, the flat-leaded roof also served as a viewing platform. The staircase (removed in ca. 1820) has now been reinstated, the new structure made of Welsh oak to the original overscaled dimensions. It has huge acorn finials and gutsy balusters modelled on a balustrade at Cornbury Park in Oxfordshire, a house by Nicholas Stone built by the Strong family of master masons, who are thought also to have worked at Lodge Park. One compromise was to re-create the upper part of the stair tower, which originally projected above the parapet, with a simpler modern alternative loosely based on a seventeenth-century form.

The banqueting room on the first floor is a perfect double cube. Nothing survives of the original Jacobean decoration, which is thought to have been destroyed in a remodelling by William Kent, who also designed furniture for Lodge Park (Sir John Dutton's accounts date this work to 1723–33). But archaeological detective work has indicated the position, if not the detail, of the original dado and entablature, and suggested that the room was hung with tapestries. The trust has reinstated certain architectural elements, including a replica of the great hooded chimneypiece that dominated the room. The original was removed to Sherborne House in about 1820 and is one of a small group associated with the area, similarly carved and probably originally richly coloured and inset with stones. The pedimented timber doorcase is conjectural but has been carefully designed in the style of the period. French glass imitates the original opaque leaded lights in a suitable glazing pattern, with new lead bars fitted into the surviving sockets, so that the tall windows are once again an impressive feature of the room.

The hall we now know was panelled at three different periods. One wall and a pair of internal porches have been re-created; the others are simply treated with traditional limewash. The handsome new front door and other timber detail were modelled on contemporary work at Bolsover Castle, which was felt likely to provide a close parallel. In the cellar, kitchens equipped with three ovens have been disinterred.

Lodge Park continued as a sporting pavilion into the eighteenth century, when racing and fox hunting, which the Sherborne estate played a leading part in popularising, succeeded the crueller sport of deer coursing. In the 1740s it was in use as a racing grandstand, as can be seen in George Lambert's splendid bird's-eye view, which shows the pavilion rising dramatically from the flat, windswept wolds to command magnificent views, much as it still does today. The deer park was remodelled by Charles Bridgeman from 1726 and, although his "Great Avenue" and serpentine canal (known from a recently discovered drawing) have disappeared, it survives remarkably intact. The deer course can also still be seen, following the line of the present long, straight road. The trust's next phase will be to restore these historic elements.

Lodge Park was gutted and recast three times during the nineteenth century for modest residential use. By 1876 it was deserted, but in 1898 it was remodelled again as a dower house for Sherborne Park. A pair of gate lodges and a tree-lined avenue and fountain court transformed its setting into that of a small country house (now replaced by open ground, so that the wall-lined racecourse is again visible). The twentieth century saw further alterations, and the building was last occupied in the early 1990s.

As a result of the trust's project, we now have a proper understanding of the history of this intriguing building, the only deer-coursing pavilion in England to be seen in its original form. It is also now a showplace for paintings and furniture formerly belonging to the Sherborne family.

[RIGHT] *The façade of Lodge Park, the most progressive building of its date in the Cotswolds, jostles with tightly packed Renaissance ornament that suggests a provincial builder/architect familiar with the work of Inigo Jones.*

[OPPOSITE, CLOCKWISE FROM TOP LEFT] *The staircase linking the grand main spaces has been reinstated, its oak balusters modelled on an external balustrade at Cornbury Park in Oxfordshire, which was possibly built by the same master masons as Lodge Park.*

The hall, with one of two new internal porches beside a portrait of Captain Sir Thomas Dutton.

A view of the banqueting room, with one of William Kent's "Mahogany settees." The new doorcase is conjectural—there may have been a stone archway here—but it has been designed in an appropriate seventeenth-century style.

A carved garden bench in the hall (not previously part of Lodge Park's contents).

Milton Manor

— OXFORDSHIRE —

ILTON Manor is an architectural historian's puzzle. Its design has much in common with country houses built by followers of Inigo Jones from the 1630s, yet the evidence, which is tantalisingly vague, points to a more likely date of around 1660. To add to the conundrum, a lawyer's statement made in 1696 refers to "the dwelling house being a new built house" in 1688, the date when it was inherited by Paul Calton and considered to be worth £400 to £500.

What makes this tall brick house so additionally fascinating is that it survives in such a remarkably complete state. Indeed, in more than three centuries it has undergone only one major phase of improvements: the addition of new wings on each side to accommodate a library and Roman Catholic chapel, internally decorated in Gothic revival style, and a dining room. This work was carried out in 1776 by Stephen Wright, a pupil of William Kent, for the lacemaker Bryant Barrett, owner from 1764. He barely touched the existing house, except to replace the mullioned and transomed windows with sashes. Since then, alterations have been minimal, one noteworthy change being the removal of three scrolled dormers that appear in a drawing of the entrance front made by Wright in the 1760s.

If, as the lawyer suggested, the house dates from the 1680s, then it was somewhat old-fashioned for its date. Five bays by five, and three storeys tall, it has a hipped roof over an emphatic cornice, raised basement, and compact double-pile plan that belongs to a tradition developed in the earlier decades of the seventeenth century under the influence of city houses built by the best masons and carpenters. A curiosity of Milton Manor is the run of Ionic pilasters across the front with raised panels at their midriffs decorated with fleur-de-lys. A similar feature was used on some houses on Great Queen Street in London of 1640 built by the bricklayer Peter Mills, who was one of the most conspicuous designers in the Artisan Mannerist style. But how loosely was the lawyer using the word "new"? A house conforming to the modern classical style might well have been described as new even if it was several decades old.

In the absence of documentation, secondary evidence has to be considered alongside the physical clues. One temptation, in favour of an earlier date, is to consider a possible connection with Sir Dudley Carleton, brother-in-

[OPPOSITE] The staircase, which rises through five floors from basement to attic, offset from the central axis.

law of Robert Calton of Milton. As Charles I's Secretary of State, Carleton would have had obvious links with the court and with the circle of Inigo Jones. However, he died in 1632 and Robert Calton did not inherit Milton until seven years later. It is possible that Calton built the house sometime between 1639 and the outbreak of the Civil War in 1642, or perhaps following the war in the 1650s (although by then he was getting old), but there is nothing to support or disprove any of this.

More plausible, perhaps, is the possibility that the house was built by Paul Calton (a forbear of the one mentioned by the lawyer), who inherited Milton in 1659. He married Susanna Ballam in the same year, and her dowry, combined with the proceeds of selling her inherited share of another estate in 1661, might have helped to finance a house for the newly married couple at this time. A hearth tax return for Milton Manor dated 1663 suggests a possible completion date. Then there is the growing number of property mortgages taken out by the family over the following few decades, suggesting straitened financial circumstances. These could have arisen from the expense of building a new house so recently, and might also explain why only one room—the drawing room—has a relatively elaborate ceiling in the manner of Inigo Jones; the decoration of Milton Manor is otherwise fairly plain.

The plan is distinctly geometric, with a central corridor running from front to back on each floor and a thick wall, containing flues and closets, running across the middle of the house at right angles to the principal axis, so that every floor is divided into four, with a single room in three of the four quarters. In the fourth, an oak staircase with sturdy turned balusters rises all the way up through the house, from basement to attic. Giles Worsley has pointed out that this plan resembles that of Ashdown House in Berkshire, which is believed to date from 1663, and also a house in Blackfriars built by Inigo Jones, long demolished but known from drawings. Another house associated with Jones is Chevening in Kent, whose original form, though slightly grander, closely resembles that of Milton Manor. It makes similar use of quoins and stringcourses, and has a raised basement for offices and kitchens, which was an Italian idea found in Palladio's work, first introduced into England in the 1620s and associated with the houses of Roger Pratt.

After examining all the various possible clues in an article published in *Country Life* in 1991, Giles Worsley suggested 1660–63 as the most likely date for the building of Milton Manor. The architect was probably a London surveyor, possibly Peter Mills, whose works show a number of similar features. If this date is correct, Milton must be one of the last to have been built to a pattern associated with houses of some thirty years earlier. Its late survival might be explained by the fact that nothing was built during the Civil War, and so during that intervening period no significant stylistic advances were made.

[LEFT] *The original central block of Milton Manor—five by five bays square and with identical garden and entrance fronts—probably dates from the early 1660s; the flanking wings were added in 1776.*

[OPPOSITE] *A detail of the main block, showing the parade of giant pilasters with their eccentric Ionic capitals, and the emphatic frieze and cornice.*

[OPPOSITE, CLOCKWISE FROM TOP LEFT] *The hall from the central corridor.*

The drawing room, with a compartmental ceiling in the manner of Inigo Jones decorated with garlands of oak and laurel leafs. The chimneypiece is late eighteenth century, with an overmantel of ca. 1740 in the manner of William Kent.

The central corridor, repeated on each of the main floors.

A view toward the staircase on the second floor.

[RIGHT] *The hall chimneypiece, with chunky garlands and an overmantel bearing the arms of Paul Calton, the possible builder of the house, and of his wife, Susanna Ballam.*

Stepleton House

— DORSET —

THERE is something to be said for the benign neglect that often accompanies long periods of tenancy. For more than a century from the 1760s, Stepleton House on the western edge of Cranborne Chase was a sleeping beauty, undisturbed except for necessary repairs, until it was revived in the twentieth century by sympathetic new owners.

At first glance it appears to be a Georgian house, built all of apiece in the Anglo-Palladian manner. Elegant and symmetrical, the central six-bay block flanked by five-bay pavilion wings has Georgian sash windows, a pedimented centrepiece on the entrance front, and, in the principal rooms, pattern-book chimneypieces and Rococo plasterwork of a distinctive Dorset strain. But this harmonious composition is deceptive. The compact central block in fact dates from the seventeenth century, as evidence of stone mullions, pairs of brick cylindrical chimneys prominent above the hipped roof, and certain internal details confirm.

The seventeenth-century house that replaced an earlier one was probably built for Thomas Fownes, who acquired the estate in 1654. In 1731 the centre was gutted by fire, and it was following this disaster that the interior was remodelled with fine plasterwork, carved woodwork, and chimneypieces bearing the characteristics of work associated with a school of skilled local craftsmen working out of the nearby town of Blandford at this time.

Work continued through the 1740s and '50s, having been started by another Thomas Fownes, a keen sportsman and pioneering foxhound breeder who also built the brick stable block. His heraldry is incorporated with his wife's into some of the fine plaster decoration, such as on the dining room ceiling. But Fownes had to sell Stepleton to pay off his creditors, and in 1745 it was bought for £12,600 by Julines Beckford, a Jamaican nabob who became High Sheriff of Dorset and M P for Salisbury.

Beckford continued the Georgian remodelling of the interiors and carried out the third significant phase of the house's development. In 1758 he added a pair of wings with Gibbs-inspired detail, whose similarity to work at Came House near Dorchester suggests the involvement of Francis Cartwright, a local master builder/architect working in the Palladian manner with the help of the popular pattern books and building guides of the day. Beckford also had the main entrance moved from east to south, where it is incorporated

[OPPOSITE] *The staircase hall with its arcaded first-floor landing, created in 1758 as a new centrepiece to the house by roofing over the small, seventeenth-century inner courtyard. The stone staircase has a handsome wrought-iron balustrade similar to work at several local houses, including Came.*

[OVERLEAF] *The north front of Stepleton. The central block was built in the seventeenth century, with a hipped roof, cylindrical chimneystacks, and classically proportioned mullioned windows. It was remodelled in the Anglo-Palladian style in the mid-eighteenth century, its pavilion wings added in 1758.*

into a fine three-bay centrepiece, the upper part of which suggests a Venetian window. This may have been designed by John Bastard—the composition of the doorway flanked by windows is very similar to that of a house by him in Poole. The Bastards were another family of architect builders who developed their skills working on a number of local houses, sometimes together with Cartwright.

The east front of Stepleton also gained a pedimented central feature at this time, and the central courtyard of the seventeenth-century house was roofed over to create a top-lit stair hall with a new cantilevered stone staircase. Beckford also created the park, having redirected the Blandford road in 1750.

From then until recent decades virtually nothing more was done to modernise the house. Peter Beckford, who inherited Stepleton in 1765, was a dilettante connoisseur of the arts who wrote classical verse, visited Italy, and brought the musician Muzio Clementi to work here from 1767 to 1774. But he hardly touched the house and was best known as a sportsman, in particular for his hunting skills and his famous 1781 book *Thoughts upon Hare and Fox Hunting*. His wife, Louisa Pitt, was the daughter of the 2nd Lord Rivers, of a family of large Dorset landowners. Their son William, who inherited Stepleton in 1811, also inherited his mother's family estates, changing his surname to Pitt-Rivers in 1828. As a secondary house of this family for much of the nineteenth century, Stepleton was mostly let out and therefore saved from any major alterations.

The present owners, who bought it in 1985, have revived the Georgian interiors, cleaning plasterwork and redecorating rooms with historic paint colours and replicas of original wallpaper. Filled with their collection of paintings and sculpture, with the gardens restored and the park replanted, Stepleton has been gently reawoken and filled with new life for the twenty-first century.

[OPPOSITE, CLOCKWISE FROM TOP LEFT] *A view toward the garden hall.*

The Hunting Room, with French Doufours-style papier peint wallpaper reproduced from a Country Life *photograph of 1932.*

The drawing room, refitted along with other main rooms in the mid-eighteenth century, with plasterwork in the Dorset Rococo manner and a pattern-book chimneypiece.

The dining room, today hung with a collection of Italian Old Master paintings. The plaster ceiling was introduced as part of Thomas Fownes's 1740s remodelling and incorporates his family's heraldry with that of his wife, Meliora Fitch of Wimborne Manor, whom he married in 1728.

[RIGHT] *The south front of Stepleton. The classical centrepiece was created when the main entrance was moved here in about 1758. The fine ashlar masonry and the roof slabs are of local stone.*

THE interiors of most English country houses are layered places, their contents and fittings reflecting the ebb and flow of the fortunes of their proprietors. However, in many houses it is still possible to find well-preserved interiors that are characteristic of their age.

❡ Thanks to decay and changes of fashion, no medieval country house retains an authentic, untouched, interior—even the most convincing ambiences in ancient manor houses usually turn out to be clever antiquarian confections. The austere rooms at Stokesay Castle, Shropshire, however, with their surviving stonework and panelling, evoke very well the domestic interiors of the Middle Ages, although they lack the vivid textiles and painted decoration that once brought them to life.

❡ Much more survives from the sixteenth century, when prosperity and comparative peace and stability encouraged wealthy landowners to commission finely carved panelling and woodwork to decorate their country houses. Perhaps most impressive are the screens that dominate the great halls of houses such as Chastleton in Oxfordshire, extravagantly carved with half-understood Renaissance ornament, the motifs often derived from contemporary engravings. Carved chimneypieces, sometimes incorporating costly imported marbles, were combined with richly carved wainscot, which would have been originally painted and gilded. Linenfold panelling was itself intended to evoke the rich hangings that clothed the walls in wealthier houses, only the tapestries of which, along with some grander embroideries and bed hangings, survive today. Elaborate plasterwork ceilings and friezes proclaimed the allegiances of their owners in a blaze of heraldry.

❡ In the seventeenth century, British country houses reflected the growing sophistication of architecture and the arts, with the importation of ideas and craftsmen from Italy and France. The magnificent interiors devised by the Frenchman Daniel Marot in the 1680s were imitated in the houses of the aristocracy and gentry, such as Belton House in Lincolnshire. Here, enfilades of lofty state rooms, lined with bolection-moulded panelling of oak or walnut, or painted to resemble exotic woods, culminated in richly appointed closets hung with tapestry of Flemish, or sometimes English, manufacture, their bracketed overmantels teeming with blue and white china imported from the Orient or Holland. Virtuoso carvings by Grinling Gibbons and his disciples framed pictures and overmantels, while ceilings sported plaster birds, fruit, and flowers enmeshed within scrolling foliage—a motif echoed in the squirming contours of the fashionable gilded Sunderland picture frames. Upholstery again played a vital role in these décors, from the suites of mythological tapestries, to the elaborate needlework on beds and seat furniture.

❡ The eighteenth century saw a grand progression

of styles in country house interiors. Experiments in the Continental Baroque championed by Vanbrugh and Gibbs were eclipsed in the 1720s and '30s by a cooler Palladian style, distilled from the treatises of Andrea Palladio under the 3rd Earl of Burlington and his followers. Burlington's protégé, William Kent, created interiors of great opulence that evoked the Italian palaces his patrons had seen on their Grand Tour, marshalling Old Master pictures and antique statuary in architectural arrangements against backdrops of damask or Genoese cut-velvet combined with monumental giltwood furniture. These, in turn, were overtaken by the lighter, prettier ornamentation of the Rococo and chinoiserie, seen in its most exaggerated form in the frenzied explosion of carved woodwork at Claydon House, Buckinghamshire, or, more typically, rooms hung with Chinese painted wallpaper. Eighteenth-century Gothic—a fanciful evocation of medieval ornament as used in the interiors at Arbury Hall, Warwickshire—emphasised the antiquity of a family and recalled the glories of our native architectural tradition. But the classical style generally prevailed, reaching the height of splendour and refinement in Wyatt's neoclassical interiors at Heaton Hall, Lancashire, or Adam's Newby Hall in Yorkshire. Here, every detail, from the lock plates on the doors to the pattern of the carpet, is part of a harmonious decorative ensemble.

❡ The wealth and prestige of Regency and Victorian Britain is reflected in the country house interiors of the age. The neoclassical interiors devised by Henry Holland at Berrington Hall, Shropshire, and Southill,

Bedfordshire, with their exquisite plasterwork and elegant furniture and upholstery, were eventually supplanted by spectacular displays such as Pugin's brazenly confident polychrome and gilded library at Eastnor Castle in Herefordshire of ca. 1849. Although the neoclassical or Rococo styles never entirely fell out of fashion—witness the opulent, clublike atmosphere that prevailed inside Brodsworth Hall in Yorkshire—such pagan or effete decors could hardly find favour with the pious merchant princes of the High Victorian era. Houses like Tyntesfield in Somerset, or the Chanter's House in Devon, had Gothic, almost ecclesiastical, interiors that reflected the tastes of their High Church proprietors, replete with polished marbles, stained and plate glass, encaustic tiles, and varnished oak, and fully equipped with all the latest technological advances. It was partly a reaction against this brashness, and a nostalgia for the traditional arts and crafts of the Middle Ages, that led William Morris to carefully restore and furnish the run-down Kelmscott Manor in Gloucestershire for his own occupation. His doctrine of simplicity and utility was to inspire a whole generation of Edwardian architects and patrons, who created evocative, comfortable country houses like Blackwell in Cumbria and Great Dixter in Sussex.

❡ Agricultural and economic depressions, two world wars, and dramatic changes in society made the story of the country house in the twentieth century one of decline and retrenchment. However, despite the abandonment, sale, and demolition of countless great mansions, the public fascination with country houses has burgeoned, fuelled by publications such as *Country Life* and the restoration and opening of houses by the National Trust, English Heritage, and dedicated private owners. Indeed, for every house lost, there were always others being newly built, decorated, and furnished by *nouveaux riches* like Sir Stephen Courtauld, who modishly restored Eltham Palace in 1933–36, or old grandees, such as the 16th Duke of Norfolk, who built Arundel Park, Sussex, after abandoning Arundel Castle to the trippers in 1958. Revealingly, both of these new houses were classical, although the red brick "Wrenaissance" exterior at Eltham Palace, which collided shockingly with the surviving great hall of the Tudor palace, concealed a series of sleek interiors in the Swedish Moderne style.

❦ The Duke of Norfolk's interiors at Arundel Park

were entrusted to the fashionable London firm of Colefax and Fowler, and it was John Fowler, "the prince of interior decorators," perhaps more than anyone else, who invented that comfortable mix of new and old furniture and textiles in an eclectic variety of historical styles known and imitated today as "the English country house style." Fowler's stylish and distinctive look can still be detected in very recent country house interiors, such as the pristine Neo-Palladian Henbury Hall in Cheshire, but the sheer variety of the country house interiors featured in this volume—from the carefully conserved dereliction of Brodsworth Hall, to the stark but agreeably rustic modernism of Baggy House in Devon—attests to the continuing vitality of the country house in the first decade of the new millennium.

Pages 136 and 141: Edwardian Damask, ca. 1901,
Hamilton Weston Wallpapers

Honington Hall

— WARWICKSHIRE —

ONINGTON lies on the edge of the Cotswolds at the unsung centre of England, where the local stone is a rich golden colour and the rolling landscape is still rural and unspoilt, but for the loss of its elms. Set in gentle parkland watered by the Stour, this handsome Caroline house presents something of a mystery, for the architect of its late Renaissance exterior remains unknown. Mellowed red brick walls, trimmed with the lovely local stone, and a steep roof, hipped and swept out over projecting eaves, convey a sense of warm, provincial domesticity, to which the doorcase at the centre of the east front and the band of Roman emperor busts set into round-arched recesses add a certain sophisticated flourish. But the measured restraint of Honington's homely exterior provides little clue to the dramatic Georgian interiors that are to be found within.

The house was built in 1682 to replace an earlier building for the MP and London merchant Sir Henry Parker. He is commemorated by a splendid marble monument in the Church of All Saints, which stands in harmony with the house and which he also had rebuilt (except the tower) to a Wren-inspired design presumably by the same architect as the house. It is a rare example of a country church rebuilt in the late Renaissance style of the last years of Charles II's reign.

The first phase of alterations at Honington dates from the 1740s, after Joseph Townsend, who bought it in 1737, had married a Yorkshire heiress. The accomplished Townsend assumed the role of amateur gentleman architect, directing the works himself, possibly with the help of Sanderson Miller, who designed a grotto and advised him on landscaping. A flanking pair of pedimented archways and screen walls was added (one survives), along with a Tuscan-columned loggia to the south, and the casements were replaced with elegant sash windows.

But it was inside that Townsend let rip his ambitions for a fashionable remodelling, with an explosion of Rococo plasterwork of outstanding brio. Depicting classical scenes and motifs, this seething riot of white stucco ornament was clearly executed by various hands, ranging from travelling craftsmen to modellers of the highest skill; it is probable that the Anglo-Danish sculptor and stuccadore Charles Stanley was responsible for the most exceptional work, which elaborated the marble-floored hall with sumptuously

[OPPOSITE] *Honington Hall from the east, showing its relationship to the Church of All Saints, which Sir Henry Parker remodelled in 1682. The fenestration is beautifully balanced, with thick, oak-barred Georgian sashes of ca. 1745 replacing earlier casements. The Roman emperors in shallow niches recall Ham House.*

143

framed bas relief panels of varying size. It is similar in feel to the decoration of the hall at Langley Park in Norfolk, which we know Stanley carried out before he left England in 1746.

In the Oak Room, Townsend retained the seventeenth-century oak wainscoting but had the ceiling refashioned and introduced a new marble chimneypiece and other detail. But what of the remarkably grand doorcase? The plaster cherubs reclining on its pediment clutch the same palms and cornucopia as those at Langley, yet it is closer in feel to Townsend's second phase of improvements at Honington, which included one of the most original

octagonal saloons of the early 1750s and a new staircase in an arcaded stair hall dripping with foliage and flowers. The Octagonal Saloon, designed by the amateur architect John Freeman, who estimated £100 "for a little carving, gilding and embellishment for the ladies," is the highpoint. It has a coved ceiling richly decorated to resemble a coffered dome, two more classical doorways with reclining figures, and luxuriant swags and garlands dropping down each angle. Two pier glasses in swirling, parcel-gilt stucco frames draw light into the room from the three windows opposite and reflect the ceiling painting by Luca Giordano as well as the flowing plaster ornament.

[OPPOSITE] *Joseph Townsend's Octagonal Saloon, which was added on the west front in 1751, to a design by the amateur architect John Freeman. The reclining stucco figures recall those by Artari and Bagutti at Mereworth Castle in Kent.*

Honington was sold in 1926 to Sir Charles Wiggin, and his descendants still live here. Together with the Historic Buildings Council, which financed extensive repairs to the house and church, the Wiggins can be credited with rescuing Honington from imminent dereliction induced by rampant dry rot and escalating costs in the 1970s. One rarity that awaits further restoration is a little Chinese closet lined with leather panels painted to imitate oriental lacquerwork. There is something very English about the way Honington contains its delights behind such an unshowy exterior.

[ABOVE] The Boudoir, which opens into the Octagonal Saloon. The cornice was restored in the 1970s, when the wallpaper, imitating the pattern of the original damask hangings, was introduced. The ceiling, with decoration that anticipates the more reserved style of Robert Adam, was probably Townsend's last addition to Honington.

Belton House

— LINCOLNSHIRE —

ONE of England's finest Restoration houses, Belton expresses the ambition and confidence of Charles II's England. It was built in 1685–87 for Sir John Brownlow and his wife and cousin, Alice Sherard, who had recently come into the inheritance of their great-uncle, "Old" Sir John Brownlow. The newly wealthy young couple launched themselves on London society and then set about building a fashionable country house on the estate that their great-grandfather, the ambitious lawyer Richard Brownlow, had bought in 1617.

They turned to the soldier/architect William Winde to draw up the plans and employed the master mason William Stanton to mastermind the building works. The architecture—beautifully proportioned, with a satisfying logical simplicity—was famously modelled on Clarendon House in Piccadilly, Sir Roger Pratt's short-lived work of 1664–67 and one of the first great classical houses in London. Belton adopted the "double pile" plan pioneered by Pratt, with suites of rooms arranged "back to back" in the main ceremonial block. It conformed to Pratt's published advice on country houses being symmetrical, with family and guest apartments separated into "pavilion" wings, and having the main floor raised up over a tall basement containing service quarters. The deep, hipped roof, with dormers, balustrated platform, and cupola, was also modelled on Pratt's Dutch-inspired designs.

[OPPOSITE] *A portrait of Old Sir John Brownlow over one of the fireplaces in the Marble Hall surrounded by limewood carving attributed to Grinling Gibbons. It was his great-nephew and namesake who built the house. Although the grained panelling feels seventeenth century, it was in fact installed by Wyatville in 1811. The spectacular wood carvings above the two chimneypieces were brought from other rooms in the house as part of the restoration of the carvings undertaken by W. G. Rogers in 1855–56.*

[BELOW] *Belton House near Grantham, built by Sir John Brownlow, whose coat of arms is carved into the tympanum of this north-facing front. The design, modelled on Sir Roger Pratt's Clarendon House and executed in rich, grey-gold Ancaster limestone, is logical and satisfying. The principal rooms have wider-spaced windows and break forward under pediments on both main fronts.*

[ABOVE] The Tapestry Room, which has been rearranged since this photograph was taken. Originally the Little Parlour or family dining room, it was furnished in 1754 with twenty walnut chairs with leather seats, a large blue and white marble cistern, and two sets of flowered cotton curtains. All that survives of Wyatville's 1811 redecoration is the chimneypiece; in 1892 G. Jackson & Sons of London re-created it as a seventeenth-century room for the 3rd Earl and Countess Brownlow, who retrieved Lord Tyrconnel's Mortlake tapestries from the attic, where they were being used as carpets, and hung them here (originally they were in the Red Drawing Room).

[OPPOSITE] The Tyrconnel Room, also rearranged since this photograph was taken. The full-length portrait is of Viscount Tyrconnel (1690–1754) in his robes as a Knight of the Order of the Bath. Originally the withdrawing room to the great parlour, this room was also used as a state bedchamber. The carved frieze is by Edmund Carpenter, a contemporary of Grinling Gibbons, but the oak panelling dates from ca. 1870, as does the painted floor.

The principal rooms on the central axis, linked by a great staircase, comprised the hall (now the Marble Hall) and great parlour (known since the 1770s as the saloon) on the ground floor, and the Great Dining Room (made into a drawing room by Wyatt in 1778 and since 1876–79 a library) and state bedchamber with dressing room (now the Queen's Bedroom and Ante Library) above. The saloon retains its original panelling and boldly pedimented doorcases; Grinling Gibbons is believed to have carved the frame of fruit and flowers over the west chimneypiece.

Among the best-preserved seventeenth-century interiors are the chapel and its anteroom. The latter, one of the most expensively furnished, is still hung with John Vanderbank's specially woven tapestries of 1691, with Mogul-inspired designs made fashionable by Queen Mary at Kensington Palace. Porcelain and lacquered furniture complement the Oriental theme.

Inventories from 1688 to 1754 chart the changing functions of Belton's rooms and the gradual enrichment of their furnishings, to both of which the ostentatious and art-loving Viscount Tyrconnel, nephew and heir of Sir John Brownlow, contributed significantly. But the house's character was dramatically transformed in 1776–78, when James Wyatt remodelled four interiors and some external elements in the fashionable neoclassical style. This was followed in 1809–20 by further work for the first Earl Brownlow by Jeffry Wyatt, who would later remodel Windsor Castle and change his name to Wyatville. His additions included the Italian garden and orangery, and two libraries in the west wing.

In the late nineteenth century Belton regained much of its Carolean splendour thanks to Adelbert and Adelaide Brownlow Cust, the third and last earl and countess, whose admiration for the period was then most unusual. They swept away much of Wyatt's work, reinstated original external features, and commissioned G. Jackson & Sons of London to replicate seventeenth-century elements of the decoration, such as the saloon's ornate plaster ceiling. Addy and Adelaide presided over a late Victorian golden age at Belton; they socialised with the aristocratic circle of intellectuals known as the Souls and were involved in politics and numerous events at a national and local level.

The next significant phase was the repair work carried out under the architect Francis Johnson for the 6th Lord Brownlow in the 1960s. In 1984 his son, the present Lord Brownlow, gave Belton to the National Trust. Since then much has been done to revive the historic interiors, particularly impressive being the restoration of the Red Drawing Room in 2004. Described as the "White Varnished Drawing Room" in 1698, this room was lavishly redecorated in 1810–11 by Wyatville and the leading cabinetmaker Gillow & Co., and further altered by the earl's third wife in 1830. Aided by a Victorian watercolour, a Gillow bill of 1810 and sketch for the swagged curtains draped over two "Reed'd & Gilt Cornices," and surviving fragments of tassels and tiebacks, the trust has now returned the room to its 1830s appearance, retaining strong echoes of the earlier Gillow scheme. The result reflects the mounting extravagance of Belton's nineteenth-century owners. Outside, Italianate and Dutch formal gardens have been re-created and parkland eye-catchers, avenues, and the Wilderness restored, so that once again the glorious work of art that unifies Belton and its landscape can be appreciated much as it appeared at its apogee around 1900.

[ABOVE] A naïve but delightfully evocative painting of Belton, believed to have been painted in ca. 1730 by Lord Tyrconnel's porter, Henry Jewel, who is seen outside the forecourt gates holding a staff. It shows how the south (entrance) front of the house was originally set behind a screen between stone piers enclosing a forecourt.

[OPPOSITE, CLOCKWISE FROM TOP LEFT] The Red Drawing Room as redecorated in 2004 to its 1830 scheme, with crimson damask newly woven by Richard Humphries to the pattern of surviving fragments found on the sofa. The damask hangs on gilt-framed wall panels and covers five chairs, a daybed, and a sofa.

A detail of the new curtains in the Red Drawing Room, which were made to a design based on surviving evidence and a sketch by Gillow of ca. 1830.

The Blue Bed Room in the southeast wing, originally occupied by Sir John Sherard, Lady Brownlow's brother. It is now named after the spectacular bed attributed to Francis Lapiere, which was reupholstered in blue in 1813 but listed in an inventory of 1737, when it was situated in what is now the Tyrconnel Room, as being covered in crimson damask. Since this photograph was taken, the room has been redecorated, the bed conserved, the cornices recovered, and the curtains remade.

Portraits by John Riley of Sir John Brownlow, builder of the house, and his wife and cousin, Alice Sherard. They hang in the saloon, originally the great parlour, which had twenty-four "Dutch chairs" around the walls in 1698 and was used for dining in state. By 1737 it had become the principal drawing room, known as the saloon from the early nineteenth century. The limewood carvings between the pictures were the work of W. G. Rogers, an authority on Grinling Gibbons, who worked at Belton in 1855–56.

Nether Lypiatt

— GLOUCESTERSHIRE —

THE ideal in miniature of a Queen Anne house, Nether Lypiatt stands high up on a ridge near Stroud overlooking the Severn Valley. To the south, a sheltered garden drops away to a beech wood; the eastern ground falls away more steeply beyond a series of low terraces to become a thickly wooded ravine. The house, wrote Osbert Sitwell in his book *Noble Essences* (1945), "is an old palace in miniature, as formal as a fugue by Bach, with its complex organisation to go with it."

Built and slated in the local limestone (the warm, grey colour of which reminded Sitwell of "guineafowl's plumage"), Nether Lypiatt has certain details that suggest the hand of a local builder or master mason. But this neat, doll's house–like box is more sophisticated than the typical Cotswolds manor house, being of the genre of polite gentry houses that sustained the classical tradition derived from Inigo Jones after the seventeenth century. The architect/builder is unknown, but he seems to have been familiar with houses such as Coleshill in Berkshire and Clarendon House in London, both by Roger Pratt. Though less grand in scale, Nether Lypiatt recalls those houses (both now demolished) with its steep, hipped roof and prominent chimneys, its raised basement and modest version of a *piano nobile*.

It was built in about 1702–05 for Charles Coxe, a judge whose wife descended from the Freame family, owners of the manor since the fourteenth century. Five bays by five, the windows have elaborately moulded architraves and would originally have all been mullioned with leaded lights (the sashes were added to keep up with fashion, probably in the mid-eighteenth century). Initially, the house stood out stark and solitary (its kitchen is in the basement), but soon after it was built, lower pavilion ranges were added to the south as counterbalancing wings, perhaps originally intended. On the left of the entrance front there was formerly just a wall, but in 1931 this was turned into another wing, adding symmetry and additional accommodation.

The plan is compact and clever, with what reads as four rooms on each of the main floors forming a U plan around an unexpectedly grand staircase and a massive central flue. Good bolection moulded panelling survives in a number of the rooms and, of the original chimneypieces, the hall has a particularly fine example carved in the Baroque style around 1730.

Over the past century, several owners have added their own layer of

[OPPOSITE] *The perfect, compact Queen Anne house, Nether Lypiatt is seen from the lane through a pair of wrought-iron gates attributed to Warren of Cambridge. Flanked by a screen of stone piers linked by wrought-iron grilles, the gates are an outstanding example of linear-patterned English metalwork of the period.*

[BELOW] *The oak-panelled study on the left of the hall. The room is seen here as it was when Nether Lypiatt was owned by Prince and Princess Michael of Kent, with a mix of furniture and paintings inherited from both sides of the family.*

interest. The house had been relegated to farm use and was virtually derelict when Corbett Woodall acquired it and commissioned the architect Percy Morley Horder to carry out the sensitive restoration of about 1920. In 1923 Gordon and Violet Woodhouse bought Nether Lypiatt, and they continued in the same vein, initiating further improvements in the spirit of Horder's restoration. The subject of a recently composed opera, Violet was the brilliant musical recitalist who lived here with two of her original *ménage à cinq*. The house became a glamorous salon, where such luminaries as Delius, Vaughan Williams, the Sitwells, Shaw, Picasso, Rodin, Ezra Pound, Wilfred Owen, and Ethel Smyth were entertained.

More recently, Nether Lypiatt was the country retreat of Prince and

Princess Michael of Kent, who bought it in 1980 and carried out a major programme of repairs and redecoration, also extending the accommodation and remodelling the garden. Princess Michael, who studied interior decorating and worked with John Fowler, chose a palette that reflected rooms of a similar date and scale in their apartment at Kensington Palace, where some of the furniture inherited from Princess Marina, Duchess of Kent, had formerly resided. These photographs show Nether Lypiatt as it was during their ownership; they sold it in 2006.

[ABOVE] *The drawing room, which extends the full width of the house but was originally two rooms, with the fireplace (its chimneypiece installed in the 1920s) on the inner wall. The wainscoting is later and simpler than that in the other rooms. The scagliola coffee table was specially made in Florence to incorporate Prince Michael of Kent's coat of arms.*

155

The Ivy

— WILTSHIRE —

ONE of the finest examples of West Country Baroque, the Ivy derives its name from the monastery of Ederose, also known as the Ivy Church, which was associated with the manor of Rowdon, to which its land belonged. The house owes its survival to its former owners, the leading landscape architects and garden designers Julian and Isobel Bannerman, who bought it as a vandalised wreck in 1981 and spent the next decade lovingly restoring it back to life and creating a glorious garden. With their inimitable verve and feeling for the period, they reinstated the series of ornate Baroque interiors, replacing decaying woodwork, introducing suitable salvaged fittings, and redecorating and furnishing the rooms to evoke the richness of the period. These photographs show the Ivy as it was when they lived here in the 1980s.

There is fabric of medieval origin in the long west range of the Ivy, which became the service wing and is now a separate house. At the end of the sixteenth century, a leading local family of clothiers called the Scotts bought the property, and they are thought to have built on the H-plan brick house that survives behind the later remodelling. A marriage settlement of 1629 provides a clue as to its date. The gables on the east front, and the steeply pitched roof and chimneystacks behind them, belong to this earlier house, as does the pair of similar gables hidden behind the segmental pediments that rise up with a swagger over the Baroque north front. Various inventories

[OPPOSITE] *The bedroom above the hall as decorated by the Bannermans, with bed-hangings of crimson moreen and walls painted the fashionable "drab" green of the Baroque period.*

[BELOW] *The north-facing entrance front, thought to have been built by the mason-architect Thomas Greenway of Widcombe. The windows, which had acquired Victorian plate glass, were remade with thick glazing bars in the early-eighteenth-century style when the house was restored in the 1980s.*

made for the Scotts during the 1600s suggest that the hall occupied the central range, with the staircase and living rooms to the east and the kitchen and other offices on the west.

So the splendid Baroque house commissioned by the lawyer John Norris after he became the owner in 1725 was not, as previously assumed, built from scratch. Instead, it encased this earlier house with a new, north-facing entrance front of beautiful Bath stone and the south range with its shell-headed doorcase, filling in the space between the cross wings to create a double-pile plan. Who designed this remodelling of about 1725–28 is not documented. However, the wealth of somewhat old-fashioned carved stone detail that enlivens the architecture suggests the hand of a local mason-architect, quite possibly the outstanding carver of Bath stone at this period, Thomas Greenway. He ran a mason's yard in the Bath parish of Widcombe, which produced an array of urns, finials, keystones with grotesque masks, and other carved stone ornament in demand all over the country. Similar details can be found on buildings by Vanbrugh, Archer, and Hawksmoor, and it is quite likely that Greenway came into contact with such architects. Widcombe Manor, also dating from around 1727, has a rich display of idiosyncratic ornament similar to that found at the Ivy—a garland of fruit and flowers over a window with a masked keystone in its round-arched moulding, for example—florid embellishments typical of a mason keen to show off his skills. The two houses also share the same relationship of staircase to hall. Greenway may have been involved in the rebuilding of Nonsuch House at nearby Bromham for John Norris's father, William, in ca. 1700, although it is much plainer than his later, more elaborate Baroque work. John Norris inherited Nonsuch in 1730, but he probably acquired and remodelled the Ivy a few years earlier in order to provide a grander residence suited to his political and social ambitions: he became an MP in 1713 and was an active Tory and opponent of Sir Robert Walpole.

Norris died in 1752; in 1758 the Ivy was sold to John Stone, and shortly thereafter to several subsequent owners, one of whom must have built on the pair of double-height bay windows on the south front and the single-storey ones on the east, which are shown on a plan of 1784.

Most of the principal internal detail—such as the staircase, the drawing room panelling, and the pair of hall chimneypieces—appears to be contemporary with the 1720s remodelling. In the hall, the great arched stone doorcase opposite the front door repeats the detail of some of the external window mouldings redolent of Greenway's work, and the drawing room has pairs of giant fluted Corinthian pilasters reminiscent of the stone ones on the façade of Widcombe Manor. The identity of the joiner is not recorded, but the woodwork is of the highest quality and similar to other work by the leading Bath joiner-architect William Killigrew. He is thought to have

The south front, with the earlier west wing to the left, overlooking the garden created by Julian and Isobel Bannerman in the 1980s.

158

[OPPOSITE] *The drawing room with a view to the library. The Bannermans replaced panelling damaged in a fire that occurred in this room when the house was derelict.*

worked for the architect John Strahan at Frampton Court in Gloucestershire, where the staircase is almost identical.

The initial shock at finding so splendid a house engulfed by urban development is allayed by the skilful manner in which the Bannermans transformed the immediate setting, building high banks to protect it from the main road. They reinstated a formal entrance court bordered by lime trees, and on the south side created a Dutch-style garden, planting the grid of box-hedged beds with a profusion of old roses, sweet peas, tobacco plants, and herbs to break the formality of the design. On the east side, from where the house formerly looked out over the "Ivy Park" and water meadows to the River Avon, they dug a long canal and built Bridgeman-style terraces.

[BELOW] *The hall, showing one of its pair of elaborately carved stone chimney-pieces, which are somewhat awkwardly positioned, and the great arched stone doorcase opposite the front door, which repeats the form of some of the external window architraves.*

[OPPOSITE, CLOCKWISE FROM TOP LEFT] *A bathroom in the reinstated space of a former dressing room/closet on the south side of the house.*

A detail of the drawing room chimney-piece, which was added in the mid-to-late-eighteenth century. Curiously, the Rococo frieze with its mask of Apollo is of marble, while the mantel and sides are of carved wood.

The Blue Bedroom showing the 1720s marble chimneypiece, which was reassembled from hundreds of surviving fragments.

A spare bedroom decorated in toile de Jouy and furnished with French walnut sleigh beds.

[RIGHT] *The Blue Bedroom as redecorated by the Bannermans. The bed, with a cornice silvered in the eighteenth-century manner, has blue and silver bed-hangings to match the vibrant blue colour scheme, which was based on fragments of old paint found on the edges of the panelling.*

Castle Godwyn

— GLOUCESTERSHIRE —

THIS small country house belongs to a lively tradition of refashioning buildings in a West Country version of the English Baroque that flourished into the 1730s. Castle Godwyn's characterful façade was the work not of an architect, but of a mason/builder armed with pattern books, highly skilled at carving the pliable local limestone known as Painswick Stone. Just as in small towns all over Southern Italy, one finds modest buildings embellished by local craftsmen with a naïve but vigorously decorated façade in a regional version of the Italian Baroque, so, here in the early 1700s, many houses were remodelled in a manner known as "mason's Baroque," which is seen at its best in towns such as Bath and Frome.

Rising abruptly from a grassy terrace in a steep Cotswolds valley, Castle Godwyn belongs to the last generation of this tradition as applied to the smaller country house. Its remodelling dates from the 1730s, when the house was owned by William Townsend, a successful clothier from Painswick who lived in the nearby Elizabethan manor of Steanbridge. This was an area enriched by the wool trade, and the surrounding valleys echoed with the clatter of cloth mills, many of which had an owner who built himself a handsome country house in the regional Baroque. But Castle Godwyn was unusual among its genre in being unconnected to a mill. Known as Paradise Farm, it had been a modest farmhouse dating from the seventeenth century, with mullioned windows that are still intact on the east and west sides. Townsend probably remodelled it for one of his twelve children.

With its new façade, the house acquired a commanding presence, which elevated it to something grander than a gentleman's farmhouse, although the property was never large enough to be a self-supporting estate. Perhaps to emphasise this new status, its name was changed to Castle Godwyn, commemorating King Harold's father, Godwin, Earl of Essex, who in 1051 established a camp on the hillside above Paradys Valley.

Who was responsible for the remodelling is not documented, but a strong possibility is John Bryan, who hailed from a dynasty of local carvers. Similar details can be found in contemporary work by the Bryans in the cloth-weaving town of Painswick, where the monuments they carved in the churchyard are particularly fine. The architectural historian Tim Mowl has pointed out the similarity of Castle Godwyn's segmental pediment with that of the stone

OPPOSITE *The entrance front of Castle Godwyn was added in the "mason's Baroque" manner in the 1730s. The sundial is inscribed with an epigram from Martial that alludes to the manufacturing interests of the owner: "He is aware that the fair days flit away and leave us / the days that are squandered by us and charged to our accounts." The porch is Edwardian.*

reredos in the south aisle of Painswick church, which John Bryan carved in 1743 when he was still very young. It is a form that reoccurs on the curious stone chimneypiece in the drawing room at Castle Godwyn, where a curved pediment is set inside a triangular one, with carved foliage in the fashionable Rococo style of the period decorating the space in between.

An alternative name possibly associated with the work at Castle Godwyn is John Strahan, a professional surveyor from Bristol. He is believed to have designed the central block of nearby Painswick House, and he built other houses in Bath and Bristol with similar detail. Whoever was responsible clearly delighted in the enrichment of classical ornament. Deeply modelled

[OPPOSITE ABOVE] *The panelled hall, with some of the present owners' collection of English furniture. The fireplace survives from the seventeenth-century house.*

[OPPOSITE BELOW] *A pair of fluted Doric columns leads to the handsome oak staircase installed by William Townsend. This was sensitively altered in 1903–04 with the addition of arched Doric screens on the first floor to link the landing with the rooms behind.*

[LEFT] *The drawing room, with its curious stone chimneypiece, described by Tim Mowl as "a little masterpiece of oddity."*

mouldings enliven the composition and create the illusion of extra height. Windows with architraves and keystones, carved panels, rusticated quoins, and the heavily profiled cornice and segmental pediment were composed and carved with the individuality of a craftsman working by eye and instinct rather than the precision of an architect using measured drawings.

In 1755, a year after Townsend's death, Castle Godwyn was advertised for sale as "A modr-built [*sic*] house, with Four Rooms on a Floor, fit for a Gentleman . . . pleasantly situated on the Side of a Hill, which affords beautiful Prospects." It was bought by William Lake, "an opulent merchant largely engaged in the silk trade" who had emigrated from America. He put in the Gothic sash windows, lengthening the lower ones so that their rooms opened into the landscape in the Regency manner, and built a castellated tower at the back for a library and study.

Following a long period of tenancy, the house was bought in 1903 by Col. Sir Francis Howard, who added the pedimented porch and remodelled parts of the interior to designs by F. W. Waller. He also restored elements of the seventeenth-century house, reviving the Cotswolds vernacular with a subtle Arts & Crafts layer.

Kelmarsh Hall

— NORTHAMPTONSHIRE —

THIS elegant Palladian house in the heart of the Shires was built to the design of James Gibbs for William Hanbury, a typical Georgian squire who inherited the estate in 1722 when he was just seventeen. Soon afterwards Hanbury demolished his great-great-grandfather's Jacobean mansion, and in 1728 Gibbs published a design for its replacement in his *Book of Architecture*, describing it as "now building."

The setting of Kelmarsh in the rolling country of the Pytchley hunt was to have a particular significance for several future occupants. One was Ronald Tree, joint master of the Pytchley from 1926, as well as MP for Market Harborough. He and his Virginian wife, Nancy, the niece of Nancy Astor, took a lease on Kelmarsh and did much to revive the house and gardens. Nancy Lancaster, as she would later come to be best known, bought the famous decorating firm Colefax and Fowler in 1944 and worked in partnership with John Fowler. Her redecoration and alterations at Kelmarsh helped to establish her reputation as a key figure in the world of country house decorating, and they contribute a significant twentieth-century chapter to the history of the house.

Unusually for this largely limestone county, Kelmarsh was built of brick, its builder, Francis Smith of Warwick, being paid £376-14s-6d for "fitting

[OPPOSITE] *The stair hall, with original plasterwork that is slightly richer than that in the hall. The bust, recently commissioned by the Kelmarsh Board of Trustees, is of the architect James Gibbs.*

[BELOW] *The east entrance front, showing the right-hand of the two flanking pavilions, which originally housed the kitchen quarters. The house as built was a modified version of James Gibbs's design, published in 1728; thirty-five of his drawings for Kelmarsh are now in the RIBA Drawings Collection.*

out the Hall" between 1735 and 1737. As constructed, it differed from Gibbs's published design in being less elaborate, with reticent stone detail. The balancing wings, connected by elegant quadrant links, are unusually large in proportion to the main block, the principal façades of which are similar in their treatment.

Three more generations of William Hanburys left their mark at Kelmarsh. The second, who inherited estates in Herefordshire through his mother, married in 1776 and sometime soon after employed James Wyatt to carry out a number of changes. These included an Adam-style scheme for the saloon, of which the fine stucco frieze survives. Wyatt also replaced the original coved ceiling with a flat one and introduced the tall arched recesses, inset roundels, and veneered doors with delicately carved architraves. Surviving correspondence suggests that around 1770 Hanbury was buying Italian and French furniture for the saloon; the marble chimneypiece came a little later, around 1800.

Hanbury's son, the M P for Northampton who became Lord Bateman, built the mansard roof in the early 1800s. But Lord Bateman's son, the fourth William Hanbury, came into other estates through his wife and sold Kelmarsh in 1865. The new owner, Christopher Naylor, was master of the Pytchley from 1872 to 1874. He added a ballroom and more convenient kitchens in 1873, using as his architect James Kellaway Colling, who also rebuilt the Kelmarsh church.

In 1902 Naylor's daughters, who were keen horsewomen and friends with the Prince of Wales, sold Kelmarsh to the Lancashire tycoon G. G.

[OPPOSITE] *The hall, entered directly from the front door (just out of the picture to the left), is lit by first-floor windows on the east front, which are echoed on the opposite wall by internal windows lighting a bedroom passage. Nancy Lancaster's colour scheme—a soft apricot copied from Rushbrooke Hall in Suffolk, with the stucco decoration picked out in off-white—is said to have been repainted by John Fowler in the 1950s, using a slightly deeper shade of pink.*

[RIGHT] *A pair of Imari jars that held gold dust taken by Admiral Anson from the Manila galleon in 1743. They are seen against Chinese export wallpaper, which Nancy Lancaster brought here from Kimberley Hall to decorate the room on the left of the front door, the most intact survival of her era at Kelmarsh.*

Lancaster. It was his son, Col. Claude (Jubie) Lancaster, who rented it to Ronald and Nancy Tree, and later married Nancy. The Trees lived here until 1933, when they bought Ditchley, another house by Gibbs famously redecorated by Nancy. They divorced in 1947, and Nancy returned to Kelmarsh having married Jubie Lancaster the following year. (That marriage lasted until 1953, after which she lived at Haseley Court in Oxfordshire until her death in 1994).

Nancy Lancaster did much to revive the Georgian character of Kelmarsh, which had been suppressed during the nineteenth century, when most of the original fittings and decorations were removed. Two exceptions were the hall and stair hall, which survived largely as designed by Gibbs, albeit filled with antlers and Oriental armour. Nancy's redecoration of this great central hall, which she furnished as a sitting room, demonstrated her skill at using colour and texture to make a visual impact. In 1928 she employed the architect Paul Phipps (Joyce Grenfell's father) to make some improvements, and she also converted the original drawing room (latterly the billiard room) into a library, and the ballroom into a dining room, using William Adams Delano as her architect. She repainted the saloon a cool olive grey, which Phipps called "the soul of blue," and introduced a monochrome palette of "old whites" to her bedroom, which she described as "like ice with a glint of gold." Nancy also remodelled the gardens and landscape at Kelmarsh with the help of Geoffrey Jellicoe and Norah Lindsay.

After his divorce, Col. Lancaster employed Sir Albert Richardson to reverse certain nineteenth-century alterations and, in 1965–56, to construct the unbuilt gate lodges that Wyatt had designed in 1778, evidence for which was provided by a recently discovered drawing. Lancaster's sister Valencia inherited Kelmarsh in 1977, and five years later she set up the Kelmarsh Trust, which now manages the estate. One recent addition has been a collection of furniture by leading eighteenth-century cabinetmakers, commissioned by the 6th Earl of Coventry for Croome Court in Worcestershire. This furniture, some of it to designs by Robert Adam, had rarely been seen since the 1940s and lacked a home, while Kelmarsh had become underfurnished. The union of the two has resulted in a handsome marriage.

[BELOW] *The dining room on the right of the hall, which Nancy Lancaster converted into a schoolroom for her two sons. It was connected by the quadrant link to new nursery quarters in the north pavilion.*

Trafalgar

— WILTSHIRE —

RESTRAINED and somewhat stern on the outside, yet bursting with Rococo plasterwork within, Trafalgar survives mercifully intact despite the vicissitudes of the past century, which saw it change hands in rapid succession and lose most of its land. Today the house combines a private and commercial role as the present owner's home and a venue for weddings and other events.

Dating from the early 1730s, it was renamed Trafalgar in 1814, when the estate was given to the clergyman William Nelson in honour of the famous naval victory that cost his brother Admiral Horatio Nelson his life. Before that the house was called Standlynch, the name of the old manor house which stood on a site close to the River Avon. The present house was built to a design by John James for Sir Peter Vandeput, a merchant of Flemish origin who had made money in the city and bought Standlynch in 1725. The attribution to James, who had succeeded Wren as Surveyor to the Fabric of St. Paul's in 1723, was confirmed only in the 1980s, when Sally Jeffery discovered a letter of 1725 stating that "Mr James is ye sefarr" [surveyor], and also a statement by James himself that he designed Standlynch, contained in the records of a court case that he brought against Vandeput in 1736 in a dispute over payment.

Vandeput's house, which was built in 1731–34, consisted of just the seven-bay central block. It has Gibbsian window surrounds and a strong cornice and quoins, but is otherwise so economic of ornament that it relies for effect on the contrast of warm red brick and pale stone dressings. The west front, which overlooks the garden terrace, has a three-bay pedimented centrepiece and is slightly less austere, but as a whole the composition reflects James's belief that "the Beautys of Architecture may consist with the greatest plainness of the structure."

In an article published in *Country Life* in 1997, Giles Worsley drew attention to the unusual character of Vandeput's house. Although on first impression it must always have resembled a country house, sited high above the river in a park laid out by Charles Bridgeman, in other respects it seems to have had more in common with an eighteenth-century villa, albeit one located far from the city. Worsley points out that the estate was relatively small at the time, and that Vandeput lived in Richmond and was not a

[OPPOSITE] *The portico, added by Nicholas Revett soon after 1766, is an important early example of the Greek Revival in England. The Greek Doric columns were modelled on those on the Temple of Apollo on Delos.*

[OVERLEAF] *The main front, facing east. The central block was built to the design of John James in 1731–34; the wings were added in 1766 by John Wood the younger of Bath, using his earlier work at Buckland House in Berkshire as a model. William Butterfield, who restored the local church, added the balustrade in front of the house in 1859.*

country squire. He argues that he built the house as a villa: a country escape in which to relax and entertain friends.

This theory is supported by the arrangement of the interior, which is dominated by one large reception room—the hall—a great cube at the centre of the house articulated by giant pilasters and smothered in Rococo plasterwork. The identity of the stuccoist is not known, but the work is similar to that found in various houses nearby, notably the dining room at Little Durnford Manor dating from around 1740.

There is an imposing staircase, but otherwise the rooms are relatively few and simply decorated. Indeed, perhaps because Vandeput realised that there would not be enough bedrooms owing to the amount of space taken up by the double-height central hall, he decided to add an extra floor in 1732, an afterthought made as work neared completion, which raised the house to three storeys.

Vandeput died in 1748, and his son sold the estate to a William Young, who in turn sold it in 1766 to Henry Dawkins, a wealthy landowner. Dawkins had returned in 1759 from Jamaica, where he owned land. He inherited two English properties and in 1767 bought the nearby manors of Tichbourne and Moore, thereby greatly enlarging the estate. As an MP married to an earl's daughter and with a large family, he clearly desired a more commodious and convenient house, and so commissioned John Wood the younger of Bath to add the pair of wings, leaving the existing house at the centre largely unaltered. Attached by corridor links and deeper than they are wide, these substantial additions of 1766 provided a considerable amount of extra space, accommodating a new kitchen, domestic offices, and octagonal first-floor dining room on the south side, and a family wing on the north.

Dawkins then commissioned Nicholas Revett, coproducer with James

Stuart of *The Antiquities of Athens*, to design certain architectural and decorative elements for his newly enlarged house. Revett was responsible for the magnificent, urn-topped portico on the east front, with its pairs of semi-fluted Greek Doric columns modelled on the Temple of Apollo on Delos, and for the impressive Doric vestibule in the north wing, both significant examples of work in the early Greek Revival style. He also designed a doorcase and ceiling, the unusual Serlian windows on the north and south wings with iron columns on the interior, and bookcases and a chimney-piece for the library. This juxtaposition of a Greek Revival layer with the earlier Rococo ornament is a particularly idiosyncratic feature of Trafalgar. The other important legacy of Dawkins's artistic input is the painted music room, something more usually associated with Baroque interiors. The splendid cycle of paintings representing an allegory of the arts is attributed to Giovanni Battista Cipriani.

It was following Dawkins's death in 1814 that the Crown bought the estate to give on behalf of a grateful nation to Admiral Nelson's brother, along with an earldom and an annual pension of £5,000 in perpetuity on condition that it was not sold. The Nelsons lived here until the mid-twentieth century, but, although they expanded the estate considerably through marriage and judicious property purchases, and the third, fourth and fifth earls all lived to ripe old ages, they did little else to leave their mark. The agricultural depression took its toll, and by 1945 the estate had been reduced to half its former size and was in a poor state.

The sale of Trafalgar in 1948 precipitated a steady decline in the house's fortunes, during which it changed hands repeatedly and lost nearly all its remaining land. The future seemed uncertain as owners came and went and the threat of insensitive development loomed. It is a familiar story: a house with decaying fabric sitting empty much of the time, with no land to support it and the property market in recession.

Then, in 1995, Michael Wade took it on and set about implementing his ambitious plans. The north wing is still derelict, but, like so many country houses today, Trafalgar has found a new role by diversifying into a more commercial market. It is a solution that can enable a house on this scale to earn its keep, while ensuring that its historic fabric remains intact.

[OPPOSITE] *The music room, decorated with an allegory of the arts painted by Giovanni Battista Cipriani in the later eighteenth century.*

[LEFT] *The west front; the attic storey was not part of the original design but was added during the course of building work.*

[OVERLEAF] *Details from the Rococo plasterwork in the sitting room and hall. The cubic hall, the one large space in the house, was conceived as a place to impress and entertain. The identity of the stuccoist is not known, but the work is similar to examples in a number of local houses. Set into the overmantel in the hall is a bust of Inigo Jones, for whom John James had declared his admiration in 1711.*

Farnborough Hall
— WARWICKSHIRE —

IT is said that William Holbech was pining for a lost love when he went to Italy as a young man in the early 1730s. He spent about two years there, certainly visiting Rome and Florence, and returning via Venice in 1734. The work that he commissioned on his return to remodel the family seat is a testament to the powerful impact made by the Grand Tour on the artistic sensibilities of a young English squire.

Farnborough Hall had been bought by his grandfather, Ambrose Holbech, in 1683. His son, also William, succeeded him in 1701 and rebuilt the west front, probably using the well-known builders William and Francis Smith of Warwick. He also created the present staircase, incorporating his arms with those of his wife into the ceiling plasterwork. When William Holbech Jr. inherited Farnborough in 1717, the seventeenth-century house formed an irregular H or U plan, with a hall at the centre flanked by ranges to the east and west.

Holbech never married, and there are no surviving documents or portraits of him, so we know little about his life and personality. But his transformation of the house and landscape at Farnborough in the 1740s suggests that he had the leanings of a gentleman amateur architect—men such as the cultivated Joseph Townsend of Honington (see p. 143), whose input into their architectural projects was considerable. He was also an early patron of the artists Canaletto and Panini. Particularly interesting is the decorative use of ancient classical busts on carved brackets and portrait medallions in the hall and over the staircase. In the hall, where this imaginative evocation of ancient Rome is counterbalanced by a contemporary view of St. Peter's in the overmantel, the marble busts are set into oval niches around the upper walls.

Holbech's structural alterations of 1749 unified the exterior of the house. They included building a new north and south front faced in richly coloured Hornton stone with contrasting grey dressings, and filling in the south-facing courtyard with the present dining room. The entrance front, which faces north, is of five bays recessed between two-bay end pavilions, with a pedimented Tuscan-columned doorway. Holbech had the entrance hall remodelled and commissioned new plasterwork and joinery of the highest quality for the interior.

[OPPOSITE] *A detail of the dining room, showing the architect's obvious feel for the architectural and decorative effects of good-quality plasterwork, executed here by William Perritt.*

[OPPOSITE] *The south front, with Holbech's saloon/dining room addition projecting slightly so as to give the room more depth, its extra height indicated by the smaller first-floor windows. The mansard roof and balustraded parapet were additions by Henry Hakewill in the Regency period.*

[THIS PAGE] *In 1742, before making any improvements to the house, Holbech began to create an extensive setting for Farnborough, which marks an important stage in the development of the Arcadian landscape. He built a long, curving terrace along the top of the ridge to provide a series of carefully composed views out over the Hanwell Valley. A series of architectural incidents in the landscape added poetic interest: an oval domed pavilion with a Tuscan loggia; a small Ionic temple; an obelisk at the far end of the terrace.*

It is not known who designed this sensitive remodelling. In an article published in *Country Life* in 1996, John Cornforth drew attention to some tantalising clues and considered some of the possibilities suggested by the links known to have existed between certain designers and craftsmen responsible for comparable work at a number of other houses at this period. Holbech's friend, the gentleman architect Sanderson Miller, is thought to have advised on and possibly designed the new north and south fronts, but another possibility is the architect John Sanderson, who was responsible for completing Kirtlington Park in Oxfordshire, where the doors he designed have the same distinctive pattern and proportions as the six panelled doors in the saloon/dining room at Farnborough. John Sanderson was also a talented designer of plasterwork, as can be seen at Langley Park in Norfolk, and had other local connections. Alternatively, the London architect William Jones might have been involved. He worked at several local houses and, in particular, supervised the construction of the octagonal saloon at Honington, where some of the plaster decoration echoes work at Farnborough. He was also involved at some of the same places as the stuccadore William Perritt, the only craftsman known for certain to have worked at Farnborough. Perritt's bill for plasterwork completed here in 1750—which included the decoration of the dining room, hall and staircase, and work in the library no longer surviving—came to a total of £434-4s-4d.

[RIGHT] *The interior of the Oval Pavilion, one of three buildings along the terrace walk that were probably designed by Sanderson Miller and built by the Warwick stonemason William Hiorns. The exuberant Rococo ornament applied to the domed ceiling is in the same style as that in the dining room.*

[OPPOSITE] *The domed skylight above the staircase dates from the 1740s but has early-nineteenth-century glass. The combination of the thick garland of flowers and monogrammed plaster ornament of the earlier ceiling, probably by the great seventeenth-century plasterer Edward Goudge, with Perritt's Rococo plasterwork, results in a wonderful fusion of styles.*

The dining room was referred to in Perritt's bill as the "saloon." This certainly fits in with the grandeur of the decoration, although it was probably also used as a dining room in the eighteenth century—the distinction between and changing uses of the principal rooms at this period are confusing. It is a remarkable early example of a room designed around a set of paintings as at Marble Hill and Castle Howard, an idea later adopted by neoclassical architects such as Robert Adam. Now replaced by copies, the four views of Venice by Canaletto and three of Rome by Panini are set high up in fixed frames of elaborate plasterwork in the manner of those at Langley Park, which were executed by Charles Stanley, who may also have

[OPPOSITE] *The entrance hall, with classical busts in oval recesses and Panini's view of St. Peter's reflecting the influence of William Holbech's trip to Rome during his Grand Tour. The wooden overmantel was probably carved in 1749 by Benjamin King of Warwick, its chimneypiece carved in the same style in stone. The pattern of the panelled stucco ceiling is repeated on the floor paving.*

worked at Honington. The plaster frames may be by a different hand to Perritt's more freely modelled Rococo ornament.

The National Trust acquired Farnborough in 1960 in a fairly early example of a house coming to the trust in lieu of death duties, with an endowment from the family. In the 1980s the trust was able to acquire the principal furnishings, including the sculpture and library books, so that Farnborough survives today as a rare example of a smaller country house still with most of its original contents in situ, and with the present generation of the family still in residence.

[LEFT] *One of the classical busts in the entrance hall.*

[RIGHT] *The dining room/saloon was decorated around a series of paintings by Canaletto and Panini.*

Claydon House

— BUCKINGHAMSHIRE —

THE surviving wing of a much larger house, Claydon represents the climax of the craze for Rococo and the chinoiserie style that swept through Britain in the mid-eighteenth century. No hint of this is suggested by the exterior, a modest Palladian composition fronted with greyish ashlar that looks out over a park laid out in 1763–66. Although conceived as an entity in its own right, this building became merely the southern pavilion of the palace built in 1757–71 by the politically ambitious Whig, Ralph, 2nd Earl Verney, to replace his Jacobean house and outdo his neighbouring rival at Stowe. When complete, this grandiose pile extended to some 256 feet, with a matching seven-bay wing at the north end housing a huge ballroom or "Egyptian Hall," and a central domed rotunda containing the saloon. Nothing of these two sections survives.

The earl's first project after inheriting in 1752 was to build the stable block, dated 1754. Thereafter, his extravagance knew no bounds. He spent recklessly on his house and a series of disastrous business ventures, which left him financially ruined and obliged to sell most of the contents in 1783 and 1784. In 1791 he died bankrupt, and the following year two-thirds of the new house were demolished.

The surviving wing, the first section to be built, contained the state rooms. Here can be seen some of the most extraordinary Georgian interiors in the country, their decoration a tour de force of eighteenth-century craftsmanship and eccentric taste. Adapted from pattern-book motifs with unbridled gusto and imagination, the Rococo ornament is not of stucco, but all of wood, carved by the brilliant woodcarver Luke Lightfoot.

Lightfoot also operated as an amateur builder and surveyor, and he was responsible for the initial building work until his dismissal in 1769. The identical north pavilion and the central block were completed after the job had been taken over by Sir Thomas Robinson, an amateur architect who thought Lightfoot "an ignorant knave, with no small spice of madness in his composition." The new hall and gallery would be "finished from the just rules of Grecian and Roman architecture" Robinson assured his client, and he brought in the stuccoist Joseph Rose (who later collaborated with Robert Adam on a number of major projects) to decorate the saloon, library, and staircase with neoclassical plasterwork. In 1771 Robinson also fell out with Lord Verney.

[OPPOSITE] *A detail of the chimney-piece in the North Hall, which was carved in the workshop of Luke Lightfoot in the 1760s.*

The plan and proportions of the principal rooms provide a Palladian framework for Lightfoot's frothing Rococo ornament. The three main rooms on the ground floor form an enfilade, the North Hall and the library on each side of the central saloon being double cubes. In the North Hall (designed as the great eating room), Lightfoot decorated with carved wood the ceiling, overmantel, overdoors, and four niches containing marble busts depicting four continents—fantastical confections crowded with birds, heads, fruit, and foliage. The busts later disappeared, to be replaced by a succession of military, sporting, and Colonial trophies, but the trust has recently had plaster copies made of a similar Italian set at Compton Verney, and the niches now look much as they did in the eighteenth century.

The library (originally the withdrawing room) is treated in a more restrained manner, with an Adam-style ceiling and doorcases with fluted Ionic columns carrying straight entablatures. But there are delicious idiosyncracies: the library steps and lectern were made from discarded fragments of Lightfoot's carvings, and the winged putti brackets in the papier-mâché frieze are surely Lightfoot's too. In the Black and White Hall, Rose's neoclassical plasterwork provides the backdrop to the delightful pattern of floriated scrolls, ears of corn, and garlanded husks climbing up the wrought-iron balustrade, so delicate that it "sings" when the staircase is in use. The stairs are a masterpiece of joinery, each step inlaid on both edges with exotic woods and ivories.

Lightfoot's woodcarving reaches its crescendo in the first-floor Chinese Room, where the chinoiserie decoration is unsurpassed. Motifs from pattern-books such as Edwards and Darly's *Chinese Designs* (1754) are transformed with outlandish fantasy for the adornment of chimneypiece and overdoors, and the pagoda-like set piece is a thing of quite extraordinary imagination and virtuosity. A starry fretwork overlaid with waves, vines, and scrolls frames an alcove originally furnished with a divan for taking tea, the breathtaking carving of which is picked out in white against a blue background.

In the nineteenth century, Claydon enjoyed a revival under the swashbuckling Sir Harry Verney, brother-in-law of Florence Nightingale. His and his son's extensive travels resulted in a fascinating collection of ethnographical curiosities coming to Claydon, and in 1893 a museum was formed within the house to display these artefacts. Many items were bequeathed to the British Museum after Sir Harry's death, but it remains one of the most atmospheric family museums to be found in any country house.

The Verney family has resided at Claydon since 1620, and there are Verneys living here still, although the building was conveyed to the National Trust in 1956. Following a careful programme of repair and restoration, the

The west elevation, which may have been derived from Isaac Ware's A Complete Body of Architecture *(1756). The southern part of a much larger building constructed in 1757–71 for the 2nd Earl Verney, this wing contained the state rooms.*

[OPPOSITE] *The saloon at the centre of the surviving block. This room has a more conventional Palladian splendour, its neoclassical stucco decoration by Joseph Rose the younger. The exuberant chimneypiece is attributed to Thomas Carter.*

[RIGHT] *The Pink Parlour, with an octagonal-glazed Venetian window and wood-carved decoration, including overdoor panels with scenes from Aesop's Fables, by Lightfoot and his workshop. The painted floorcloth is a recent introduction.*

[OPPOSITE] *One of the four niches in the North Hall with a carved surround by Luke Lightfoot and a bust representing America. The yellow and green colour scheme by John Fowler dates from 1976.*

trust brought in John Fowler, the doyen of country house decoration, to redecorate the state rooms in 1956 and again in 1976. He introduced a series of striking, original schemes, devised not as historicist re-creations, but rather to enhance the architectural and sculptural qualities of rooms long deprived of their original furniture. Fowler's work at Claydon was among his best, and the rooms have subsequently been refreshed rather than redecorated in order to preserve this interesting twentieth-century layer. With portraits, archives, and other items loaned by the Verney family on display, and many improvements and discoveries made over recent decades, Claydon's unusual atmosphere has been recaptured and the house is now much better understood.

[ABOVE] *Lightfoot's grotto-like alcove in the Chinese Room, which framed a divan or day bed for taking tea. Inside is a frieze of a tea ceremony carved in high relief, and niches to display porcelain. The present colour scheme dates to 1956 and is the work of John Fowler.*

197

Hovingham Hall

— YORKSHIRE —

Hovingham is as idiosyncratic a creation as any in this book, conceived as the result of the twin passions of its creator: horses and architecture. There are many examples in Britain of stable courtyards later converted into country houses—Studley Royal, not far away, is perhaps the grandest—but Hovingham is unique in having been conceived as a riding school and stables, only to be modified to incorporate a country house as building work progressed.

Thomas Worsley, amateur architect, professional horseman, and builder of Hovingham Hall, inherited the estate from his father in 1751. The Worsleys hailed originally from Lancashire but had settled in Yorkshire on the edge of the Vale of Pickering in about 1610. Here, in the 1680s, Thomas Worsley's grandfather, also Thomas, built a manor house near the present site, and it was through his and his son's success in forging good marriages and connections at court, acquiring more land and carrying out public duties, that the family became well established in the county.

Thomas Jr. trained at the Swiss Academy in Geneva, where he learned the science of schooling horses and was also taught draughtsmanship, for which he showed considerable talent. His deep interest in architecture was nurtured further by his peregrinations on the Continent, after which he returned to England in the 1740s. During this time, Worsley developed his architectural skills, sketching out imaginary schemes and sometimes finding the opportunity to implement his designs—a stable block for John Hutton in 1741, for instance, and a temple for his father in 1750.

When he inherited in 1751, Worsley immersed himself almost immediately in an ambitious building programme. Fortunately, many of his drawings and bills survive at Hovingham, as does his correspondence with such friends as Lord Bute, and part of his impressive collection of architecture books. These give a fascinating insight into the approach of an intelligent amateur intent on designing his own house, and they also provide an important source of information about the development of this complex building.

It is clear that Worsley's initial plan was to build a new stable block and riding school, after which he would replace the late-seventeenth-century house nearby with a new, more fashionable residence. He conceived a quadrangle in the Palladian manner, with equestrian buildings lit by Diocletian

[OPPOSITE] *Looking from the Tapestry Hall, which was built as a stable, through to the dismounting room known as the Samson Hall.*

[OVERLEAF] *The west front of Hovingham Hall, showing one of the oldest private cricket pitches in England. A south (right-hand) wing for additional stables was intended but never built.*

[LEFT] *The drawing room at the centre of the north range.*

[RIGHT] *The dining room, originally the State Bedroom, hung with family portraits. The carved chimneypiece and Corinthian columns are works of high quality by leading craftsmen with whom Worsley came into contact after he became Surveyor-General of the Office of Works in 1760.*

windows in blank arcades arranged around three sides as a handsome backdrop to a courtyard or open-air manège in which the horses would be exercised. There were other proposals too, but Worsley's father had left him with "many Thousands in debt," and he was obliged to compromise. "Pro viribus non pro votes erexit T W" reads an inscription on the house—he built according to his means not his wishes.

In 1755 Worsley abandoned the idea of creating two separate buildings and decided instead to integrate them as one. The result, though eccentric and impractical, was a handsome and imaginative solution born of a love for horses combined with a sophisticated knowledge of the classical orders and the inspiration of Italian and Greek architecture. In a design suggestive of an early Roman villa, Worsley planned to have the domestic accommodation incorporated as three pavilions: one in the centre and one each at the ends of the two wings (the southern wing was never built). The central pavilion, intended to house the state rooms, is derived from a drawing by Palladio, which was also adapted by William Kent for the Horse Guards in London of 1750.

The house has a most unconventional relationship to its village, for, unlike most English country houses, it is set not at a polite distance surrounded by parkland but stands right in the village itself, where a pedimented archway signifies the entrance. Arthur Young, visiting in 1769, described the approach: "The entrance is directly out of the street for coaches, through a

[OPPOSITE] *The Ionic Room, the architectural detail of which suggests that William Worsley was looking at Stuart and Revett's* The Antiquities of Athens *(1762–1830) when he made alterations to it in the 1830s.*

narrow passage into a large riding house, then through the anti-space of two stables and so up to the house door."

The route through these spaces is marked by a progression through the classical orders, each of which can be traced to a specific source. The riding school has pairs of Doric columns forming loggias at each end, from which guests could watch horses performing. In the Samson Hall, which opens off its far end, baseless Roman Doric columns support a fine-groined vault in what was originally intended to be a dismounting hall, modelled on Palladio's entrance halls in Vicenza. From here, one turns right to pass through the Tapestry Hall, like the Hunting Hall on the left (also originally designed as stables) vaulted over Tuscan columns, before entering the house proper in the north wing, where the Corinthian order is used in the library, dining room, and drawing room. And then there is the Ionic room at the head of the staircase, one of the first-floor state rooms in the main east range.

Another notable feature of Hovingham is the obvious delight in the textural qualities of its materials, the way stone is used with great subtlety to express the functions of the building's different parts. Thus, the entrance arch in the village leading into the riding school is set into a wall of great undressed blocks of stone, and the ground floor arcade of the original equestrian quarters is rusticated, whereas the domestic end pavilion and upper storey are of contrasting smooth ashlar.

"My neighbours visit me as an exotick out of curiosity" wrote Worsley in a letter to Lord Bute, and in 1765 his nephew, Thomas Robinson, noted: "To Hovingham, two days there were as much as were necessary and more than was agreeable.... The house he has built is very strange, he has made it uncomfortable if not uninhabitable by trying to blend his favourite amusements, the place is very fine and pleasing, but animus deficit equis [his

mind is weakened by horses]." But Worsley cared little what his neighbours thought and showed the same lack of convention in his private life. Unlike his father and grandfather, both of whom married heiresses, he chose to wed his sister's maid.

In 1760, as the interiors were being fitted up and decorated by specialists such as the leading London wallpaper supplier Thomas Bromwich, the new king, George III, appointed Lord Bute as prime minister and chose Thomas Worsley as his Surveyor-General of the Office of Works. This was a remarkable advance for a Yorkshire squire, albeit one of such refined interests, and he took it seriously, moving to London and receiving a good income. On his return to Yorkshire in 1764, work on the house was resumed, and by 1766 the Ionic Room and ballroom (unusually on the first floor, lit by a Venetian window) were complete. By now, the local craftsmen formerly employed were replaced by leading specialists—names such as the plasterer Joseph Rose and the carver Richard Lawrence, whom Worsley had encountered working in London on projects such as Somerset House.

For practical reasons, the stables were soon moved, and in 1769 Worsley filled them with statues, tapestries, and other works of art. But as illness and bereavement took their toll, his interest in the house waned and, although work continued, it remained unfinished on his death in 1778. Not until his grandson William inherited it in 1830 was anything further done. He made some sensitive alterations, mostly to the principal rooms, and demolished the old house. Since then, the only notable alteration has been the insertion of plate-glass windows. Still the home of the Worsleys, Hovingham survives today much as Thomas Worsley left it, the impressive creation of a man Horace Walpole described as "a rider of the great horse and architect."

OPPOSITE *The staircase, hung with tapestries in the 1930s, and with ornamental ironwork added to the plain iron balusters by William Worsley in the 1830s.*

ABOVE *A Corinthian capital in the dining room.*

[ABOVE LEFT] *A detail showing Worsley's subtle use of contrasting stone textures—rusticated stone versus smooth ashlar—to denote the equestrian and domestic uses of the building.*

[ABOVE RIGHT] *The view through the riding school towards the village.*

[RIGHT] *The entrance front from the village, its great undressed blocks of stone recalling the work of Giulio Romano in Mantua, and conveying Worsley's delight in the texture of masonry. The archway leads into a coffered, barrel-vaulted passage opening into the riding school.*

OPPOSITE *The Samson Hall, originally for dismounting. The finely vaulted stone roof supported on a forest of baseless Roman Doric columns gives it a feeling of an undercroft. The hall takes its name from the marble group of Samson and the Philistine by Giovanni da Bologna, which was given to Sir Thomas Worsley by George III and is now in the Victoria and Albert Museum in London.*

Wrotham Park

— HERTFORDSHIRE —

EW of the villas that ringed London in the eighteenth century still stand protected by their original landscape setting, and fewer still have remained in the hands of the family that built them. Wrotham Park, just fourteen miles from the city's centre, is a remarkable exception. Known to many as the house that featured in the 2002 film *Gosford Park*, it was built by Isaac Ware for Admiral the Honourable John Byng, who bought the estate in about 1750. Though altered and redecorated in the nineteenth century, Wrotham appears today much as Ware designed it, an important example of the English Palladian villa made fashionable by architects such as Lord Burlington. Owned by Robert Byng, it is an outstanding example of a country house still in private hands within the environs of London.

But Wrotham's early years were darkened by misfortune, for Admiral Byng was responsible for the loss of Minorca and in 1757 he was executed on the deck of HMS *Monarque* in Portsmouth Harbour. The "martyr admiral" died before his new house was finished and probably never lived here.

Ware's design for Wrotham, commissioned in 1754, was published in his influential *A Complete Body of Architecture* (1756), and also in the fifth volume of Colen Campbell's *Vitruvius Britannicus* (1771). The engravings showed the restrained symmetrical villa enlivened with Rococo touches that can still be seen today: on the entrance front, a pedimented centrepiece with a columned portico flanked by Venetian windows; on the west-facing garden front, a detached, pedimented Ionic portico approached by a pair of curving staircases. Domed octagonal pavilions were connected on each side by wings.

On the death of Admiral Byng, his nephew George Byng inherited Wrotham and probably completed the internal fitting-up. He also extended the park and improved the landscape with advice from Capability Brown in 1765. The house was built of red brick with stone dressings, but sometime before 1816 his son, a Whig MP who succeeded in 1789, rendered over the brickwork above the rusticated basement. This George Byng also raised and extended the wings and pavilions, and made other additions, such as the elegant stable block and an elaborate flower garden.

Then in 1854 another George—George Stevens Byng, who became the 2nd Earl of Strafford in 1860—inherited Wrotham and over the next two

[OPPOSITE] *Isaac Ware's Palladian villa for Admiral the Honourable John Byng. The garden front from the northwest, with its pedimented Ionic portico above a rusticated stone basement.*

[LEFT] *The stair hall, rebuilt after the fire of 1883 to the original form designed by Ware. The impressive collection of Byng family portraits includes, below the stairs, works by Sargent and de Laszlo.*

[OPPOSITE] *The east-facing entrance front showing the flanking wings and pavilions raised and extended by George Byng sometime before 1816.*

decades implemented an extensive programme of alterations. These included raising the attic storey to accommodate more bedrooms, applying short Tuscan colonnades to the connecting links on the entrance front, adding the pair of canted bays flanking the portico on the garden front, and remodelling the interior. All this work was carried out by William Cubitt & Co., collaborating in 1857 with the London firm Morant & Boyd for the upholstery and interior decoration. The earl commissioned the architect S. S. Teulon to design a Gothic clock tower in 1863 but fortunately this was never built, for it would have clashed dreadfully with the smooth symmetry of Ware's house. Teulon did, however, build the Gothic gate lodge, gates, and estate church.

In 1883 disaster struck in the form of a devastating fire, which completely gutted the house. Almost immediately, Cubitt & Co. was called in to repair the damage, and the survival of Ware's plan today owes much to the fire insurance company's insistence on a replica reconstruction. Not everybody was satisfied: Lord Strafford's daughter-in-law complained in her memoirs that he "declined to consult his heir in any way on the subject, but had nearly every fault that had existed in the old house reproduced." To exacerbate her disapproval, on his death in 1886 Lord Strafford left only the estate and important heirlooms to his son, the 3rd Earl; his fortune and all other possessions went to his widowed second wife. She and her daughters stripped the house of its furniture and all movables "down to the most homely items," such as doormats, and took it all off in eight van loads.

On moving into Wrotham, the 3rd Earl and his wife commissioned the London decorator Frederick Muntzer to re-create the Morant & Boyd schemes and brought in items from the family's London house to refurnish the rooms. The Victorian remodelling of Wrotham was particularly interesting for the way it respected the original Georgian character of the rooms. The neoclassical strain continued through to the post-fire reincarnation, so that today the interior can be regarded as a fine example of late Victorian "neo-Georgian."

Within this spectacular setting is a collection of superb quality, the majority of the valuables having mercifully been rescued from the fire. Among the paintings, most of the best examples of which were collected by George Byng who succeeded in 1789, is an outstanding collection of Old Masters, including works by Van Dyck, Murillo, and Kauffmann, and there is also an important collection of family portraits. George Byng was a regular visitor to the Paris and London auctions, and he enlarged the collections that his father had established with many treasures, including fine French furniture and Sèvres porcelain.

Many of these items have been professionally restored in recent years, and some of the principal rooms redecorated by James Finlay to the existing scheme. However, some of the objects seen in these photographs were sold by Christie's in 2004 The present owner lives in the house and hires out the principal rooms for films and private parties.

[LEFT] *A view of the dining room, which occupies the entire south end of the main floor. The walls are decorated with restrained plasterwork framing family portraits, many by Sir Francis Grant. Over the eighteenth-century chimney-piece is Field Marshal the 1st Earl of Strafford, flanked by his grandsons. The décor is wonderfully faded today, which adds greatly to the room's atmosphere.*

[OPPOSITE] *The drawing room as it was before the 2004 sale, containing George Byng's French furniture, many pieces mounted with Sèvres plaques. The ornamental plasterwork, curtains, mirrors, and upholstery introduced by Morant & Boyd in 1857 were replicated after the fire. On the right of the chimneypiece is Murillo's* Rest on the Flight into Egypt.

[LEFT] One of a pair of Rococo gilt-wood console tables with matching mirrors in the saloon, possibly part of the original eighteenth-century contents rescued from the fire.

[OPPOSITE, CLOCKWISE FROM TOP LEFT] The library, re-created after the fire as a more elaborate version of the room remodelled by George Stevens Byng in the mid-nineteenth century.

The entrance hall, faithfully reinstated in the 1880s, with family portraits and statues of Venus and Diana saved from the fire (though the latter have now been sold). The gilded table supported by ormolu dolphins was once at Malmaison.

A portrait by Thomas Hudson of Admiral the Honourable John Byng, the "martyr admiral" and builder of Wrotham Park. The gilded Rococo frame bristles with cannon, anchors, rigging, and weaponry surmounted by the mask of a sea god—references to his naval career. It is believed to have been designed by Isaac Ware and carved by Matthias Lock.

The billiard room, added along with an additional library by the 6th Earl of Strafford in 1938 and hung with some of the paintings of horses and racing subjects collected by the 2nd Earl, a keen racehorse owner and breeder.

Newby Hall

— YORKSHIRE —

Newby has an unrivalled pedigree: attributed to Sir Christopher Wren, it is best known for the outstanding neoclassical interiors that Robert Adam created between 1767 and 1774 in collaboration with some of his favourite artists and craftsmen. The house was built between 1685 and 1693 for Sir Edward Blackett, who inherited his father's coal- and lead-mining fortune and acquired the estate in 1677 (he demolished the old house in 1690).

Kip's 1707 engraving provides an excellent bird's-eye view of Blackett's new mansion and extensive formal gardens, which were much admired by contemporary visitors. Celia Fiennes, in her journal of 1697, described Newby as "the finest house I saw in Yorkshire." Daniel Defoe was the first to mention Wren's name in connection with Newby: "Sir Christopher Wren laid out the design, as well as chose the ground for him," he wrote in *A Tour Through the Whole Island of Great Britain* (1724–26). Many architectural historians have since questioned this on stylistic grounds: Christopher Hussey, writing in *Country Life* in 1937, thought Newby's design "quite jejune, the kind of thing a local master mason would produce when told of Hampton Court," although by 1967 he had changed his mind. John Cornforth, in his articles of 1979, rejected the attribution. Certainly a Yorkshire squire was not typical of Wren's clients, but we now know that the architect was in contact with Blackett, who in 1694 made a payment to "Sr. Chr. Wren's Servts." The two men also probably had dealings through the import of coal from Newcastle to London, the taxes from which financed Wren's London churches.

Blackett's red brick house, stone-quoined and with projecting corner pavilions, conformed to the Baroque manner made fashionable by Wren at Hampton Court Palace. Newby had the latest arrangement of an attic storey with a flat roof behind a balustraded parapet (since altered), and was almost certainly the first house in Yorkshire to have "sash windows on all ye 4 fronts." This use of the latest technical developments being pioneered in London by Wren and the Office of Works strengthens the claim that Wren was involved, although provincial masons must also have had a hand.

In 1748 Newby was sold to Richard Elcock Weddell, who employed John Carr of York to reorient the house. Carr remodelled the east side as the entrance front and built the pavilion wings (originally single-storey and

[OPPOSITE] *The central rotunda of the sculpture gallery looking towards the marble sarcophagus in the apsed east end, which evokes all the antique splendour of the catacombs in Rome. One of Robert Adam's most brilliant creations, the gallery retains its original arrangement of Roman pieces mixed with some copies made in the eighteenth century, when it was acceptable to heavily restore and even complete antique statuary. Adam also designed many of the pedestals, some of which conceal heating ducts. The Weddells enjoyed "elegant breakfastings" in the portico off the rotunda.*

detached). When Weddell died in 1762 he left the estate to his second son, William, a member of the Society of Dilettanti and a man of exceptional taste with a passion for collecting.

William Weddell engaged Robert Adam to redesign and decorate the principal interiors as a showcase for his treasures: paintings, furniture, and other artworks commissioned from leading artists and designers, and an outstanding collection of sculptures and other antiquities acquired during his Grand Tour. The result was a succession of neoclassical interiors that are regarded as among the finest of their date.

Adam was not, as often assumed, responsible for the architectural alterations at Newby. These were carried out by John Carr and by William Belwood, a protégé of Adam's who had worked with him at Syon House and supervised the building of Harewood from 1760. Belwood designed the east portico and raised the wings to their present height; he executed Adam's designs and did other internal work, and was responsible for the pair of gate lodges, with their theme of antiquity, and the fine stable block long attributed to Adam.

Weddell must have had a sculpture gallery in mind before he departed for Rome in 1765, for George Dance had prepared a design for "a public gallery for statues, pictures, etc." two years earlier. On his return in 1766, he consulted William Chambers but then commissioned Adam to create a suitable setting for his nineteen chest-loads of newly purchased antiquities. Using Dance's concept for the space formed by joining the south wing to the house, Adam created a grand Roman interior inspired by his sketches of Hadrian's Villa at Tivoli and other Roman ruins and catacombs, and also clearly influenced by the drawings of Clerisseau and Piranesi.

In 1767 his brief was extended to the entrance hall and other principal rooms, where he designed ceilings, friezes, and panels, harmonising and articulating the spaces with his brilliant use of colour. His favourite stuccoist,

[LEFT] *The Tapestry Room, remodelled by Adam in 1775–76 as a setting for Weddell's Gobelins tapestries, which incorporate medallions of Boucher's "Loves of the Gods" and are the only one of the six sets woven for English patrons to remain intact in their original location. Adam enriched his finely balanced design for the room with lavish gilding and festoon curtains, originally of green watered tabby. A blander palette has since been introduced to tone in with the now-faded tapestry grounds. The pair of giant French neoclassical pier tables and glasses imported from an anonymous Parisian maker are similar to designs by Neufforge; Chippendale made the seat furniture, and the painted ceiling medallions are by Zucchi.*

[OPPOSITE] *The library, designed by Adam as the dining room in 1767–69, with a smart livery of French grey, black, and buff (and, originally, a suite of Etruscan-style furniture to match). Converted to the library in 1807, it was later furnished as a sitting room. The ceiling, with a pattern of recessed and relief panels, is centred on a painted oval of Bacchus; arabesque wall panels resemble those in the dining room at Osterley. In the niche at the far end can be seen one of the original translucent alabaster vases designed to hold candles.*

Joseph Rose, modelled the plasterwork; Antonio Zucchi painted medallions and panels, and Thomas Chippendale designed furniture to the tune of £7,000, which survives in situ.

In the cool-toned entrance hall with its enriched Doric frieze, Piranesian martial trophy panels contrast effectively with the Greek Revival–style of James "Athenian" Stuart's organ case. By contrast, the drawing room created from the original entrance hall on the west front is a sumptuous Louis XV–style setting for a set of Rococo tapestries commissioned from Gobelins in 1763. The Tapestry Room is a triumph of brilliantly orchestrated detail within a coherent overall scheme, Adam's designs for ceiling, carpet, chimneypiece, and frieze all carefully coordinated and every pattern and shade chosen to tie in with the tapestries and glamorous Parisian pier tables and mirrors. Chippendale supplied the richly detailed mahogany doors, giltwood pelmets and frames, as well as the furniture—the only set still with its original fabric (tapestried by Gobelins).

The south range, overlooking the river, was replanned as the dining room and sculpture gallery, with a magnificent vista through both. Converted to a library in 1807, the former remains a room of the purest Adam style, with Rose's stucco panels and mouldings, screened apses with niches that held alabaster vases emanating candlelight, and Zucchi's inset Bacchic scenes.

In the sculpture gallery, Weddell's purchases from the Rome antiquities dealer Thomas Jenkins are brilliantly assembled to complement each other in scale and grouping, and to enhance the tripartite space of apsed chambers centred on a domed rotunda. Terminating the vista at the east end stands a great sarcophagus of Pavonazzo marble. There is no finer ensemble of Roman statuary in its own neoclassical setting in private hands in Britain.

Following Weddell's death in the Roman Baths in the Strand in 1792, Newby passed to his cousin, Thomas Robinson, the 3rd Lord Grantham and later Earl de Grey. An amateur architect, Robinson created the library, orangery, and Regency dining room; his descendants still own the house today.

After a long period of decline, Newby has undergone a resurgence and is a family home again. Richard and Lucinda Compton, who took over in 1999, have continued the work begun in the 1970s by his parents, who redecorated the house, radically replanned the gardens, and dramatically increased visitor numbers. Lucinda, a conservator, has cleaned and repaired the marbles herself as part of an important conservation programme. Newby now attracts 140,000 visitors a year and is also hired out for weddings and other events.

[ABOVE] *A detail of the decoration in the library. The room was redecorated in the late 1970s, using evidence taken from paint scrapes and Adam's coloured drawings. The chimneypiece dates from 1769.*

[BELOW] *Grotesque decoration in the Circular Dressing Room, which, according to tradition, was painted by William Weddell's wife, Elizabeth Ramsden, a friend of Sir Joshua Reynolds.*

[OPPOSITE] *The south bedroom, with a bed by Thomas Chippendale and a fine eighteenth-century serpentine chest of drawers in the manner of his workshop. The principal bedrooms at Newby were opened to the public for the first time in 1978.*

THE ENGLISH COUNTRY HOUSE AND ITS COLLECTIONS

THE nineteenth-century American writer Washington Irving wrote of the joys of civilisation as encountered in the home of an English gentleman: "He manages to collect around him all the conveniences and elegancies of polite life, and to banish its restraints. His country seat abounds with every requisite, either for studious retirement, tasteful gratification, or rural exercise. Books, paintings, music, horses, dogs, and sporting implements of all kinds, are at hand."

❦ The extraordinary refinement in the provision of these requisites was the result of centuries-old habits of patronage and connoisseurship, of a self-conscious attempt to make country houses centres of civilisation. As H. G. Wells noted in the early twentieth century, the contribution of the minor nobility and gentry to the world of culture was considerable: "within these households, behind their screen of deer park and park walls and sheltered service, men could talk, think, and write at their leisure." From the Middle Ages, country houses had a public face, however, and often served as territorial law courts and as county hotels for royalty and other people of rank. It is important to recognise that their collections were not developed just for private enjoyment; visiting other country houses was a long-established social convention amongst the gentry from the seventeenth century onwards.

❦ This is shown by the observant diaries of the 1680s–90s of Celia Fiennes; for instance, at Burghley in Lincolnshire: "you go thence into parlours dineing rooms drawing roomes and bed-chambers, one leading out of another at least 20 that were very large and lofty and most delicately painted on the top, each roome differing, very fine Carving in the mantelpieces and very fine paint in pictures, but they were all without Garments, that was the only fault, the immodesty of the Pictures especially in my Lords apartment; the bed chamber was furnish'd very rich the tapestry was all blew Silke and rich gold thread."

❦ The contents of an English country house have perhaps two key threads: objects of use—without which a country house could not function as a centre of elite family life—and objects of display—representing the culture and dynastic status of the house. The latter often refer specifically to the real (and occasionally romanticised) lineage of the family, or to its royal or military service. This is particularly so with portraits—heirlooms bound to pass with the house by inheritance, be they Jacobean full-lengths, or the works of Van Dyck in the seventeenth century (as at Wilton House, page 477)) or Gainsborough from the eighteenth (as at Althorp, page 27), which are frequently a dominant element of a country house picture collection.

❦ In the Middle Ages, the furnishings of the English country house were by necessity movables. Most landowners might expect to move regularly from one house to another. Tables would still have been largely demountable trestle tables that could be brought out as required. William Harrison, in his 1577 *Description of England,* wrote of the "abundance of arras, rich hangings of tapestry, silver vessel" that could be seen in "nobleman's houses." Tapestries were eminently movable and often depicted hunting scenes, or scenes from classical mythology. Much of the seat furniture was in native oak.

❦ By the mid-sixteenth century, elaborately carved chairs with arms began to appear in the furnishing of great halls, used by the lord of the manor or his principal guest. On the walls, armorial banners and displays (or "trophies") of arms and amour were exhibited (although many that we see today are the result of judicious nineteenth-century collecting). Tester beds had finely carved posts and headboards, and were hung with curtains for warmth. By the end of the seventeenth century, the principal furnishings had become highly decorative, made of walnut, inlaid with marquetry or lacquered ("Japanned"). Upholstered furniture was also immensely popular, most notably in the high-backed armchair and state bed, which provided opportunities for the display of costly textiles and decorative trimming.

❦ In the 1720s the influence of French and Italian examples also brought elaborate gilded pieces to the English house, for instance the glorious pier tables designed by Lord Burlington's protégé, William Kent, for Houghton Hall in Norfolk (see page 476). The sheer elegance and variety of the work of mid-eighteenth-century cabinetmakers and upholsterers is illustrated in Thomas Chippendale's famous

Gentleman and Cabinetmaker's Director, which was published in 1754 and provided patterns that could be imitated anywhere in the world.

❦ Few English country houses are untouched by Italy, many paintings and works of art collected in the mid-to-late eighteenth century reflecting the well-established conventions of the Grand Tour, the period of travel through Europe and particularly to Rome which represented the final part of the education of a gentleman. Classical sculpture and Romantic landscapes dotted with classical ruins, and portraits painted by artists based in Rome, become a defining feature of the country house interior (as at Holkham Hall), as did the ubiquitous use of classical iconography in the details of furnishing and interior decoration.

❦ The neoclassical style of furniture of the later eighteenth century, associated with Robert Adam and others, culminated in the familiar and comfortable solidity of furniture of the Regency period (the equivalent of the Federal in the United States), often made in exotic woods such as mahogany imported from the West Indies. Stout dining room furniture was provided for many houses, reflecting changing habits, with the large dining room becoming a permanent feature. Suites of bedroom furniture were also supplied for country house weekends revolving around shooting parties and race meetings. Such weekends became an element of English life admired around the world, reaching a peak of reputation in the Edwardian era.

❦ While in the late seventeenth and eighteenth centuries the furniture of grander apartments was often formally arranged around the edge of rooms, paintings and inventories show that the early-nineteenth-century country house drawing room had a noticeably more informal arrangement, with sofas and smaller tables arranged in the middle of the room, and intended for comfortable amusements. This was part of what country house historian John Cornforth dubbed "the quest for comfort," which defined the arrangement of rooms for the next century. It led to the plush, crowded interiors of the late Victorian country house, as seen in early *Country Life* articles.

❡ Ornate Gothic revival furniture, such as that at Eastnor Castle in Herefordshire, was the result of a new nationalism and historicism in English taste. By the end of the nineteenth century, this fascination for the Old English past led to an interest in original furniture of the Tudor and Jacobean age, and thus began the taste for collecting genuine antiques, which shaped the presentation of country house collections in the twentieth century. This is exemplified by the collections of Tudor and Stuart paintings and oak furniture at Parham in Sussex, formed in the 1920s and '30s.

❡ Country house collections were often enriched from surprising sources, such as the spending power of American heiresses married by British aristocrats, or the transferral of furnishings from London to country houses as the social habit of maintaining a grand town house declined in the early twentieth century. The interwar years were also a period of renewed interest in high Georgian culture, which set a standard of taste and elegance that still pertains today.

❡ The political and economic upheavals of the twentieth century have, perhaps, played their part in emphasising the attractions of surviving country house collections. Sir Ernest Gowers wrote in the 1940s about death duties leading to the dramatic dispersal of the contents of country houses. He compared it to the dissolution of the monasteries and called for the protection of this heritage: "an embodiment of our history and traditions, a monument to the creative geniuses of our ancestors and the graceful serenity of their civilisation." The National Trust, founded to preserve landscapes in the public interest, had also been extended in 1935 to embrace country houses and their collections. It now preserves three hundred such houses, many with their original contents.

❡ There are still thousands of country houses in private family hands that play a vital role in preserving the graceful serenity of their, and our, civilisation (the collections of many were celebrated in the great 1986 exhibition *Treasure Houses of Britain*, held at the National Gallery of Art, in Washington). From Chatsworth in Derbyshire (see page 474) at the grandest end of the scale, to small manor houses such as Eyam Hall in Derbyshire—which has passed in an unbroken line for three hundred years—and Mapperton in Dorset (see page 479)—which became the repository of an ancient family collection only in the 1950s—they are enjoyed by millions of visitors. England is extraordinarily rich in such houses. Their diverse and diverting collections reflect the history and taste of both individual families and of the nation.

Pages 223 and 229: Royal Crescent, ca. 1775,
Hamilton Weston Wallpapers

Heaton Hall

— LANCASHIRE —

EATON Hall was James Wyatt's first major country house, and this neoclassical masterpiece is arguably his most important. Wyatt, a member of the great architectural dynasty, had found early success through his rebuilding of the Pantheon in London, which opened to wide acclaim when he was just twenty-six, in 1772. That same year, at the Royal Academy, he exhibited his designs for the remodelling of Heaton Hall. Payments recorded in the accounts for 1773 indicate that his brother, Samuel, with whom he was in partnership until 1774, was involved at Heaton as clerk of works, while James masterminded the designs.

The house that Sir Thomas Egerton, later 1st Earl of Wilton, had inherited in 1756 at the age of seven was a plain, three-storey brick building remodelled in the 1680s. His decision to refashion it on a grander scale coincided with his marriage in 1769 to his cousin, the heiress Eleanor Assheton, who had family connections with the Curzons of Kedleston, where Samuel Wyatt had worked from 1759 to 1768, and with the Curzons of Hagley, for whom James Wyatt designed an octagonal drawing room in 1771. (James also worked for Eleanor's brother-in-law at Gunton in Norfolk in 1770.) Already a fashionable architect, James now had the opportunity through new, young clients to put into practice certain ideas that challenged those of his rival, Adam, whose fussier decorative treatment he was also adept at imitating. Wyatt could master any style, and his genius as a designer can be seen in the range and variety of his work, from the Georgian Gothic to the "antique." His designs for Heaton are the key to his early development of a classical idiom.

What he created here was really a grand villa with wings. The house is entered through a portico on the pedimented north front, but it is the ashlar-faced south elevation that is Wyatt's masterpiece. Restrained in its decoration, with capitals and relief panels of crisply moulded Coade stone, it has a satisfying sense of balance combined with Picturesque movement. The centre is dominated by a broad domed bow—a recurring feature of Wyatt's classical houses—between Venetian windows, flanked by straight, colonnaded links to projecting octagonal pavilions. These house the library (completed by Lewis Wyatt in 1823) and kitchen, and contribute to the beautifully articulated rhythm of the whole composition, which proved highly influential.

[OPPOSITE] *The staircase, described by John Cornforth in* Country Life *as forming "a fulcrum around which everything appears to revolve in a way that is novel in a country house." Starting as one flight and then branching into two, it has an elegant balustrade of iron, lead, and brass, as well as tripod lamp standards based on one discovered in Herculaneum.*

Inside, the space and decoration are handled with a similar sense of control and aesthetic unity, and the early development of Wyatt's distinctive vocabulary can be detected, for example, in his inventive capitals and ceilings. The use of Graeco-Roman detailing, strong colours, and lavish marble and scagliola elements played an important part in his development of a Regency classical style. The plan, too, is significant, for this was Wyatt's first country house to have an enfilade of state rooms on the ground floor.

After the relative austerity of the shallow, apse-ended hall, the imperial

staircase rising up to three landing galleries screened by Corinthian columns comes as an unexpected thrill. With a cast-iron girder replacing the need for supporting columns below, this glamorous set piece fills the whole centre of the house with a sense of spatial drama comparable to designs by Sir William Chambers, the master of powerful staircases.

The central bowed room houses the saloon, entered through a screen of columns—another typical Wyatt arrangement more commonly found in his halls and dining rooms. Complete by 1778, it was probably used until 1789 as the music room; lyres feature in the friezes. The long walls are unadorned, setting off elaborate plasterwork by Joseph Rose II, which includes reliefs over the fireplaces based on engravings from von Stosch's *Gemmae Antiquae* of 1724. Grisaille overdoors, and, in the dining room, painted ovals, achieve a similar decorative effect. The saloon's present colour scheme dates from the 1980s.

The dining room has an apsed sideboard recess at its inner end furnished with three specially designed serving tables reminiscent of Adam's dining room at Kedleston. The room is balanced to the east by what must originally have been a drawing room, with plasterwork of the highest quality and a distinctly feminine style of decoration. Now the billiard room, it has a cycle of paintings after subjects from Ovid by Michael Novosielski, a Polish painter whom Wyatt had used at the Pantheon. The room is furnished with a billiard table supplied to Heaton by Gillow in 1771 (before the present house was built); a room in the west wing may originally have been intended to be the billiard room.

The grand staircase leads up to the climax of the house: the mirrored Cupola Room over the saloon, with Biaggio Rebecca's gilded and painted "Pompeian"-style decoration enriching walls, pilasters, and the domed ceiling.

This decoration is well preserved, although the background colour scheme is somewhat out of balance with Rebecca's work, and not as it would have been in 1775.

Egerton's fortune escalated on the profits of coal mining, and he filled the house with furniture by leading makers, such as Gillow, and Ince and Mayhew, and works of art acquired on trips abroad. His lifelong interest in music culminated in celebrating the completion of Samuel Wyatt's music room with an inaugural performance of Handel's *Acis and Galatea* in 1789. The bedroom ranges on the northeast were added in the 1820s by Lewis Wyatt to accommodate guests during the Heaton Park races, which were established by the 2nd Earl in 1827 and later succeeded by the Aintree races.

Unlike the majority of houses in this book, Heaton Hall has lost its original contents and long been out of private ownership, having been sold by the 5th Earl to the Manchester Corporation in 1902. As a result, the rooms feel somewhat museum-like, and William Emes's Brownian landscape has changed (though £10 million has been spent recently to restore its early nineteenth-century appearance). But Wyatt's masterpiece can still be appreciated despite the fact that it stands in the midst of what for more than a century has been a municipal country park.

[OPPOSITE] *The Cupola Room, designed in the mid-1770s as a boudoir for the dowager Lady Egerton, whose palm-tree bedroom and dressing room were en suite. The room was fitted out with a circular carpet, a set of gold and white painted chairs supplied by Caleb Jeacock in 1777, and torchères. It was painted in a style reminiscent of Adam's Etruscan Room at Osterley by the Italian decorative artist Biaggio Rebecca, who worked for Adam at Kedleston and Harewood. The present background colour scheme is not original.*

[RIGHT] *A watercolour of 1802 by William Marshall Craig, showing the south front of Heaton Hall in its landscape setting.*

[LEFT] *The saloon, its 1980s redecoration informed by a sketch for the ceiling by Sir Thomas Egerton. It is unlikely that the room would have been gilded in 1778, as gilding was then out of fashion, but it probably was a decade later, when gilding was once again in vogue. None of the furniture is original to the room.*

[OPPOSITE, CLOCKWISE FROM TOP LEFT] *A capital in the saloon. Notice the lyre motif in the freize; the room was probably originally used as the music room.*

An enriched door case with double mahogany doors—a dominating feature of the music room, where it is situated on the west wall with Samuel Green's organ facing it at the other end.

A detail of the saloon ceiling pattern designed by James Wyatt.

The apse in the dining room, inspired, along with Wyatt's design of the three serving tables, by Adam's dining room at Kedleston. The oval medallions of bacchantes were painted by Biaggio Rebecca.

Beckside House

— LANCASHIRE —

SHELTERED by a woodland garden on the edge of the small, fellside village of Barbon, Beckside exemplifies that rich English tradition of modest-scaled provincial gentleman's houses built by skilled local craftsmen familiar with the popular builders' pattern books of the day. Some are plain and polite, but many, like Beckside, have florid embellishments in plaster, carved stone, or wood—somewhat old-fashioned for their date but infused with a distinctive regional character and style. Further south, modest-scaled Georgian houses of this quality are quite common, but here on the edge of the fells in the northern county of Lancashire, Beckside is a rarity, of particular interest for the survival of so many original fittings. Notable, too, is the exemplary restoration carried out in the 1990s. This included the addition of the two pedimented wings, which balance the main block and are thought to have been originally intended.

Once part of a medieval manor, the land on which Beckside stands was acquired in the eighteenth century by a local family named Turner, who built the house in 1767. They sold it to the Gibsons in 1859, and it was from that family that the present owner bought it in 1989. Although not documented, the exceptionally high quality of the woodwork suggests that Beckside is almost certainly the work of the local joiner turned architect, John Hird of Cartmel. Hird's hallmarks included the pattern resembling a St. Andrew's cross stretched between quatrefoil heads that decorates panels on the elliptical arch in the hall and elsewhere in the house, and can be seen on the gateposts at nearby Witherslack Church, where he worked in 1768. Other idiosyncratic carved details redolent of provincial craftsmanship include the rustic version of an egg-and-dart moulding seen around the front doorcase and on the drawing-room chimneypiece.

The south-facing entrance front is well proportioned, with a certain architectural pretension, but there is a charming naïveté about the overall composition, which is not as symmetrical as it at first appears and includes stone-mullioned windows. The spirited doorcase is richly carved but old-fashioned for its date, based on a design in James Gibbs's *Book of Architecture* (1728).

We know from details of buildings with which Hird was certainly involved—Leighton Hall near Lancaster, for example—that he subscribed

[OPPOSITE] *The front doorcase, with chunky egg-and-dart–moulded architrave, foliated frieze, and modillioned pediment supported on bold decorated consoles, was based on a design in James Gibbs's* Book of Architecture *(1728).*

[OVERLEAF] *Beckside House is a rare survival of an eighteenth-century Lancashire gentleman's house, built of stone rubble, lime-rendered, and washed in the local tradition. Standing shoulder-on to the open hill, it is sheltered by a woodland garden that drops down to the Barbon beck. This photograph was taken in 1998, before the left-hand wing was added to achieve a Georgian-style symmetry.*

[LEFT] The view from the staircase hall to the entrance. The pattern in the wooden panels of the arch is a characteristic detail by Hird that reoccurs in other places.

[RIGHT] The unusual built-in china cupboard in the original dining room (now the drawing room) with Gothick glazed doors.

to publications such as James Paine's *Plans . . . of Noblemen and Gentlemen's Houses* (1767). At Beckside, his familiarity with Batty Langley's fashionable pattern books is evident in the design of the stair balusters (unusually, the main staircase ascends all the way to the attic floor) and the chimneypieces, notably those in the drawing room (originally the dining room) and guest bedroom (originally the first-floor drawing room).

By 1989 the house had been empty for more than two decades and was nearly derelict. But it remained in a remarkably unaltered state, probably because for much of the past two centuries it had been let out to tenants, and the present owner has been able to gently repair the existing fabric, and even to bring the old kitchen back into use. The new wings, designed by the local architect Michael Bottomley from an initial idea sketched out by the artist Glynn Boyd Harte, house a library on one side and boot room on the other. Each has a Venetian window with characteristic Gothick glazing in the manner of similar wings by Hird, such as at Abbot Hall near Kendal. Conceived in the spirit of the eighteenth-century classical vernacular, they represent the best sort of gentle, unpretentious accretion to a historic building.

[OPPOSITE, CLOCKWISE FROM TOP LEFT] The view from the hall through the eating room to the library in the new wing, which was designed by Michael Bottomley.

The drawing room on the left of the hall, originally the dining room.

The eating room, with a carved chimney-piece probably taken from a pattern-book design.

Berrington Hall

— HEREFORDSHIRE —

A PROPERTY of the National Trust since 1957, Berrington is the perfect ensemble: a handsome Georgian house and courtyard of domestic offices set in a landscape laid out by Capability Brown, with panoramic views of Wales and the Black Mountains. The controlled severity of Henry Holland's exterior hides the colour and elegance of his exquisite interiors in the French neoclassical taste, to which an overlay of Edwardian decoration and more recent input by the trust have added layers that are generally sympathetic and restore certain elements of the original composition.

Berrington has a significant place in the history of this border country, which was dominated by the Harleys, an old Herefordshire family with seats at Brampton Bryan and Eyford. Thomas Harley, a younger son of the 3rd Earl of Oxford and Mortimer, married an heiress and went to the city, where he was Lord Mayor of London in 1768. He acquired wealth and prominence as a banker, merchant, government contractor, and politician, and in 1775 returned to the country to buy the Berrington estate and become the local MP.

From 1778 Harley employed Capability Brown, who designed the site and grounds for his new house. The task of architect was handed to Henry Holland, Brown's thirty-three-year-old son-in-law, who was shortly to become the Prince of Wales's architect at Carlton House. Although Holland did not visit France until 1785, he was already pioneering the plainer French neoclassical style that became fashionable from the 1770s. His designs for Berrington Hall and its triumphal-arch gate lodge, with their sense of geometry and external restraint, have strong Continental overtones. The exterior of the house, built of reddish sandstone, is dominated by a huge portico with four Ionic columns framing a wide central bay, above which is a pediment pierced by a segmental lunette.

Behind the house, the service courtyard encloses three ranges originally connected by quadrant links, approached through a pedimented archway in the Palladian manner. Here are the laundry, kitchen offices, and a tiled dairy, which Lady Sykes of Sledmere described in 1796 in an unpublished journal as "furnished with two sets of china milk bowls, one of foreign coloured, the other of English blue and white."

[OPPOSITE] *The library, with grisaille roundels in garlanded surrounds creating a very French effect. The colour scheme belongs to Lord Cawley's redecoration of ca. 1908.*

[OVERLEAF] *The Palladian-style service court, aranged around three sides of a courtyard at the rear of the house.*

Visiting Berrington in 1784, Lord Torrington found it "gay, just finish'd and furnish'd in all the modern elegance . . . throughout a scene of elegance and refinement." The enrichment of the principal rooms to a more elaborate degree than originally intended coincided with the marriage in 1781 of Harley's favourite daughter, Anne, to the eldest son of Admiral Lord Rodney.

The principal rooms are arranged around three sides of the main and secondary staircases, which rise up through the centre of the house in a geometrical plan similar to Holland's design for Claremont in Surrey. Lit from above by a glazed dome, the staircase hall is a masterly achievement, compact yet spatially dramatic. Exciting Piranesian effects are created by the distortion of the axis, the perspective of two superimposed coffered arches—a smaller one set inside a great supporting span—opposite the void of the staircase, and the contrast of light and shade. The eye is drawn up to the colourful screens of scagliola columns and pilasters around the stairwell and between the landing and galleries.

The vestibule, known as the Marble Hall, lies at the centre of the main enfilade, flanked by the drawing room and library. Its circular, domelike ceiling on four pendentives and shallow segmental arches is redolent of John Soane, who was an assistant in Holland's office until 1778 and involved at Claremont, where the hall is very similar. The doorcases and overdoors, with their trophies in plaster roundels and arrangement of mouldings and corner

[LEFT] *The library, with pedimented bookcases and wall decoration designed by Holland to resemble classical façades, and a ceiling almost the same as one at Claremont in Surrey. Lord Rodney turned it into a billiard room, but it was reinstated in the early 1900s by Lord Cawley, who filled it with books bought at the sale of Heaton Hall.*

[BELOW] *The entrance front, with its giant Ionic portico and widely spaced entrance bay with an oddly narrow and elongated doorway. Originally the frieze was decorated with the Harley coat of arms, but it became so decayed that Lord Cawley replaced it with the present acanthus pattern.*

rosettes, show the influence of French decoration of a generation earlier, suggesting that Holland was looking at books such as Neufforge's *Recueil Elémentaire d'Architecture* of 1757. Little is known of his use of colour, but it is likely that the original decorative scheme would have been plainer, probably in shades of stone and white and ungilded, which would have tied in better with the architectural elements. Berrington was redecorated in the early twentieth century, and it is the colour schemes of that period, skilfully painted and gilded, that the trust has carefully preserved.

The drawing room has its original gilt pelmets and curtains, pier glasses surmounted by framed panels decorated with light sprays and garlands, and a marble chimneypiece flanked by caryatids very similar to one Holland had made for Claremont. The panelling is later—in 1796 Lady Sykes noted that "the room and furniture deserved better hangings, being only papered with a four-penny paper, or some paltry stuff." She also mentioned "the chairs in Chenille composed of bunches of Flowers, all different, and from Mrs Wright's patterns by the Miss Harleys extremely fine. The housekeeper lamented they could not prevent gentlemen sitting down on the chairs, tho' there are a second set for use!" Today the room is furnished with a bequest of eighteenth-century French furniture, clocks, and other pieces. The "gilt ceiling" referred to by Lady Sykes is one of Holland's most elaborate, with plasterwork, possibly by William Pearce, featuring putti with sea horses, and painted medallions attributed to the Italian decorative artist Biaggio

Rebecca, who worked for Adam on several projects. Indeed, this ceiling is more in the spirit of Adam's earlier style than Holland's spare, French-inspired neoclassicism.

The blue grisaille roundels over the doors and mirrors in the library, and the tablets in its frieze and over the chimneypiece, are also attributed to Rebecca, as are the portrait medallions of men of letters in the ceiling. Thomas Harley, whose great-grandfather, the 1st Earl of Oxford and Mortimer, created the finest private library in Britain, had his own book collection here, but it was sold by the 7th Lord Rodney, and the room was turned into a billiard room.

The dining room commemorates the Rodney connection, with paintings by Thomas Luny of the admiral's victorious sea battles. On Harley's death in 1804, the 2nd Lord Rodney succeeded, but the 7th Lord Rodney gambled away much of the inheritance and in 1901 Berrington had to be sold. It was bought by the future 1st Lord Cawley, a Lancashire cotton tycoon who had made his money selling patent black dye on the death of Queen Victoria. The Cawleys redecorated the house and reinstated the library.

Berrington passed to the National Trust in 1957, although Lady Cawley remained in residence until her death at the age of one hundred in 1978. The trust has carried out many repairs and improvements, including the removal of an ugly Edwardian water tower, the replanting of the walled garden, and the restoration of the parkland and Victorian gardens.

Cronkhill

— SHROPSHIRE —

VIEWED across the Severn valley, to where it stands looking down over the river to Wroxeter and the Wrekin, Cronkhill might be a Tuscan farmhouse or a building in a Claudian landscape. Designed by John Nash in 1802 for Francis Walford, the 2nd Lord Berwick's agent on his Attingham estate, it represents a significant landmark in the story of the smaller English country house.

Cronkhill was conceived as a *villa rustica*, and its informal composition of shallow-roofed, stuccoed ranges, arcaded loggia, and round tower played a key role in the development of Picturesque design. Nash had probably met Richard Payne Knight and was certainly familiar with his theories. He had experimented with Picturesque massing and asymmetry in some of his earlier villas, but his adoption of the Italianate vernacular style for Cronkhill, and the way he grouped the house with its model farm to create a Picturesque ensemble, were entirely new to English domestic architecture.

Nash was probably introduced to Lord Berwick through his partnership with Humphry Repton, who between 1797 and 1801 was redesigning the landscape at Attingham Park. After the partnership ended in acrimony in 1800, Nash set up in independent practice, becoming one of the most fashionable architects of the day. A favourite of the Prince Regent, he was best known for designing villas and country houses; Lord Berwick continued to employ him, both on his Mayfair house and at Attingham.

The first design for Cronkhill was shown in a perspective view by George Stanley Repton at the Royal Academy in 1802. Work started about a year later, and the house was complete by 1808. The plan is a development of one Nash devised for his Welsh houses of the 1790s. Informal and modestly scaled, it comprises three ground-floor reception rooms and a sequence of porch, outer hall, and stair hall, with a curving staircase rising to the first-floor bedrooms, all plainly decorated in the neoclassical style.

This innovative villa/farm complex became a model for other rustic villas conceived as Romantic expressions of the Virgilian ideal during the great age of agricultural improvement. Cronkhill's design was also to influence the development of the suburban villa, which Nash himself, through his houses at London's Regents Park, was instrumental in pioneering.

[OPPOSITE] *Cronkhill, John Nash's pioneering Italianate villa, or ferme ornée, was intended as an eye-catcher visible from Lord Berwick's Attingham House and park in the Severn valley. It is viewed here from the east.*

[ABOVE] *The main staircase ascending from the hall, with the library beyond.*

[BELOW] *A view of the octagonal drawing room, which has a bow window at the base of the round tower.*

[OPPOSITE] *A detail of the dining room chimneypiece.*

Angeston Grange

— GLOUCESTERSHIRE —

ANGESTON Grange, a romantic, rambling *cottage orné* in the manner of Jeffry Wyatt's Endsleigh in Devon, is a perfect expression of the Picturesque ideal. Looking down over the Uley valley, it stands dramatically elevated on a south-facing hillside, from where it both enhances and commands the glorious view.

The house was built in about 1811 for Nathaniel Lloyd, a cloth manufacturer. Although the architect is not recorded, it is quite possibly an early work by George Repton, son of the celebrated Humphry Repton, who designed the landscape at Endsleigh. Certainly the way Angeston Grange relates so well to its setting suggests the hand of somebody familiar with the work of landscape designers. George Repton was apprenticed to John Nash at the time, and worked at Blaise Hamlet in Somerset, where the almshouses have similar pattern-book detailing to Angeston Grange, with its decorative bargeboarded gables, neo-Tudor chimneys, and rustic verandah. Repton also worked on a number of other buildings in the county, including the Ridge, a neighbouring cloth manufacturer's house, since demolished.

[OPPOSITE] *Dramatically sited above the Uley valley, Angeston Grange was designed in the romantic Regency cottage style known as cottage orné both as an eye-catcher and as the chief residence of a working cloth mill.*

[BELOW] *The drawing room, one of the original rooms, was extended in 1874 for John Hamlyn Borrer.*

Unlike Endsleigh, which was built in 1809 as a shooting box for the 6th Duke of Bedford, Angeston Grange's romantic appearance disguised the fact that it was originally attached to a working cloth mill—unique for a house sited so spectacularly as an eye-catcher in the landscape. The house is deceptive, too, in being only one-room deep: this, and the way its gabled ranges angle around the face of the hillside, give a false impression of size, and impart a certain stage set–like quality. It is almost as if the house has been designed as a screen to distract attention from the owner's industrial business, while at the same time making a stirring visual statement.

In 1826 Lloyd went bankrupt, and Angeston Grange was later owned by John Hamlyn Borrer, who extended it in a similar style in 1874 (originally the ground-floor reception rooms had comprised just a dining room, billiard room, and library). The interior plan reflects the changing axis of the building, at the hub of which is an octagonal stairwell with an elegant cantilevered staircase.

[OPPOSITE] *The garden front, its decorative bargeboarded gables, Neo-Tudor chimneys, and rustic veranda typical of the sort of pattern-book detailing employed by Humphry Repton's son, George Repton, who may have designed the house.*

[RIGHT] *The elegant cantilevered staircase in an octagonal stairwell at the hub of the house.*

257

Arbury Hall

— WARWICKSHIRE —

ARBURY Hall is arguably one of England's finest early Gothic revival houses, though less famous than Horace Walpole's Strawberry Hill. Begun in 1748 and not finished until more than fifty years later, the Gothicising of Arbury represented a lifetime's commitment on the part of its owner, Sir Roger Newdigate, whose complex personality is reflected in the house. Although he involved several different architects, Newdigate produced accomplished architectural drawings himself, and his close involvement in the project resulted in a remarkable stylistic unity and consistency of finesse.

The family had owned the estate since 1586, and Newdigate succeeded in 1734. The existing house, built on the site of an Augustinian priory, was a courtyard-plan complex of ca. 1580, but he swept most of this away, keeping little but the long first-floor gallery, which he Gothicised and treated as a museum, retaining some original features and the chimneypiece from the former great hall.

The first rooms to be remodelled were a dressing room and the library. The south front of Arbury is symmetrical, with a pair of two-storey bow windows mirroring each other at either end. These were built eight years apart, probably with input from Newdigate's neighbour, Sanderson Miller, whose own Radway Grange featured similar "Gothick" bows of 1746–48, built to his design. The earlier of the two at Arbury, completed in 1752, lights the library at the west end, the interior of which was being "fitted up" in 1755 by the mason-architect William Hiorn, who also worked at Radway. With its ogee-arched bookcases set within panels of late Perpendicular-style tracery, this room echoes the library at Strawberry Hill, which had been completed the previous year.

Newdigate then engaged Henry Keene, surveyor to Westminster Abbey, who supervised the fitting out of the drawing room at the other end of the south front in 1762–63. This remarkable room is smothered in a lacework of crocketted ogee-patterned panels, which incorporate full-length portraits at intervals along the walls, and, on the barrel-vaulted ceiling, painted coats of arms. (The panelling continues transversely across the ceiling in the manner of the vestibule to Henry VII's chapel in Oxford.) Newdigate had a set of new Gothic furniture made for this room.

[OPPOSITE] *The saloon, with its great east-facing bow window, richly decorated by the plasterers William Hanwell, G. Higham, and Robert Hodgson in 1786. The room was furnished with contemporary Italian furniture and paintings.*

After an interlude of about six years, during which owner and architect were engaged with projects in Oxford, Keene returned around 1770 to oversee the remodelling of the former great hall into Arbury's most spectacular Gothic space: the double-height dining room, with a billowing fan vault, canopied niches, and a tomblike canopy over the fireplace. Newdigate had the original external wall replaced with a Gothic screen to his own design, beyond which the room projects as an aisled bay lit by the three huge windows at the centre of the south front. He had acquired some plaster casts of classical sculptures in Italy, which he set into the Gothic niches, possibly believing that the unity of Gothic and classical art through the moral absolutes they expressed was more important than any differences of style.

After Keene's death in 1776, Newdigate designed many of the alterations himself, collaborating on structural work with builder-architect and quarry owner Henry Couchman of Warwick. Couchman was responsible for the battlements on the south front and for constructing the east façade, with its principal room—the saloon. Here, the playful design of the fan vaults and the great bow window frothing with stucco decoration were derived from Henry VII's chapel at Westminster Abbey. The saloon was "in the same style of florid pointed Gothic as the dining-room, but more elaborate in its tracery, which was like petrified lace-work picked out with delicate and varied colouring," wrote George Eliot in one of the stories published in her *Scenes of Clerical Life* (1857). Eliot's father had been agent to the estate, and she knew Arbury well. She described the house in intimate detail in several atmospheric passages of *Mr. Gilfil's Love-Story*, in which it features as the fictional Cheverel Manor. The saloon retains one of the few surviving original decorative schemes: Joseph Alcott's scagliola work, based on the colours of the marble-topped tables bought by Newdigate in Italy.

One room left unchanged was the chapel, where wonderful classical plasterwork and panelling survives from 1678, introduced shortly after Christopher Wren supplied designs for the stable doorway. Perhaps Newdigate felt it was still relatively up to date—it is important to remember that he thought of Arbury as a modern house; he was not Gothicising it purely for antiquarian reasons. Nor was he simply indulging in the frivolity of a fashionable Rococo-Gothic restyling. To Newdigate—scholarly, pious, hard working, and political minded—Gothic stood for the ancient authority that underpinned the constitution and the church, and Arbury was therefore a symbol of his political and religious ideals. Perhaps, too, it helped to reconcile the inherent inconsistencies of a man who was loyal to the Crown and the Church of England, but also a secret sympathiser of the Jacobites and the Church of Rome (as the three stained-glass roundels above the dining room arcade, with their symbols of the exiled Stuarts, attest).

Newdigate died in 1806, and Arbury has been little altered since then. In the 1950s the house was threatened with destruction owing to the National Coal Board's plans to mine underneath it, but fortunately it was given a reprieve in 1954. Today the house is the home of Newdigate's direct descendant, the 4th Viscount Daventry.

[LEFT] *A detail of the saloon plasterwork and scagliola columns.*

[OPPOSITE] *Arbury Hall from the south. The bows (library on left completed 1752; drawing room on right of 1760) are very similar to ones by Sanderson Miller at his own home, Radway Grange. Between them, the dining room is lit by the three Gothic windows in the centre.*

Views of the dining room, which George Eliot described in Mr. Gilgil's Love-Story as having "aerial curves and cream-coloured fretwork touched with gold." Sir Roger displayed casts of classical statues acquired in Florence and Rome in the delicate Gothic niches.

[ABOVE LEFT] A cast of the Capitoline Museum's relief of sleeping Endymion above a classical frieze from a sarcophagus above the sideboard recess

[ABOVE RIGHT] Cupid and Psyche over the chimneypiece, with Apollino on the left and, on the far left, The Dancing Faun. These last two were on show in the Tribuna of the Uffizi.

[RIGHT] Celestial Venus on the right of the chimneypiece, and some of the superb collection of early portraits now hung in the dining room.

[OPPOSITE] The drawing room, its "ceiling heavy with carving and blazonry" (George Eliot). The chimney-piece canopy designed by Henry Keene was modelled on Aymer de Valence's tomb in Westminster Abbey. It was carved in 1764 by amateur sculptor and neighbouring squire Richard Hayward of Weston Hall, for the price of £90.

Renishaw Hall

— DERBYSHIRE —

RELATIVELY few country houses remain in the hands of the family that built them, but happily the Sitwells still own Renishaw after nearly four hundred years, for it is impossible to contemplate it without them. The house exudes the unorthodox enthusiasms, cultivated tastes, and eccentricities of one of the more extraordinary scions of the English aristocracy, and in particular of the inimitable Sir George Sitwell (1860–1943). The idiosyncracies of this hybrid pile overlooking the Rother Valley not only reflect the personalities of its patrons but also helped to shape the characters and output of their offspring, notably Sir George's three children: the celebrated aesthetes and writers Edith, Osbert, and Sacheverell Sitwell.

Associated with the area since 1301, the family acquired the present site near Sheffield around 1600. It was here, in about 1625, that George Sitwell built a Jacobean manor house with a three-storey centrepiece that can still be seen on the garden front. The plan took the conventional form of a hall with a great parlour to the east (now the library, still with its original ribbed plaster ceiling incorporating animal heads in its design) and on the floor above, the great chamber, now a drawing room.

The first significant alterations were carried out around 1729 by Francis Sitwell, a scholarly bachelor who became "immensely rich" through coal and iron. He replaced the old mullioned windows with fashionable sashes and elaborated the gardens, which his forbear "Mr. Justice" George Sitwell had planted with lime and elm avenues in ca. 1698. With Francis Sitwell's death in 1753, the direct male line was broken and Renishaw passed to a cousin and then to his sister's son, Francis Hurt Sitwell, who employed John Platt to carry out some alterations. These included the creation of the first-floor drawing room in 1777.

Francis Hurt Sitwell died in 1793, and it was his son, Sitwell Sitwell, the first baronet, who employed the Sheffield architect Joseph Badger to extend the house in 1793–1808. This remodelling transformed Renishaw into the long, rambling edifice we see today, a Regency Gothic confection of dark Derbyshire sandstone mixing castellated parapets and Georgian sash windows. On the north side, a new entrance hall and Gothic porch filled in the area between the original cross wings.

[OPPOSITE] *The drawing room of 1803, with a fine chimneypiece by William Chambers of ca. 1772, its classical frieze possibly by Joseph Wilton. Sir Sitwell Sitwell bought it from Marlborough House (now Albany) in London in 1802 for the new drawing room he was creating at Renishaw.*

[OVERLEAF] *The south front, which looks down over terraces and a lake to the valley of the Rother. From 1887 Sir George Sitwell carried out a masterly re-creation of the Jacobean gardens, reintroducing topiary, wide green allees, Baroque statuary, and a new pool.*

[OPPOSITE] *The view of the ballroom from the anteroom, the latter originally used as a billiard room but remodelled to its present rather formal appearance by Lutyens in 1909. Dominating the ballroom is Salvator Rosa's* Belisarius in Disgrace *in an ornate frame by William Kent. Some of the exotic carved and decorated Italian Baroque pieces acquired by the eccentric Italophile Sir George Sitwell can also be seen, including one of two Venetian Rococo chairs attributed to Brustolon, which bear the arms of Doge Marc'Antonio Giustinian (d. 1688).*

[ABOVE] *The drawing room, with its rich blend of English and Italian pieces, a Regency gilt bronze colza-oil chandelier, and two of the three tapestries in this room from the set of five by Judocus de Vos acquired by Sir Sitwell Sitwell on a trip to France in 1802. The painted floor by Jane and Paul Czianski dates from 1988 and was modelled on the floor of the state bedroom at the Pavlovsk Palace in St. Petersburg.*

Sir Sitwell was a Regency buck, a friend of the Prince Regent, and a leading sportsman with a celebrated stud. His enjoyment of life is reflected in an undated letter reminding a friend to come over for "coursing, dining, whisting, drinking, sleeping," and he created a series of suitably elegant neoclassical rooms at Renishaw in which to entertain. The Adam-style dining room in the west wing was completed in 1793; then came the east wing with the great drawing room of 1803 and the ballroom of 1808, interconnected by an anteroom which served as a billiard room. Sir Sitwell spent lavishly on furniture and fittings. He also built new stables and a Gothic temple, and transformed the old gardens as landscaped pleasure grounds. After his death at the age of just forty-one in 1811, Renishaw went through a decline in the hands of his son, Sir George Sitwell, who lost much of the family fortune.

During the minority of Sir George's grandson and namesake, who inherited Renishaw in 1862 at the age of two, the estate recovered from bankruptcy thanks to the careful management of his widowed mother. In the autobiography of his son, Osbert, Sir George's reputation as one of England's

most eccentric aristocrats is affirmed. He is portrayed as domineering and difficult; his wife, Lady Ida, as "irresponsible, sensual, and extravagant."

But Sir George was fascinated by history, architecture, and design, and in particular Italian sixteenth- and seventeenth-century art and gardens, which he pursued with great devotion. The interior of Renishaw was already dramatised by the juxtaposition of intimate Jacobean and grandly scaled Regency interiors; now a new, exotic element was introduced with Sir George's eclectic acquisitions, the decorative effect of which Osbert Lancaster would later describe as "Curzon Street Baroque." This concentration of grand Italian Baroque pieces, unusual for the turn of the nineteenth century, was intended to heighten the senses. The objects obviously appealed to Sir George for aesthetic reasons, but they also helped to fill impossibly large rooms. He furnished the ballroom as a sitting room and in 1909 had the billiard room remodelled as its anteroom, to Lutyens's rather formal design. But Sir George's greatest legacy at Renishaw was his re-creation of the Jacobean gardens, with new terraces, topiary, allees, and a pool.

[LEFT] *The ballroom, which Sir George Sitwell turned into a sitting room in 1906. On the left of the door is one of three ornate seventeenth-century Italian cabinets on stands, between a pair of enormous candlesticks said to have come from Lucca Cathedral.*

[OPPOSITE] *The dining room, with its distinctive apsed sideboard recess and Adam-style decoration, was added by Joseph Badger for Sir Sitwell Sitwell in 1793. Christopher Hussey, writing in* Country Life *in 1938, described the walls as retaining "their original colour, a light Pompeian red, described in the accounts as pink."*

The numerous pieces of ornately carved Italian Baroque furniture that he introduced, along with the sumptuous Brussels tapestries in the drawing room and ballroom, must have had a strong effect on his son Sacheverell, whose *Southern Baroque Art* of 1924 remained one of the most influential books on its subject for years. The writings of Edith and Osbert were also influenced by growing up at Renishaw, the atmosphere of which is vividly captured in Osbert's autobiography. They knew all the literary and artistic figures of their day, many of whom were regular visitors to Renishaw. Cecil Beaton's famous photographic portraits of the family capture the Baroque flavour of their surroundings in the 1930s.

Osbert, who with his brother promoted avant-garde art and mixed it boldly with decorative Venetian furniture, inherited his father's eclectic eye; some of the more theatrical pieces at Renishaw were his acquisitions. In 1965 he passed the estate on to his nephew, the late Sir Reresby Sitwell, who with his wife, Penelope, brought the house into the twenty-first century. In addition to an extensive programme of repairs and modernisation, they redecorated all the rooms, introducing colours evocative of the Jacobean period and carefully redisplaying many paintings and objects. Lady Sitwell designed new curtains and pelmets, and embroidered new seat covers herself. They further improved the gardens re-created by Sir Reresby's grandfather and opened them to the public. A performing arts museum, restaurant, and art gallery have given the Regency stable block a new lease of life.

[ABOVE] *John Singer Sargent's celebrated portrait of Sir George and Lady Ida Sitwell and their children, Edith, Osbert, and Sacheverell, in 1900. Seen in the picture is the famous inlaid Chippendale commode that stands just below the painting in the drawing room. This may be the one that was supplied in the 1770s to Melbourne House (now Albany) in London, and sold along with the rest of the contents in 1802, although Sitwell family tradition holds that it has been at Renishaw since the 1760s. Its companion piece is at Harewood in Yorkshire.*

[OPPOSITE] *The Sitwells' friend John Piper was a regular visitor, and many of his paintings can be seen at Renishaw, including this one over the hall fireplace depicting Venice, on which his signature appears.*

Knepp Castle

— SUSSEX —

KNEPP Castle on the Sussex Weald is an inspiring example of a country house that has overcome the vicissitudes of the past century to be revived and refreshed in the hands of a new generation. When in 1985 the present owner, Charles Burrell, inherited it from his grandfather, the house had become dour and fusty—"reminiscent," he says, "of an abandoned boarding school." Since then, he and his wife, Isabella (daughter of Michael Tree, who owned Colefax and Fowler and whose mother was the famous decorator Nancy Lancaster), have redecorated the house with panache and restored important elements of the landscape.

Knepp was one of a pair of houses designed by John Nash for two brothers, Sir Charles and Walter Burrell. Viewed from the south, Knepp possesses something of the appearance of a toy fort or stage set: its symmetrical front, punctuated by thin, octagonal turrets and fringed with crenellations, seems rather two-dimensional. But a series of long service wings transforms the composition into a Picturesque grouping of castellated ranges that sit well in the landscape—a model of the Regency "castle" style. It was Nash's skill at relating architecture to its setting that was his strength, rather than any scholarly attention to detail, and his informal-looking arrangement of wings at Knepp give it not only a Romantic, castle-like appeal, but also a false impression of size.

Knepp's landscape, originally a medieval deer park, was redesigned as a park in the manner of Repton from 1806. The lake, although smaller now than in 1835, when it was described as "the most extensive piece of water south of the river Thames," is still a remarkable feature, appearing to flow past the house like a great river. Across the water stands a fragment of old Knepp Castle, probably a medieval hunting lodge, an eye-catcher in the landscape recorded by various antiquarian artists.

The Burrells' roots in this area go back to the fifteenth century, when they were vicars and farmers, and later ironmasters. But it was Sir Merrik Burrell, a prosperous merchant and governor of the Bank of England, who reestablished the family's presence here in the mid-eighteenth century, buying back former Burrell lands. On his death, he left the West Grinstead estate to his great nephew, Walter, whose house by Nash (demolished in 1964) was less flamboyant and built a few years earlier than his brother's at Knepp. When

[OPPOSITE] *A Regency Gothic "castle" designed by John Nash in ca. 1808, Knepp stands in a medieval deer park relandscaped from 1806 in the manner of Humphry Repton.*

Walter died childless in 1831, West Grinstead was amalgamated with Knepp to form a five-thousand-acre estate.

Sir Charles Burrell inherited Knepp in 1803 on the death of their mother, Sophia, whose father, Sir Charles Raymond, had acquired it in 1787, though he never actually lived here. The sales particulars described it as extending to 1,600 acres and having, near the upper end of its eighty-acre "fish pond," an "elevated and beautiful spot, to build a house upon."

By 1808 Nash had already designed "a mansion house and offices" for Sir Charles, which he estimated would cost "about £13,500 exclusive of the charge of the architect and carriage of materials." This estimate was to prove rather unreliable: by the time the interior had been decorated and the stables and other works completed, the bill came to £33,000. The house was built of stuccoed brick, the works superintended by Alexander Kyffin. George Repton, son of the great landscape designer Humphry Repton and Nash's assistant at the time, may have been involved, though this is not documented.

The apparently casual grouping of ranges that characterises Knepp's exterior belies the fluency of Nash's geometric plan. Typically, he composed a sequence of well-lit rooms opening off a long, central axis comprising a hexagonal vestibule and an octagonal hall and lobby, with an impressive can-tilevered circular staircase ascending a tower with a great Gothic window at the far end.

[LEFT] *The drawing room, redecorated by the present owners with a double damask wallpaper from Colefax & Fowler.*

[RIGHT] *The oak-panelled library, with a new chimneypiece carved by Emily Young to a design by Chester Jones, whose wife, Sandy Jones, designed the carpet. Among the paintings are works by Augustus John, Graham Sutherland, and Lucian Freud.*

In 1904 a devastating fire reduced all but the servants' quarters to a roof-less shell. Among the contents destroyed was a prized collection of Holbeins and Van Dycks, a fine library, and rare manuscripts. Remarkably for the time, a full and faithful rebuilding was carried out almost immediately, using a firm called Longleys. Jacksons reproduced Nash's decorative plasterwork from surviving fragments, so that the rooms still have their charming Gothick friezes and cornices decorated with tiny groin vaults and cusped interlacing tracery. The architects A. W. Blomfield & Sons introduced a number of Arts & Crafts elements, notably in the library; some rooms acquired panelling and chimneypieces salvaged from other houses.

The recent redecoration was carried out in collaboration with Chester Jones, who designed some of the furniture, wallpaper, and a chimneypiece, and introduced playful elements, such as grained niches with trompe l'oeil Gothic panels, and overscaled theatrical curtains. Nash's loosely Gothic rooms have lent themselves well to the stylish blend of bold contemporary colours and fabrics and older pieces and antiques, including some from Ditchley Park in Oxfordshire, Nancy Lancaster's former home.

The Burrells removed a lot of Edwardian furniture and introduced a fine collection of twentieth-century paintings and other pieces inherited by Isabella. From the kitchen, which they made out of a passage and butler's pantry, a new bay window opens onto a lawn shaded by a Cedar of Lebanon, where the reclining chairs are copies of the original Art Deco sun-loungers at Mirador, Nancy Lancaster's family plantation house in Virginia.

Meanwhile, in the park, the Burrells have established a herd of fallow deer and created a thriving polo club. And on their 3,500-acre estate they have introduced a revolutionary approach to estate management that aims to reverse the effects of recent decades of intensive agriculture by reestablishing a natural wilderness. They have removed nearly all the fences so that deer, cows, and pigs now roam free, and re-created wildflower meadows in the parkland, so that the birds, butterflies, animals, and plants that were once common here are now returning.

The entrance front from the south. Nash disguised the symmetry by adding long, thin service wings, which contribute to the picturesque grouping and give a false impression of size.

Eastnor Castle

— HEREFORDSHIRE —

O F all the country houses that have succeeded in casting off the shackles of twentieth-century decline, Eastnor stands out triumphant. Revived to its Victorian splendour and sustained by new-found commercial success, it is a model of how a grand country house can be made to earn its keep in the twenty-first century.

Built in 1812–20 by Robert Smirke, architect of the British Museum, this fortress-style mansion is an arresting vision rising above wooded pleasure grounds on the edge of the Malvern hills. Although Smirke's public work is associated with the Greek revival, he built a number of country houses in the Regency castle manner, and Eastnor is the best surviving example. It retains the symmetry of a classical house, but the roofline breaks out in a series of castellated towers to create the romantic silhouette of a medieval fort, alleviating the austerity of Smirke's neo-Norman architecture. So grandly overscaled, Eastnor must have seemed a fitting showpiece for the autocratic John Somers Cocks, the future 1st Earl Somers, who built it to replace his former ancestral seat with the profits of the development of Somers Town in London and the sale proceeds of another estate.

[OPPOSITE] *A detail of the Gothic drawing room ceiling, showing Augustus Welby Northmore Pugin's heraldic decoration.*

[BELOW] *A vision of crenellated towers designed to resemble a medieval Welsh border fortress, Eastnor Castle dates from the early nineteenth century, when aristocratic confidence was at its peak. The deer park that flanks its Victorian pleasure grounds was originally part of the Royal Chase of Malvern.*

The building takes the form of a rectangular main block with quatre-foil-shaped corner towers and a taller central "keep." A castellated gatehouse affords access to a forecourt, from which the house is entered, somewhat incongruously, through a porte cochère. The principal rooms and stair hall open off the top-lit great hall, which is sixty feet high and leads at its far end into an octagonal saloon overlooking the garden terraces and lake. Smirke's decoration of these rooms was plain and somewhat stark, and when the 2nd Earl inherited Eastnor in 1841, he initiated a programme of enrichment in the High Victorian style.

The most remarkable legacy of this period, carried out in 1849–50, was the redecoration of the drawing room by the great Gothic revival architect A. W. N. Pugin. With the exception of the Palace of Westminster, this is the best surviving complete domestic interior by Pugin, and, restored now to its former glory, it shows how brilliant the architect was at adapting medieval forms to domestic use. Though some of the existing features of the room conflicted with Pugin's ideals—Francis Bernasconi's plaster decoration of the fan-vaulted ceiling, for example, and the seventeenth-century Gobelins tapestries—he cleverly incorporated them into his designs. A polychromatic scheme of heraldic decoration reflected the earl's fashionable interest in genealogy; it included a new, ogee-arched chimneypiece surmounted by a huge coat of arms and richly coloured family tree. Pugin used the same firms that had worked with him at Westminster to make up his designs: Minton for the tiles; Crace for the painted decoration, furniture, and carpets; and Hardman for the metalwork and stained glass. Amazingly, he was paid just £20 for all his design work at Eastnor.

Another great Gothic revival architect, George Gilbert Scott, was involved here from about 1850. He rebuilt the local church and began work on a dramatic scheme for the great hall, but then in 1852, three weeks after Pugin's death, the 2nd Earl died and his son Charles had different ideas. A keen traveller and collector, he filled the house with Italian Renaissance art and the grounds with exotic specimen pine trees. Around 1866 he commissioned George E. Fox to redecorate some of the interiors as appropriate settings for his collections, and so the great hall became a Moorish-Gothic backdrop for his displays of armour, and the Gothic library was refashioned in a rich quattrocento manner, the theme adopted for the redecoration of a number of other rooms.

The 3rd Earl's death in 1883 brought about complicated inheritance and financial problems. The Agricultural Depression took its toll, as did the world wars and heavy death duties. Land was sold, rooms closed up, furniture put into storage, and the family restricted to occupying smaller rooms at the south end. With little spent on repairs for nearly a century, Eastnor's situation was grave, and there was even a suggestion of demolition (rejected on the grounds of cost).

Then, in the 1980s, the sale of a major artwork and English Heritage grants made it possible to carry out certain repairs. In 1989 the present owner, who inherited from his mother, moved in and, with further generous grants and earnings from the estate, continued a challenging programme of repairs, including the whole of the roof coverings. Over the next few years, many abandoned rooms were brought back into use, with new heating, wiring, and plumbing. Furniture was retrieved from attics and cellars and also bought. The principal rooms were redecorated or restored with respect to their different historic schemes in a manner that revived their rich, textural qualities and sense of antiquity without sacrifice to modern comforts. Most successful has been the refurnishing of the great hall as an Edwardian living hall, using photographs of ca. 1900 for inspiration.

All this has found strong appeal with a new type of user, and the castle is now regularly hired out for a range of corporate and social activities. With the family living privately at the south end and the principal rooms—indeed, the entire estate—enjoying a thriving commercial life, Eastnor may now be in better shape than ever before.

[OPPOSITE] *The Gothic drawing room, Pugin's best surviving domestic interior, now restored and refurnished with furniture designed by Pugin for the room. The Brussels tapestries, somewhat incongruous in this Puginian setting, came to Eastnor through marriage from Wimpole Hall in Cambridgeshire. The chandelier was made by Hardmans to Pugin's design, modelled on one he had seen in Lorenzkirche in Nuremberg.*

[LEFT] *The library as redesigned in the 1860s by George E. Fox, who stripped out Smirke's Gothic fittings and refashioned it as a room in the Italian Renaissance style for the 3rd Earl Somers. With the recent programme of redecoration at Eastnor, the library is now more densely furnished.*

[OPPOSITE, CLOCKWISE FROM TOP LEFT] *The Little Library, redecorated by George E. Fox in the Italian Renaissance manner, with seventeenth-century bookshelves acquired in Sienna.*

The Gothic-style chimneypiece, which replaced Smirke's original in the drawing room, carved and painted with the Somers arms.

The principal bedroom, with Italian Renaissance furnishings and a baldacchino for the bed created from a nineteenth-century Italian bookcase, hung with heavy drapes.

A leather-topped writing table with carved decoration and polychromatic marquetry, made by John G. Crace to Pugin's design.

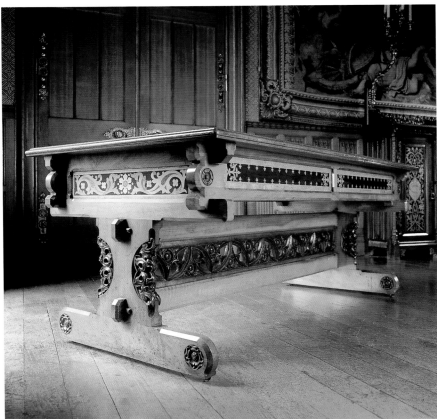

[LEFT] *The great hall, remodelled in a Moorish Gothic style by George E. Fox, with wall decoration said to have been copied from a Saracen banner in Toulouse Cathedral. In contrast to its appearance in 1968, when the* Country Life *photographs showed it unfurnished and hung only with armour, the hall is now filled with big sofas, rugs, and stuffed birds, in the manner of an Edwardian living hall.*

[OPPOSITE] *The plain Gothic architecture of Smirke's dining room has now been enhanced by the present owner's revival of a bolder colour scheme and a denser hang of family portraits. The mirror was bought through Bonhams from a Salvation Army hostel.*

Bolesworth Castle

— CHESHIRE —

THE Picturesque movement of the eighteenth century took root in the Welsh borders, and here, overlooking the Cheshire plain, is an epitome of those ideals. Bolesworth Castle stands boldly turreted and castellated on a great platform cut into the wooded slope, a commanding eye-catcher against the Broxton Hills. From its bowed and canted west front, wonderful views extend over the terraces, park, and lake to the distant mountains of Wales.

An 1820s rebuilding of an eighteenth-century house, Bolesworth was remodelled for the present owner's great-grandfather in the 1920s by Clough Williams-Ellis. This work is of considerable interest in its own right, for it transformed the interior with an urbane, classical elegance, to which Nina Campbell's more recent redecoration has added a stylish contemporary layer.

The original house, built for James Tilson and altered by Robert Mylne in 1777, was a rambling pile in the Georgian Gothic castle style. It was remodelled to its present form for George John Walmesley, who bought it in 1826 and initiated the work two years later; since then, the exterior has been little changed. Walmesley's architect was William Cole, who had succeeded Thomas Harrison of Chester as county surveyor. Bolesworth was his only country house, and he exhibited the designs at the Royal Academy in 1831.

It seems likely that Cole, who was Harrison's pupil, may have been involved with the Citadel at nearby Hawkstone, a castellated and turreted Gothic dower house in a dramatic landscape, built in 1824–25. Certainly Bolesworth echoes it in a number of respects, and, like the Citadel designed by Harrison (a Greek revival architect), it is essentially symmetrical.

After just seven years, Walmesley sold the estate. It was bought twenty years later by a rich Manchester businessman, Robert Barbour, who extended the castle and built several model farms, as well as a lodge designed by Alfred Waterhouse.

By the time Barbour's grandson inherited Bolesworth it was 1919 and the Gothic revival style was derided. Major Robert Barbour might well have chosen to demolish, but instead he turned to his friend and relation by marriage, the architect Clough Williams-Ellis, and, with "no fixed ideas" of his own, asked him to come up with some suggestions for updating the house.

[OPPOSITE] *The west front, behind which is a sequence of five reception rooms forming an impressive enfilade. At the right-hand end is the drawing room, followed by the morning room, library (behind the canted central bay), dining room, and finally the circular billiard room, which Clough Williams-Ellis converted into a servants' hall in the 1920s. Clough inserted the mezzanine at the top of the semicircular bay, removing Tudor Gothic hood moulds from all the windows at this end to avoid overcrowding.*

[LEFT] *The 1920s inner hall, looking through to the central saloon, with a Regency colza oil lamp, and scagliola columns simulating Siena marble. It recalls the work of Lutyens, whom Clough admired.*

[RIGHT] *The early Georgian-style dining room, created in the 1920s from the Gothic library, which had the most elaborate of the original interiors.*

The commission was well timed, for Clough had just reestablished his practice after the hiatus of the First World War and, although he is best known today for the quirky seaside village of Portmerion in Wales, which he developed from 1926, he was beginning to carve out a reputation as a skilful adaptor of large country houses to suit modern needs. His tactful remodelling of Bolesworth is an admirable early example. "I have generally done my best to keep anything that I could of earlier work even against my clients' wishes, for the sake of history and continuity, so long as it was good of its kind, no matter what the period, and provided it could be reasonably harmonised with the overall mood of the new deal," he wrote in his autobiography *Architect Errant* of 1971.

Despite a row over fees in 1920, client and architect remained good friends: "My dear Bob" Clough's letters all begin, and in 1924 Barbour wrote, "we very much do know that Clough is absolutely the It in the world of architecture particularly when utility and beauty are wanted together."

Clough's classical interventions at Bolesworth synthesised well with the earlier Gothic work. The main external alteration was to create a new

entrance on the east front, with a modern version of a porte cochère in the form of a long glass canopy over three round-headed glazed openings. This led into a smart inner hall with black and white marble flooring, walls painted to simulate masonry, and a pair of scagliola columns screening the entrance into the saloon.

The saloon, which was created at the centre of the house behind the enfilade, comprised two parts: one half was formed from the Gothic hall, with three new south-facing windows replacing the Gothic-arched entrance, and the other half was new, with an iron-balustraded gallery admitting light from above. These features, and the emphatic classical decoration supplied by G. & A. Brown of Hammersmith, gave the saloon "something of the atmosphere of a fashionable hotel or a setting for a house party in a Noel Coward play," concluded David Watkin in *Country Life* in March 2000, although, as redecorated by Nina Campbell and furnished as a sitting room, it has become more comfortable and visually cohesive.

Clough converted the library into a dining room, replacing spikey Gothic canopies with early Georgian-style panelling. Again, the effect has been

[LEFT] *The drawing room, with the original early-nineteenth-century Gothic vaulting and doors. Previously brown-grained and rather ecclesiastical in atmosphere, the room was redecorated by Nina Campbell in the late 1990s.*

enriched by Nina Campbell, whose gold-printed cotton moiré curtains and swagged pelmets now frame the bay window. The octagonal drawing room was in a lighter, more elegant Gothic style, and so the rib-vaulted ceiling was preserved, though the chimneypiece was replaced with a classical eighteenth-century one bought at Harrods. Clough opened up the end wall with a large window, terminating the enfilade with a view over his new garden on the south side, the former entrance front. His many other improvements at Bolesworth included installing heating, lighting, and bathroom fittings from the best London firms, remodelling the gardens and terracing, and building kennels, stables, garages, and estate cottages.

[ABOVE] *A view of the Cheshire plain, with the Welsh mountains beyond. In 1922 Clough offered the Barbours "a pair of urns or two trophies of basketed fruit or flowers" to adorn the terrace steps "in memory of gratitude for two years of very pleasant cooperation with two nice people."*

Oakly Park

— SHROPSHIRE —

OAKLY Park is a rare example of an English domestic building in the Greek revival style. Designed by Charles Robert Cockerell, who would later succeed Soane as architect to the Bank of England, it demonstrates how skilfully this brilliant architect could synthesise fluent archaeological detail with the more homely characteristics of a Georgian country house.

The remodelling of a much-altered eighteenth-century brick house, Oakly was commissioned in 1819 by Cockerell's friend and fellow Travellers' Club committee member, the Hon. Robert Henry Clive. The two young men were almost the same age and shared similar intellectual and artistic tastes, notably a passion for the newly rediscovered arts of ancient Greece. R. H. Clive had inherited Oakly in 1817 from his widowed grandmother, Lady Clive, whose husband, the great Clive of India, had bought it from the Earl of Powis in the 1760s. In 1819 Robert Henry married Harriet, Baroness Windsor, younger daughter of the 5th Earl of Plymouth, and it was her income from extensive properties in Cardiff, combined with the proceeds of Indian nabobry, that funded the remodelling of Oakly.

The house stands in a park approached via the old bridge over the Teme, with Cockerell's neoclassical gate lodge of 1826–27 at its entrance. To the north, the ruins of Bromfield Priory form a picturesque group with the gatehouse and church, and in the east rises the distinctive landmark of Clee Hill.

Cockerell's considerable knowledge as a classicist was acquired by studying Greek and Roman architecture firsthand. During his Grand Tour of Hellenistic sites in Asia Minor, he was among the group that discovered the Aegina Marbles in 1811, followed shortly by the Phygalean Marbles at Bassae. He also studied sites in Sicily and Rome, and had only recently returned from his travels when R. H. Clive asked him to remodel Oakly, the first of his few country house commissions.

Work was carried out in two stages, first in the early 1820s, then in the mid-1830s. Cockerell created a perfect Regency plan: a series of grand reception rooms interconnecting around two sides of the original house, on the site of which he formed a new central stair hall. On the west front, which J. H. Haycock had designed with nine principal and three additional bays in

[OPPOSITE] *A detail of the dining room, with a portrait by Burne-Jones of Lady Windsor. The Grecian bust of the 5th Earl of Plymouth (first creation), a pair with one of his wife, was carved in Rome in ca. 1800.*

1784–90, he replaced the central porch with a portico in the archaic Doric order of the Temple of Apollo at Delos. Then, in 1836, he heightened this front with a Greek Doric attic storey and redesigned the porch with twin columns *in antis*, duplicating it with another to the left and filling in the space between with an extension to the dining room; he also added a further two bays to the left (the study). In Cockerell's own words, Oakly was "almost unadorned, except by minor features, beside those solid proportions, shewing a refinement that would escape vulgar eyes . . . of low proportion & Doric in all its character."

On the south front, he disguised the join between the earlier left-hand section (which became the drawing room) and the new three-bay library to the right with a pedimented centrepiece, inserting a blank panel surmounted by a niche where one would expect to see a door. To the east, he created a parterre with an orangery, supplied by Jones & Clark of Birmingham in 1824, projecting at right angles to the house. This cast-iron framed structure was dismantled in ca. 1930, but its stone urn-topped colonnade has been re-erected on the terrace.

In 1823–24 Cockerell remodelled the existing circular entrance hall with an unusual flat-ribbed saucer dome, and with wide double doors designed to disguise the fact that the openings are misaligned owing to surviving earlier fabric. He created the top-lit stair hall as a spectacular space in which to display some of the largest paintings in the Clive collection. A cantilevered stone staircase sweeps up to the landing, which is supported on columns with unusual Ionic capitals modelled on a fragment he had found in the Temple of Apollo at Bassae, which Ictinos, architect of the Parthenon, is said to have designed. The climax is the colonnade of fluted columns that towers above the staircase, their simplified Corinthian capitals derived from the Tower of the Winds in Athens, the frieze belonging to a set of plaster casts that Cockerell had made from the Phygalean Marbles.

[BELOW] *The west front (on the left) and the south front (on the right), as remodelled by Cockerell. The picturesque entrance front, with its rhythm of recessed and advanced sections, was remodelled in two phases; the twin porches (the one on the right the entrance, the one on the left for symmetry) date from the 1830s. The south front incorporates the earlier dining room wing to the left and Cockerell's library extension to the right, with a pedimented centre-piece masking the join.*

[RIGHT] *The drawing room, originally the dining room, in the southwest corner, the most important surviving room from the earlier house. Created for Clive of India's wife, and still much as it was in her day, it has delicate Adam-style plasterwork by Joseph Bromfield of ca. 1785 and is hung with family portraits. The mid-eighteenth-century marble chimneypiece was possibly brought here from the Clives' London house at 45 Berkeley Square, built in ca. 1745.*

The circular entrance hall, remodelled by Cockerell with a shallow, flat-ribbed saucer dome modelled on coffering thought to have been in the Temple of Apollo at Bassae.

The upper level of the stair hall, its walls canted to provide space for hanging some of the largest paintings in the Clive collection. The frieze is one of a set of plaster casts made from the Bassae Marbles (the others are on the staircase of Cockerell's Ashmolean Museum in Oxford). The colour scheme was devised by John Fowler.

The east parterre, laid out by Cockerell in 1824, with the colonnade that fronted the now-dismantled orangery, re-erected here in the 1970s.

Cockerell's spacious stair hall of 1824, showing his first use of the Ionic order derived from the Temple of Apollo at Bassae, which he later used on other buildings such as the Ashmolean Museum in Oxford; the capitals have spiral tendrils instead of the usual volute. The staircase has a newel resembling the truncated shaft of a Bassae column and a balustrade of slender brass colonettes, which curves back on the landing to make room for Benjamin West's huge painting, Clive Receiving the Diwani of Bengal from the Moghul. This was painted for Clive of India's dining room at Claremont in Surrey, part of an unfinished cycle of Indian paintings begun in 1774.

[ABOVE] The library of 1822–23, the purest Greek revival interior at Oakly, with its unusual chimneypiece of white marble colonettes with Indian lotus leaf capitals against green marble slabs, recessed mahogany bookcases, and a restrained Grecian frieze.

The beautifully proportioned library is a perfect expression of the Greek revival style at its most understated and refined, as well as a testament to the scholarly interests of R. H. Clive. After his death in 1854 Oakly became a dower house until it was requisitioned in the Second World War. Today, it continues to be occupied by Clive's descendants. In the 1980s the 3rd Earl of Plymouth (of the second creation) did much to revive the former appearance of the interiors, guided by a set of photographs taken in 1892 by Bedford Lemere. The photographs shown here were taken in 1990, since when his son, Viscount Windsor, has restored the dining room and bought back some of the original contents as part of an ongoing programme of improvements.

WRITING in 1624, Sir Henry Wotton called a gentleman's house "an epitome of the whole world": not the world as it often was, in all its disorder and squalor, but the world as it ought to be, hierarchically ordered, with due attention paid to social rank and "degree." This was an ideal that has persisted down to modern times, and it goes a long way towards explaining how we perceive the country house today.

❧ In the Middle Ages, the greatest houses were those we now call castles. A visitor to a castle first passed through a haphazard assemblage of farm buildings—barns, perhaps a dovecote—before arriving in an outer courtyard, with stables, lodgings for members of the lord's household, and perhaps a chapel. Then came the inner courtyard: the ceremonial centre of the whole complex. Here were the great hall and kitchen, the lord's own apartments, and more lodgings. This pattern was repeated with variations in less-fortified courtyard houses like Haddon Hall, Derbyshire (see page 13), and Baddesley Clinton, Warwickshire. Magnificence went hand in hand with mundanity, and when the lord departed, mundanity—the everyday life of an agricultural community—took over.

❧ As Renaissance ideas of symmetry began to take hold in the sixteenth century, and as houses began to look out to their surrounding landscape rather than in on themselves, the design of the outbuildings began to be integrated with that of the main house. This can be seen at Hardwick Hall in Derbyshire, which is approached through a lodge directly in front of the main entrance, giving access to a walled forecourt. At Montacute in Somerset (see page 13) the corners of the forecourt are occupied by gazebos with pagoda-like roofs, to which members of the household could retreat for privacy. Farm buildings could now be tidied away to one side of the entrance courtyard, kitchens to the basement of the main house. This meant that the forecourt could be laid out in an orderly manner as one of a number of outdoor rooms visible from the upper storeys of the house, as at Chastleton in Oxfordshire.

❧ The tendency to integrate house, outbuildings, and gardens developed further in the second half of the seventeenth century. This was partly because of the new cult of horsemanship and the growing use of carriages. Stables, carriage houses, and riding houses were not mere utilitarian adjuncts to a house; they needed to be visually related to it. The approaches to great houses were therefore formalised, giving a greater sense of unity and Baroque magnificence. Houses now looked out onto open courtyards flanked by the ancillary buildings, with iron gates at the far end: a fashion that originated in Italy and France and reached its apogee at Burley-on-the-Hill in Rutland and Blenheim Palace in Oxfordshire (see page 479). Parks and gardens were meanwhile enlarged by swallowing up small farms. This meant that straight avenues could be driven from the house into the depths of the surrounding landscape—an effect that can be seen at Cirencester Park in Gloucestershire.

℆ Stables themselves increased in size, perhaps justifying the French quip that England was "a hell for women, a paradise for horses." At Belton in Lincolnshire, they were arranged around a service courtyard to the side of the house, and this practice became more popular in the eighteenth century. At Houghton in Norfolk (see page 28) and Althorp in Northamptonshire (see page 27), the importance of the stable blocks is emphasised by their arched and pedimented gateways. Often, as at Chatsworth in Derbyshire (see page 474), there was a cupola with a clock. In these equine palaces the human inhabitants had a secondary role, living in the attics, like the servants in the main house.

℆ As formal gardens went out of fashion in the mid-eighteenth century, so too did the formal arrangement of outbuildings flanking the entrance to a house. The approach to a house was now expected to be oblique, along a winding drive, the house isolated among lawns with only the stable block and perhaps the parish church for company, as at Compton Verney in Warwickshire. Here, though, the medieval church was deemed to be an unsuitable component of Capability Brown's carefully contrived view, and was replaced by a new one behind the house. Inconvenient cottages were sometimes swept away, too, and the more utilitarian ancillary buildings—brewhouse, washhouse, laundry, and increasingly the kitchen—were placed behind the house, as at Attingham in Shropshire, or to one side, as at Erddig in Wales and Tatton Park in Cheshire. Ideally, service quarters were not seen at all by visitors, and when Mrs. Lybbe Powys visited the newly built Thames-side villa of Harleyford Manor in Buckinghamshire in 1767, she was pleased to find that they were "so contriv'd in a pit, as to be perfectly invisible."

℆ The late-eighteenth-century house presided over a largely self-sufficent world screened off from the ordinary agricultural landscape by sheltering belts of trees, or even a wall, and approached through a gate lodge. Earlier lodges had been built for hunting or as private retreats, like Sir Thomas Tresham's unfinished Lyveden New Bield in Northamptonshire, begun in ca. 1594. Now the aim was to control access to the park and to announce the importance of the owner to the outside world. The lodge therefore became a miniature epitome of the house, sharing its architectural characteristics, as in the splendid Italianate lodge of 1834–38 at Bowood in Wiltshire.

℆ Some landowners lavished equal care on their home farms. For people like "Squire Coke of Holkham" in Norfolk, and the 5th Duke of Bedford at Woburn Abbey in Bedfordshire, the home farm was both an essential part of provisioning the household and a model for future improvers, to be shown proudly to guests. So barns and other agricultural buildings achieved monumental proportions, as at Wimpole Hall in Cambridgeshire, where the farm buildings were designed by Sir John Soane.

℆ Though often hidden away from public view, the great house spread its influence to its surrounding villages. Some early estate villages, such as Milton Abbas in Dorset, were built to house workers evicted from their homes by landscaping schemes; others, like the "hamlet" designed by John Nash for retired workers on the Blaise Castle estate near Bristol, were more genuinely altruistic in intention. Both can be seen as idealised versions of the "Old English" village, appealing to the romantic yearning for the past and for the simple life. Such villages proliferated throughout the nineteenth century, and in Victorian times they acquired the institutions thought to be essential for a contented and deferential workforce: schools, churches, and even a village pub. These buildings can still be seen outside the gates of places such as Bearwood, Berkshire, and Ripley Castle, Yorkshire.

❆ The architectural form of nineteenth-century estate villages was deeply affected by the cult of the Picturesque, with its anticlassical emphasis on irregularity and asymmetry. Picturesque principles also lay behind a growing tendency to group country houses and their outbuildings in a single loose and informal composition, as at Ashridge in Hertfordshire, externally evoking the vanished medieval abbey on the site, and at the turreted and crenellated Caerhayes Castle in Cornwall. By the time these houses went up in the early nineteenth century, basements had gone out of fashion and, as domestic tasks became more minutely differentiated, the number of service rooms proliferated. This is why the service quarters of Victorian country houses usually take up as much space as the house itself.

❆ As formal gardening came once more into vogue, lawns retreated from the immediate surroundings of the house, to be replaced by terraces and flower beds, sometimes overlooked by a conservatory, such as that at Sezincote in Gloucestershire (see page 14), an Orientalist fantasy built in circa 1805 for an East India nabob. With gardens becoming larger and more complex, walled enclosures sprang up, often at some distance from the house, surrounding working landscapes of sheds, greenhouses, vegetable plots, and cottages or bothies for garden workers.

❆ New technology also made its mark on the nineteenth-century country house, and not just in the design of conservatories. Water towers went up, often next to stable yards, enlivening the skyline of houses like Cliveden in Buckinghamshire, where the tower can be seen from a distance rising above trees. Hot water heating and better lighting—gas and, later, electricity—demanded boiler houses and power plants, usually discreetly hidden behind walls or among plantations. Cragside in Northumberland, the technologically sophisticated but externally reassuringly "Old English" country retreat of the engineer and armaments manufacturer Lord Armstrong, was lit from 1878 by electric light supplied by a hydroelectric plant on the estate.

❆ The building of Cragside coincided with the onset of an agricultural depression, which continued until after the Second World War. New country houses continued to be built, but they tended to be smaller than their nineteenth-century predecessors, to employ fewer servants, and to have less complex or extensive gardens. Outbuildings contracted, though space was usually found for garages and sometimes for an outdoor or even an indoor swimming pool. In recent years estates have become less self-sufficient, farms have been sold off, stable blocks turned into business centres or tearooms, walled gardens into garden centres. The surroundings of country houses have always demonstrated the relationship between the house and the wider world in a particularly vivid way, and that is as true in the rapidly changing world of the early twenty-first century as it was in the more distant past.

Pages 300 and 305: Archway House, ca. 1800,
Hamilton Weston Wallpapers

Southill Park

— BEDFORDSHIRE —

SOUTHILL is a perfect expression of the restrained elegance of the Regency, a period described by Christopher Hussey as "the most civilised decade in the whole range of English domestic architecture." This remodelling of an earlier house was the work of Henry Holland for Samuel Whitbread, a prominent Whig politician whose father, also Samuel, had made his fortune in the London brewery. Of yeoman roots, Samuel Whitbread I was a humanitarian and reforming Tory, progenitor of five successive generations of Whitbreads who served as members of parliament. Having risen from apprentice to partner in the brewery, he returned to his country roots to become a squire and in 1795 bought Southill from George Byng, the 4th Lord Torrington. But within a year he was dead, and it was his son who was responsible for Southill as it appears today.

Samuel Whitbread II was a complex personality. Eton-educated and married to the daughter of the 1st Earl Grey, he was idealistic and nonconformist, a friend of Fox, Cobbett, Sheridan, and other radical Whigs belonging to the circle that revolved around the Prince Regent. His wealth and love of political oratory were tempered by a certain puritanical moral fervour and a neuroticism that led ultimately to his suicide in 1815.

Through the simplicity, solidity, and refinement of Holland's mature style, Southill perfectly embodied the ideals of liberty and pacifism upheld by Whitbread and his set. A favourite among the Whig aristocracy, Holland owed his reputation as the fashionable choice of architect to the Prince Regent, whose celebrated Carlton House in London he reconstructed from 1783. That this house no longer survives makes Southill, with its remarkable survival of contents, all the more important as an example of the refined, French-inspired taste associated with the Regency.

Work began around 1797, and Holland supervised the reconstruction and decoration until his death in 1806. (He is commemorated by a bust in the hall carved by George Garrard and engraved with a poem composed by Whitbread.) The work involved encasing the existing brick house in stone and reorienting it with a new entrance on the north, although not on the central axis. Holland kept the earlier Palladian pavilions, adding Ionic-colonnaded corridors to their linking wings, and reduced the number of windows on the main façades. The design relies for its effect on this harmony

[OPPOSITE] *A detail in the drawing room, showing part of a "Grecian" sofa made by Marsh and Tatham to a design showing the influence of Thomas Hope's severely classical manner. It was reupholstered in the 1990s with a "red striped Tabby" specially rewoven in Naples. Visible too is part of the spectacular picture frame for Romney's* Blind Milton Dictating to His Daughters.

of proportions and the clean simplicity of lines. The interior was replanned to a more practical and comfortable arrangement, with rooms for entertaining in the main block, private family rooms in the east wing, and the library, billiard room, and breakfast room in the west wing. The service quarters were in the basement.

In his articles for *Country Life* in 1930, Hussey described Southill as "a complete work of art to an extent that is true of few other great English homes of any period. Its furniture, its pictures and its ornaments are of the first order. . . . Above all, its exquisite internal decoration . . . is of a quality that makes almost every other house appear a little overdone or a little barbaric in contrast."

Holland synthesised Graeco-Roman and French elements with characteristic simplicity and restraint. The French influence is seen, for example, in Garrard's bronzed overdoor plaster reliefs in what is probably the least altered room—the hall. The library, with its distinctly French chimney-piece, shows Holland at his most masculine and archaeological, although the ornamental detail remains exquisitely delicate and refined.

The discovery of severe outbreaks of dry rot in 1989 resulted in an extensive programme of structural repairs, providing an opportunity to rethink elements of the interior decoration. Research showed that Holland's exquisite decorative schemes had been altered a few years after his death, in keeping with a taste for greater opulence. The drawing room and ante-room were redecorated in a more flamboyant, feminine style, probably by Holland's former assistant, C. H. Tatham. An estimate survives of 1808 from Robson and Hale, "Paper-Hanging Manufacturers to . . . the Prince of Wales," for twenty-five pieces of wallpaper for the panels of the two rooms, "Hanging & Colouring Geranium Red," and for green velvet borders. All this was replaced in the late nineteenth century with a scheme dominated by beige damask.

Now, as a result of a programme of redecoration carried out in the 1990s, the panels of boldly coloured fabric and gilt mouldings have been

[RIGHT] *The south front under reconstruction in a painting by George Garrard, a protégé of Samuel Whitbread. Garrard also modelled the plaster overdoors of the entrance hall with horses, bulls, camels, lions, and deer, and made a marble bust of the architect Henry Holland for the hall.*

[OPPOSITE] *The dining room (the drawing room in the eighteenth-century house), as redecorated in the 1990s by Alec Cobbe and Edward Bulmer to a scheme dating from about 1809, which replaced Holland's simpler pale greens and whites. Almost all the furniture listed in the inventory of 1816 is still here, including five mahogany sideboards on "curved Chimera legs."*

[OPPOSITE BELOW] *The south front, as remodelled around 1800 by Henry Holland, whose façades at Southill are regarded as among his most refined and satisfying compositions. Holland filled in the recessed centre of the eighteenth-century house with a projecting, pedimented frontispiece and colonnaded portico, reduced the number of windows, and added Ionic colonnades to the lateral wings. He also clad the whole building in stone, texturing the pavilions and lower storey of the central block with rusticated masonry.*

reinstated, and the curtains of "Red Sarsnet" lined with green calico remade by Melissa Wyndham using specially woven silk damask. The original gilt pelmet boards with eagles to hold up the swags of "green Manchester velvet drapery" survived; they were probably inspired by the Rose Satin Drawing Room at Carlton House.

The dining room occupies the centre of the north front, with a bay window added by Holland where one expects to see the front door. Although it is now redecorated to a later scheme of about 1809, evidence of Holland's pale green and marbled decoration was discovered by Alec Cobbe and Edward Bulmer during cleaning and restoration. Almost all the furniture listed in the 1816 inventory is still here.

The furniture at Southill belongs to three main periods, including earlier Georgian pieces sold with the house by the Byngs. The fine Regency furniture was supplied by leading London firms such as Marsh and Tatham— Tatham being a brother of C. H. Tatham, which may partly explain the remarkable harmony that continued to exist between the interior decoration and the furniture in schemes carried out after Holland's death. Large bills from Marsh and Tatham dating from 1809–13 suggest that much of the "Grecian"-style furniture in the house came from them.

The pleasure grounds at Southill are noted for their fine collection of sculptures, many by Cheere. On the north side of the house, with views to the lake and its fishing temple on the far bank, are terraces and balustrades designed by Holland, who was also paid for "ground work" in the park. It is perhaps not surprising that the architect's influence should have extended to the landscape, given that he was the son-in-law of Capability Brown.

[LEFT] *The drawing room, with new damask wall panels bordered in green velvet, reproducing Tatham's ca. 1810 scheme. Alec Cobbe has rehung the paintings, returning Hoppner's huge portraits of Samuel Whitbread II and his wife, Lady Elizabeth, to their original positions on either side of the chimney-piece. On the far wall is Romney's* Blind Milton Dictating to His Daughters, *which Whitbread bought in 1794. The writing table in the foreground belongs to a set of furniture supplied by Marsh and Tatham, featuring lion masks.*

[RIGHT] *The curtain draperies in the drawing room, remade in the 1990s by Melissa Wyndham. Between them is one of the "rosewood Pier Tables with shelves for china" now returned from a corridor and arranged with most of the same pieces of Chinese and Japanese porcelain listed in the 1816 inventory. Above it is Garrard's painting of the Whitbread Brewery in London.*

[LEFT] *Looking towards the hall through the double doors in the dining room, with a Hellenistic motif of lion and vase decorating the panel above. The porphyry-coloured pilaster strips were a later addition, made to increase the apparent height of the room.*

[OPPOSITE] *A detail of one of the porphyry-painted pilaster panels in the dining room, its scrolling vine tendrils alive with snails and insects. The accounts do not reveal the identity of the painter, although Crace was paid about £15 in March 1806, maybe for this work. Alternatively, it could be by the French artist Louis-Alexandre Delabrière, who had worked at Carlton House and painted the decoration of the family rooms at Southill before 1800.*

The Chantry

— SOMERSET —

THE Chantry was the home of the novelist Anthony Powell from 1952 until his death in 2000, and it survives little altered as an atmospheric memorial to the tastes and personality of this leading British author. But it is also a fascinating social document of the changing fortunes of a local family of ironmasters turned squires, the story of which might well have provided the theme for one of Powell's novels.

The Fussells hailed from the Mendips, where they made and exported agricultural tools. By the early nineteenth century, they had acquired six ironworks and sufficient wealth and social ambition to enable James Fussell and his brothers to set themselves up as gentlemen, each with a country seat. James acquired some land believed to have belonged to the fourteenth-century chantry chapel of the Whatley church, and in about 1826 he built himself a handsome Regency house. Later, in 1846, he built a new church on the edge of the park to the design of Scott & Moffatt (Scott being the future Sir George Gilbert Scott, the famous Gothic revival architect) and had a parish specially created for it.

[OPPOSITE] *Family portraits and miniatures in one of the spare bedrooms.*

[BELOW] *The south front, with a handsome bow emphasising its height. The lower extension (now the kitchen) was built in the 1930s and used as a chapel.*

[LEFT] *Anthony Powell's writing room on the first floor, with Osbert Lancaster's cartoons, framed covers to his first four novels in the* Dance to the Music of Time *series, and caricatures of their characters by Mark Boxer seen on the walls.*

[OPPOSITE] *The library, with 1950s Cole & Son wallpaper in a black and white striped design by Edward Bawden. The portraits are of Powell ancestors.*

Although no documentary evidence survives, it has been suggested by Mark Girouard that the architect of the Chantry may have been John Pinch, who built many of the fine early-nineteenth-century terraced houses and villas in Bath, just eighteen miles away. Alternatively, H. E. Goodridge, who designed a number of that city's handsome outlying villas and possibly also worked with Soane, may have been involved. Whoever was responsible created a dignified neoclassical edifice that responds to its sloping site with façades of strikingly different scale. The north-facing entrance front, of two storeys with a raised attic in the central bay, has the appearance of a polite villa, the refined detail of its curving Doric porch and the shallow recession of planes giving it a distinctly Soanian air.

On the other side, where the ground drops away, the house reads as four storeys, its height emphasised by a tall central bow and surmounting tower-like attic block. The principal floor, raised up over a rusticated basement, has long sash windows to take advantage of the views across the valley. The park drops down to a lake, which was created not only as an ornamental feature but also to supply power for the Chantry ironworks. A pair of grottoes created in the 1840s provides an enjoyable diversion.

Fussell left the house to his nephew, also James, who became the local vicar and in 1857 established a school here. He married the daughter of Sir John Dalrymple of North Berwick, and their son, educated at Eton and Cambridge, became a barrister. But by the 1890s the mills were bankrupt, and on James's death in 1927 the Chantry was sold. It lent itself subsequently to a number of uses, including as a refuge and a chocolate factory. When the Powells bought it in 1952, the house was in a state of disrepair and the grottoes were completely overgrown.

As a child, Powell had lived in Regency villas in St John's Wood and Chester Gate in London, so it is perhaps not surprising that he developed a love of neoclassical elegance. Over the years, he built up a collection of early–nineteenth-century English and French Empire furniture for which the Chantry provided a perfect setting.

The plan has a certain informality characteristic of villas of the period. At the centre of the principal floor, facing south, the elegantly bowed drawing room doubles as a library, flanked by a small sitting room (used as a study) and the dining room, which runs the full width of the house. The plan is echoed on the floor above, where three south-facing bedrooms open off a corridor. The original kitchen and service quarters were in the basement.

The spirits of Anthony Powell, and of his wife, Lady Violet, a sister of the late Lord Longford, are still very much alive at the Chantry, which is now the home of their son John. Powell's collection of Regency furniture; his paintings, ranging from inherited portraits to caricatures of friends and fictional characters; and the atmospheric writing room and library tell us much about his tastes and character, his family roots, and the social and literary circles in which they mixed. He had a good eye for architectural detail, although his fictional descriptions of country houses tend to be unflattering. His son recalls that his most frequent observation about the Chantry was that it was like a town house set down in the country. He describes it briefly in his autobiography of 1982, *The Strangers All Are Gone*.

[RIGHT] *The north entrance front, which has a rather Soanian air. Three of the windows are blind.*

[OPPOSITE, CLOCKWISE FROM TOP LEFT] *The hall and landing are hung with a hand-blocked wallpaper in a Second Empire design that reflects Powell's love of the neoclassical style. He bought it from Cole & Son's London factory in the 1960s. The huge portrait of him is by Henry Mee.*

The dining room, with mostly Regency furniture. Among the pictures in this room are portraits of Anthony Powell by Augustus John and Rodrigo Moynihan.

A view of the boot room in a corner of the basement boiler room. The original kitchen and former service quarters were located on this floor.

A detail of the floor-to-ceiling collage in the basement boiler room, which Anthony Powell made over several decades.

Sandon Hall

— STAFFORDSHIRE —

WILLIAM Burn was the doyen of the Victorian country house. Nobody had greater experience in the planning and building of these great machines for domestic living than this Scottish architect, who moved his practice to London in 1844. Sandon Hall, which he built in 1852–55, epitomises the genre. In Michael Hall's June 13, 1991, article for *Country Life*, excerpts from a letter written in 1859 by a Polish visitor, Cecylia Dzialynska, provide a fascinating contemporary record of the degree of specialisation and social segregation that went into the planning and running of a house on this scale. Every domestic function was accorded its own space: "Separate room for cleaning lamps, separate for cleaning shoes, another only for silver, lined by green felt covered shelves behind the matching curtains, further on a place for washing china, and still further for ceramics, and then again a little room for all maids' paraphernalia, i.e., all brooms, rugs, pails, dusters, everything so clean and neatly arranged it's a pleasure. But all this is nothing compared to the kitchen and cellars. . . . Masses of equipment, no end of utensils, in one place a roasting jack—a mechanical spit wound up like a clock, turns round by itself and thus roasts the meat. Further on 'au bain marie' is being cooked, and then puddings and tarts, and nobody can enter the kitchen, it is a very strict rule, everything is served through a hatch. Then there are cellars, swept, washed, light and clean, lighted by gas like a ballroom, then servants' common room, where they have their dinners, and then came the tea room, where they drink their tea, then the housekeeper's kingdom, her various stores, stoves, jars."

Sandon Hall was built for the 2nd Earl of Harrowby, the first nobleman to get a double first in classics and mathematics at Christ Church, whose grandfather had bought the estate in 1776. It replaced a late eighteenth-century house that had succumbed in 1848 to a devastating fire. Miraculously, most of the contents, including chimneypieces and plate glass, were saved and the house had recently been insured.

Burn designed the new house in his familiar Jacobethan style, with shaped gables and a turreted centrepiece over a porte cochère on the north front. Much of the detail was derived from such places as Broughton Castle and Cranborne Manor—houses that featured in John Nash's *Mansions of England in the Olden Time*—while the unusual strapwork banding on the

[OPPOSITE] *Lord Harrowby's room, with a desk almost certainly made by Chippendale for the 1st Lord Harrowby.*

[OVERLEAF] *The drawing room combines Jacobethan plasterwork and an early-eighteenth-century Chinese paper of peacocks and butterflies. The room has splendid eighteenth-century furniture and a chimneypiece salvaged from the earlier house.*

porch columns and quoin stones probably came from a sixteenth-century northern European source. Typical of Burn's planning was the segregation of family rooms and state rooms; here the lower family wing is on the west, screening the service court, and the state rooms form two enfilades to the north and south.

Running along the north front is the hall, a vast and opulent space divided by screens of columns into three parts: the staircase, the saloon, and, at the far end, a space originally used as a billiard room. Cecylia Dzialynska described it as "huge, long, with family portraits hanging round the walls, a . . . beautiful fireplace with a huge fire, and then oak stairs, but what kind of stairs! Huge, wide, smooth like a mirror, glazed and highly polished—and so magnificent, heavy, and 'massive.'"

Superb plasterwork by James Annan of London included the drawing room and library ceilings. The Jacobethan style of this work and other architectural detail did not, however, extend to the furnishings, which featured

[ABOVE] *The oak staircase at the end of the long hall, which Cecylia Dzialynska described with great admiration in a letter to her mother of 1859.*

[RIGHT] *The hall seen from the staircase. The far end originally served as a billiard room.*

pieces of the Georgian and Regency periods. Among them were a satin-wood suite with painted decoration made between 1787 and 1792 by Ince and Mayhew, and a pair of spectacular Louis XIV Boulle commodes. George Trollope & Sons made the library bookcases, and also supplied carpets and curtains. The drawing room was hung with an early-eighteenth-century Chinese paper.

The family's continual interference in the project culminated in Burn's resignation in 1855. The conservatory, built on the east side and attached by a curved link in 1864–65, was designed by Stevens and Robinson of Derby. It is a splendid Victorian survival, with a soaring iron and glass roof and a floor of Minton tiles.

Thanks to Cecylia Dzialynska's letter to her mother, we have a vivid picture of Sandon in the 1850s: its servants lined up in red and white livery, and its owners, Lord Harrowby, "small, thin, grey, wearing glasses" (he had been disfigured by smallpox), and his wife, a daughter of the 1st Marquess of Bute, "thin, quiet, dark and sad . . . with a silent, slow and gliding step . . . such a beautiful head, such features as if cast in white marble."

These photographs of Sandon were taken in the early 1990s, around the time that the 7th Earl reorganised the house and moved into the family wing. The state rooms are now used for private functions, and private tours of some of the main rooms and the family museum are available by appointment.

[ABOVE] *The north front of Sandon
Hall, with the family wing on the right
and the conservatory on the left.*

Brodsworth Hall

— YORKSHIRE —

[OPPOSITE] *The inner hall, where pairs of scagliola columns and marbled and painted decoration set off and frame Charles Thellusson's collection of contemporary Italian marble sculpture. The marble group of a girl teaching her little brother to read—Education—is by Giuseppe Lazzerini of Carrara.*

IT would be difficult to find a more atmospheric example of opulent 1860s classicism than Brodsworth Hall near Doncaster. Little altered since it was built, the house stands all of a piece with its formal terraced gardens, the ambience of the interior intensified by its air of arrested decay. "The 1860s have been miraculously preserved in the amber richness of its rooms," wrote Mark Girouard when he first brought Brodsworth to public attention in *Country Life* in October 1963.

But the impression that nothing has ever been touched is deceptive, and the vicissitudes of the past century and a half have left their mark. English Heritage acknowledged this when it acquired Brodsworth in 1990 and set about implementing a radical new approach to its conservation and interpretation. This shifted the focus from the more conventional presentation of the house as an architectural showcase for important paintings and furniture, to place equal emphasis on its social role and fluctuating fortunes. Brodsworth's comprehensive collection of household contents charts a changing way of life for family and staff over 120 years, and it is this story that English Heritage has endeavoured to tell. Thus everything, from paintings and sculpture to irons and frying pans—nearly 17,000 objects—was subjected to the same painstaking "conserve as found" policy: photographed, catalogued, and conserved using minimal intervention. Stabilised and deinfested of bugs, the interiors and their contents still look romantically distressed, so that the house appears just as it did when it was last occupied in 1988.

Brodsworth was built by Charles Sabine Thellusson, who inherited the estate in 1859 following six decades of lawsuits—the consequence of his great-grandfather's infamously controversial will. Between 1861 and 1863 Thellusson demolished a Georgian house and replaced it with the present Italianate mansion using a little-known London architect, Philip Wilkinson. Despite Wilkinson's obscurity, and the reputation the Victorian Italianate style has for being dull, Brodsworth is a better building of its type than many and differs from others in being boldly symmetrical, with a rectangular main block that is visually distinct from the lower service wing. Inside, a sequence of generous circulation spaces flows along the central east/west axis, leading from the entrance hall at the east end, through a columned screen into a larger staircase hall, into the pillared South Hall, and from there down an

[OVERLEAF] *The east-facing entrance front with its bold porte cochère. The increasingly common Victorian arrangement of moving the entrance to one end allowed the principal rooms on the main front to enjoy more privacy and a garden view.*

arcaded and mirrored corridor to the drawing room and library at the far end.

A high point of Brodsworth's interior is the arrangement of Thellusson's fine collection of contemporary Italian sculpture against the richly marbled and painted backdrop of these hallways. Its purchase in 1865 from the Chevalier Casentini, a Tuscan architect and sculptor who also supplied garden statuary and further drawings for architectural sculpture for the house, led to the longstanding belief that he was the architect of Brodsworth. Most of the furniture and other fittings were supplied by Lapworths, the London furnishing firm and carpet specialists, while some doors and chimneypieces were reused from the old house in an unexpected gesture

[OPPOSITE] *In the once-opulent drawing room, Lapworths' hand-knotted Axminster carpet and silk upholstery are now much faded. The crimson damask wall hangings have been conserved with their patches, but their matching curtains have not survived. The ceilings are painted with arabesque designs similar to those at Grimston Park in Yorkshire and Locko Park in Derbyshire, the latter painted by an Italian artist called Romoli in 1861–64.*

[LEFT] *The dining room combines furniture from Lapworths and an eighteenth-century chimneypiece from the earlier house with family portraits, including Dutch Old Masters and a Lawrence.*

[RIGHT] *The billiard room is a Victorian period piece with its original padded red leather banquettes raised as a platform for spectators and a fine collection of equestrian pictures, including four by James Ward dating from 1812–33.*

of respect for earlier taste. This sympathy towards Georgian architecture is evident, too, in the arrangement of the drawing room as two splendid interconnecting spaces on the principal front. Here, gilded frames, huge gilt-framed mirrors, and crystal chandeliers glitter in the diffused light against walls of now-faded crimson damask.

Beyond the green baize door, washboards, mangles, electric clothes spinners, and antique vacuum cleaners tell their own "below stairs" story of hard work and dwindling staff numbers. Modern accretions, such as Tupperware, Formica, and an Aga cooker, have all been carefully preserved, as have such improvisations as brown paper stuffed into unused fireplaces as draught excluders, and numerous "quick fix" patchings to the interiors and their contents.

Brodsworth's last occupants were Sylvia Grant Dalton, whose husband was Charles Thellusson's grandson, and her cook/housekeeper Emily Chester. After Mrs. Grant Dalton's death in 1988, her daughter gave Brodsworth to English Heritage, and it opened to the public in 1995. Outside, the "conserve as found" approach was less appropriate: decaying stonework and leaking roofs had to be repaired, and the 1860s garden layout was resurrected from choking undergrowth. As it mellows, the exterior of Brodsworth sits more comfortably with its fragile, intensely atmospheric interiors.

Bishops Court

— DEVON —

BISHOPS Court near Exeter is charged with the fervour of High Victorian Gothic. A high-minded exercise in the interpretation of Gothic architecture for a domestic building, it expresses the aesthetic and moral vision of its pious mid-nineteenth-century owner and architect—both committed Goths. The house's origins as the thirteenth-century Episcopal palace of Clyst, which until 1546 was the country residence of the bishops of Exeter, adds a special dimension to William White's Tracterian remodelling, which he carried out for John Garratt in 1860–64.

Secularised as a gentry house since the seventeenth century, this was the home of the Beavis family from 1651 until 1800, and throughout that time much of the medieval palace survived. But in the early nineteenth century the house was Georgianised by Thomas North, the 2nd Lord Graves, whose father, the famous admiral, had bought it in 1800, and much of the remaining thirteenth-century fabric was destroyed. Graves replaced the north range of the courtyard with a new wing, demolished the tower, and created a symmetrical entrance front on the site of the great hall. New sash windows were introduced—square-headed, with Gothick glazing bars. Although the architect for this work is not recorded, it is possible that James Wyatt may have been involved: he had remodelled Plas Newydd on Anglesey for the Earl of Uxbridge, who was Graves's father-in-law.

In 1833 John Garratt (of the tea and coffee merchants Garratt and Miller) bought Bishops Court. A former sheriff and Lord Mayor of London, Garratt was a city magnate and a committed Anglican of strongly evangelical persuasion, who, on becoming a widower, decided to retire to the country. Although he did little more than redecorate and refurnish the house, he embellished its setting considerably, adding an ornamental lake, hothouses, lodges, and improved farm buildings. He also provided a new village school and financed the rebuilding of Sowton Parish Church.

His son, also John and equally religious-minded, moved into Bishops Court in 1846. A High Anglican, he was a supporter of the Ecclesiological Movement and a keen advocate of the revival of Gothic architecture in English churches. His driving inspiration in remodelling Bishops Court was to see the chapel, long relegated to the role of servants' hall and laundry, restored to its religious function.

[OPPOSITE] *A view along the corridor that opens off the entrance hall to the richly moulded chapel doorway at the far end. The lavish treatment of the walls with geometric-patterned stencilling is a key part of William White's architectural composition.*

[OVERLEAF] *A view showing the contrast between the severe north wing (on the right) and the asymmetrical entrance front.*

335

William White, whom Garratt knew through the Diocesan Architectural Society, transformed the house to its present, highly individual appearance with a boldly massed, asymmetrical, and richly polychromatic design. To the chapel wing on the south side he added lancets and a bell-turret and, behind it, a picturesque cluster of gabled service buildings. The north wing is striking for its rectilinear severity, an oriel over a buttress on the east side and a polygonal, spireletted observatory tower on one corner being almost the only adornments. The flatness and austerity of the west front, which overlooks a garden terrace from beneath a long, unbroken parapet, is broken only at the chapel end by a pair of tall, round-arched recesses flanked by flying buttresses. In striking contrast, the entrance front is enlivened with an irregular rhythm of bold forms and shifting planes. Between the two wings is an eccentric composition of buttress, massive double chimneystack, and arched windows, with the entrance and lean-to conservatory pushed up against the north wing on the right.

Inspired by William Butterfield, White had a particular interest in the architectural use of colour. This is demonstrated on the exterior of the house, where the lovely mottled patina of the medieval masonry is enhanced with a variety of stones ranging in tone from warm ochre to reddish brown, creating a subtle counterbalance to the muscularity of the architecture. Eastlake commented on it in his *History of the Gothic Revival*.

Inside, colour is used more boldly and decoratively as a key part of the architectural composition. The entrance hall, created from the former billiard room, and the spine corridor opening off it through a Gothic arcade, are covered with stencilled patterning, and White's fascination for geometric ornament is revealed in his treatment of a sixteenth-century window recess, making it the focus of the corridor.

The decoration of the corridor intensifies as it nears the chapel, climaxing with a richly moulded doorway. When one enters, the scale and mood changes, for the chapel, unlike its medieval predecessor, rises full height under an open timber roof, and the nave walls are painted white, with just a simple masonry-pattern outline in red. Over the altar is a triptych by Westlake. White designed the Pre-Raphaelite-style stained glass, which was made by Lavers and Barraud, and most of the fittings. He also designed other fixtures and furniture for the house.

The staircase, which turns around a giant column carrying stilted Gothic arches over the two main flights, is another distinctive feature of White's interior. He left the first-floor rooms largely unaltered but made a dining room where the former hall had been, and turned the old dining room in the north wing into a library. Although the library and drawing room acquired new windows at this time, they remain essentially early-nineteenth-century in character.

After a period from 1958 to the 1990s as the headquarters of a family firm, Bishops Court is now a private house again, remaining well preserved and much as it appeared following White's remodelling.

[OPPOSITE, CLOCKWISE FROM TOP LEFT] *White's fascination for geometric ornament is revealed in his treatment of a sixteenth-century window recess, making it the decorative focus of the main corridor.*

A detail of the staircase, which climbs around a giant column carrying stilted arches over the two principal flights. In contrast to the muscularity of the column, the capital is delicately carved with naturalistic foliage and little birds.

White's chimneypiece and overmantel in the entrance hall.

Looking towards the front door from the entrance hall, which was created out of the old billiard room.

Tyntesfield

— SOMERSET —

THAT beautiful house was like a church in spirit, I used to think so when going up and down the great staircase. . . . At the bottom, after prayers, Mr. Gibbs in his wheeled chair used to wish everybody good night." So wrote the Victorian novelist Charlotte M. Yonge in a letter to a friend, describing the home of her cousins, William and Blanche Gibbs, as she remembered it in the 1860s. Were she to return to Tyntesfield today, she would find the atmosphere of this remarkable Gothic revival house little changed: it is as if the family has just stepped out for a few hours, perhaps to attend church, and the servants have temporarily abandoned their duties, leaving everything in place.

This enthralling Victorian time capsule was virtually unknown until 2002, when it was put on the market following the death of the bachelor 2nd Lord Wraxall. So complete was the ensemble of art, architecture, gardens, and landscape that the prospect of it all being broken up seemed unthinkable, and Tyntesfield became a cause célèbre. Faced with what seemed an impossible deadline, the National Trust launched a campaign and in just fifty days succeeded in raising £20 million to buy the house, most of its contents, and 148 acres, including gardens, stables, lodges, and the home farm. As a result of this triumphant feat, Tyntesfield has survived intact, and the trust is in the process of conserving this fragile document of Victorian country house life, which since 2002 has been open to the public.

When in 1843 William Gibbs bought the estate, he acquired a small Regency Gothic mansion built by the Reverend George Turner Seymour in 1813. Of Devon gentry stock, the Gibbses were enterprising business-men whose family firm, Antony Gibbs & Sons, had trading and banking interests in Spain and South America. In 1842, the year William took sole charge, the firm signed contracts to import guano for use as fertiliser from the Chincha Islands off Peru. Over the next two decades, William and his partners amassed a fortune, and it is a fact much relished by visitors today that this astonishing house was largely funded on the proceeds of this enter-prise—the mining of bird excrement.

Not until he was in his seventies did William embark on a major recon-struction of Tyntesfield. The architect was John Norton of Bristol, who had trained with Benjamin Ferrey and was best known for his High Gothic

[OPPOSITE] *The stair hall, remodelled in 1887–88 by Henry Woodyer, who removed the central Y-shaped staircase and reorientated it around the walls, reusing Norton's iron balustrading and extending the balcony to a three-sided landing. Also dating from this time is the painted and stencilled decoration, echoing the green of the Connemara marble in the columns. The bust is one of a pair of portraits of William and Blanche Gibbs, commissioned when they were in Rome from the sculptor Lawrence Macdonald. The picture arrangement of portraits and maritime paintings dates from around 1908.*

churches, and the job was carried out by the London builders Cubitt & Sons in 1863–65. Norton retained the general disposition of the earlier house but scaled it up to create an exuberant Gothic pile embellished with traceried windows, pierced friezes, and an array of naturalistic carved stone detail, its skyline enlivened with turrets, finialled gables, pinnacles, and ornate chimneystacks. With the exception of a domed conservatory, demolished in 1916, and the great, tourelled clock tower that loomed over the entrance porch until 1935, Norton's picturesque composition survives largely intact. So too do the extensive Victorian gardens, with their formally planted terraces, shaded walks, and shrubberies encircled by parkland, from which views extend over the Land Yeo Valley to the distant Mendips and Bristol Channel.

Inside, the principal rooms are grouped around a great top-lit stair hall, their tile and metalwork, stained glass, inlaid marble, and elaborate carved stone and timber decoration displaying the finest craftsmanship. The richness of all this architectural ornament is complemented by furniture, fittings, paintings, and textiles of exceptional quality, many belonging to the original ensemble, to which three subsequent generations of Gibbses made sympathetic additions. The key figure responsible for Tyntesfield's interior decoration was the leading house furnisher John G. Crace, famous for his earlier collaboration with Pugin. Only Eastnor Castle (page 281) retains a comparable amount of Crace's Puginian furniture; here at Tyntesfield, the dining room and library preserve particularly good examples. The house also has the largest collection of Gothic revival furniture by the excellent Warwick cabinetmakers Collier & Plucknett, while many of the bedroom and more utilitarian pieces came from Laverton and Co. of Bristol.

The atmosphere of Tyntesfield is charged with the High Church sensibilities of William Gibbs, whose wealth and confidence went hand in hand with a deeply religious nature and public-spirited munificence. His beautiful, oak-lined library feels almost ecclesiastical, with its churchlike roof and traceried windows, and the bookcases are filled with texts of the Oxford movement, of which Gibbs was a generous patron, as well as seminal works by Ruskin and Pugin. But the Gibbses' piety and emphasis on reading, music, and the contemplation of art and nature, was tempered by a sense of fun and enjoyment of their seven children; far from feeling sombre, Tyntesfield was a cheerful family home, its schoolroom and nursery "crowded with romping good-hearted boys and little girls in brown-holland pinafores." It was also technologically progressive for its date, with central heating, gaslight, and, from the 1880s, electricity. Much of the equipment required to work these utilities survives, along with the remarkable kitchen garden—one of the few of the period to have remained continuously in cultivation.

William Gibbs was a generous patron of church buildings, paying for at

The south front, showing the balanced asymmetry of Norton's composition. The three traceried windows on the right light the library; on the ground floor of the mighty central block is the music room, and at the far end is the drawing room, its veranda added by Henry Woodyer in 1885.

least nineteen during his life, including the chapel at Keble College, Oxford, by William Butterfield. His last addition to Tyntesfield was the impressively scaled chapel, designed by Arthur Blomfield on the model of Sainte Chapelle in Paris and completed in 1875, the year of William's death. The interior is a wonderful celebration of Victorian High Church craftsmanship, with mosaics by Salviati, marble paving and stained glass by Powell, stone carving by James Forsyth, and metalwork by Barkentin & Krall.

William's eldest son, Antony, shared his tastes and temperament, if not his business acumen. He commissioned the High Church architect Henry Woodyer to remodel the staircase and enlarge the dining room, introducing to the latter a superb carved doorway and triple-bay window with arcaded screen. He also altered the billiard room, adding an inglenook fireplace, a centrally heated table, and an electronic scoreboard. This room, used for smoking, was very much the male domain of the house.

The barrel-vaulted drawing room, approached through an anteroom displayed with sculpture, was hung with Gibbs's collection of Old Masters. Originally stencilled by Crace, it was redecorated in 1908 for Antony's son

George (the 1st Lord Wraxall) and his first wife, Via, whose anti-Gothic tastes are represented at Tyntesfield by various alterations in a Renaissance revival style, and by quantities of seventeenth- and eighteenth-century English and Continental furniture.

George's second wife, Ursula, lived here as a widow until her death in 1979. She and her son, the 2nd Lord Wraxall, cared devotedly for the house and grounds and were together responsible for ensuring that they survived so intact. A particularly rare and fascinating dimension of Tyntesfield is the survival of the service quarters—a warren of specialised rooms, such as brew house, dressed meat larder, game larder, and still room, that have hardly been touched since the 1880s. Virtually all the domestic household contents remain, and the kitchen has been in continuous use since the house was built. The challenge now is to preserve the magical atmosphere while ensuring that the house becomes more widely known. Tyntesfield is also a pioneering example of the trust's new approach to involving the public more directly in its work. Visitors can observe and participate in all its conservation projects here, both in the house and the wider landscape.

[LEFT] *The library, with its open, churchlike ceiling and traceried Gothic windows, reflects the deeply religious nature of its patron, William Gibbs. The warm tones of the oak fittings and leather bindings are beautifully offset by Crace's brilliant-coloured carpet, Minton tiles, and a collection of Imari porcelain. The deep-buttoned sofa and chairs, still with their original wool and silk upholstery, were made by Crace for the drawing room in ca. 1855.*

[CLOCKWISE FROM TOP LEFT]

The night nursery, decorated by Ursula Wraxall for her children.

The drawing room, arranged today as an Edwardian drawing room. It was given its current Renaissance revival appearance in 1908 by George Gibbs and his first wife, Via. Bellini's Holy Family hung here but is now in the Bristol Museum and Art Gallery.

The billiard room, showing part of John Norton's ingenious clerestoreyed pine roof structure. The room was remodelled for Antony Gibbs in the late 1880s, when Henry Woodyer added the inglenook fireplace. Also dating from this period is the centrally heated billiard table supplied by James Plucknett, carved with sporting scenes and connected directly to the electronic scoreboard. The moose, whose head is on display, was shot by Via Gibbs in Canada in 1911.

[LEFT] *The entrance hall or cloister, with a stand made by Collier & Plucknett for Blanche Gibbs in 1878. Tyntesfield has the largest group of Gothic revival furniture by these Warwick-based cabinetmakers, who also supplied some of the carved panelling in the house.*

[OPPOSITE] *The dining room, remodelled in 1887–90 by Henry Woodyer, who added the arcaded screen and triple-bay window, the lavishly carved doorway, and gilded and lacquered wall covering imitating Spanish leather. The room contains important examples of furniture by Crace modelled on designs by Pugin.*

The Chanter's House

— DEVON —

SELDOM has a building reflected so atmospherically the mutual interests of its architect and patron as the Chanter's House in Ottery St. Mary. The architect William Butterfield and John Duke Coleridge were close friends; both were brilliant, scholarly, similar in temperament, and ardent High Churchmen. A legal high-flier, Coleridge was elevated to the peerage in 1873 and became Lord Chief Justice of England in 1880. As befitted his new rank, he set about remodelling the family home he had inherited in 1876, turning to Butterfield, whose "great skill and abilities . . . and the masculine severity of his taste" he had already admired in the architect's restoration of the fourteenth-century collegiate church of St. Mary of Ottery, in whose shadow the Chanter's House stands. Butterfield's name is associated with High Victorian churches; he was one of the most original exponents of the genre. Of his few country houses, only one other—Milton Ernest Hall in Bedfordshire, built for Coleridge's brother-in-law in 1854–58—was substantial, but the Chanter's House was his most ambitious domestic work.

[OPPOSITE] *Butterfield's boldly diapered brick extensions enclosing two sides of a courtyard: his new main entrance on the east side, and a long service wing at right angles replacing an earlier range. The huge, stone-mullioned and transomed window is the principal feature of the outer entrance hall.*

[BELOW] *The dining room in the seventeenth-century part of the house, its elm panelling dating from about 1910. Still known as the Convention Room, this is where in 1645, according to a lead plaque over the sideboard, "Oliver Cromwell presented General Fairfax with a fair jewel for his valour at Naseby fight."*

These photographs, taken in 1990, show the house when it was still the home of the Coleridges. It was sold in 2006, and since then most of the contents have been dispersed.

Of medieval origin, the Chanter's House was the largest of the collegiate houses grouped about St. Mary, the grandest parish church in Devon. The buildings stand on a hill at the edge of the little town, with open views to the southwest over the valley of the River Otter. Butterfield's work here, which dates from 1880–83, involved remodelling what was essentially a nineteenth-century house behind a plain Georgian façade. At the time it was known as Heath's Court after the family that had owned it in the eighteenth century, but in 1900 the house reverted to its original name.

The Coleridges first came to Ottery St. Mary in 1760, when John Coleridge became master of the King's School and vicar of St. Mary's. He

had a large and talented family, many of whom were successful in a range of traditional careers, though none with such lasting fame as his youngest son, the poet Samuel Taylor Coleridge (1772–1834).

It was James, one of Samuel's older brothers, who had fought in the Peninsular War and married a local heiress, who bought Heath's Court in 1796. His son, Sir John Coleridge, was a brilliant graduate of Oxford, where his friends included Thomas Arnold and John Keble, and later became a judge. Sir John's scholarly High Church circle made a strong impression on his son, the future 1st Lord Coleridge, who also went to Oxford and had similar literary, ecclesiastical, and artistic interests. As a student in about 1840, he met Matthew Arnold and John Henry Newman and became inextricably caught up in the Oxford Movement, which was then at its height.

Coleridge's High Victorian tastes, shared by Butterfield but so very

[ABOVE] *The west front, with the parish church in the background. This wing, built to house Coleridge's huge library, has been described by Michael Hall as "Butterfield at his most effortlessly monumental."*

351

different from the lighter "Queen Anne" style then in vogue, permeated the Chanter's House. His wife, Jane, had died suddenly in 1878, and so the remodelling was conceived in part as a memorial to her, with her own paintings grouped on the walls of the outer hall and library, and a life-size cast of her effigy, which Frederick Thrupp had carved for the church, laid in a small, chantry-like room off the library gallery.

Butterfield designed his extensions around the existing building, which housed the dining room, old library, and drawing room. The Georgian south façade he encased in brick, adding an extra half-timbered storey with three elongated dormers (its present, rather top-heavy appearance is the result of the later cladding of the half-timbering with shingles). As Michael Hall so eloquently pointed out in the January 10, 1991, issue of *Country Life*, Butterfield stressed rather than played down the idiosyncratic union of the different parts, leaving the Georgian building visible "like a fossil in a High-Victorian cliff-face."

The forecourt is enclosed on two sides, with the entrance range on the east and a more extensive replacement of the 1840s service wing to the north, all characterised by bold diapering in blue against red brickwork. On the west side, overlooking the terrace, is the tall, gabled library wing, beyond which was a conservatory (now dismantled) and the aviary, billiard room, and skittles alley enclosing another courtyard.

The house is entered through a sequence of spaces progressing with right-angled turns from the porch into a tall, narrow outer hall with a huge Gothic window and painted coat of arms, and then through a little lobby into the (altered) inner hall with the staircase. Directly ahead is the library, the high-point of Butterfield's work here, built to house Lord Coleridge's collection of 18,000 books. It is a remarkable space—a long, two-storey room, beautifully lit by a pair of full-height bay windows. Bookcases incorporating carvings from the church's old pews project at right angles and a first-floor gallery runs along one side. Two marble chimneypieces are inset with reliefs carved by Thrupp, and the room was peopled with bronzed plaster casts of classical statues, busts of heroes and friends, and Lady Coleridge's drawings after Michelangelo.

Despite schemes by later generations of Coleridges to de-Victorianise the house, some of Butterfield's original interior decoration survives, including several painted ceilings, areas of coloured tiling, gas light fittings, marble and iron radiator cases, and other details. The new owners are restoring as much as possible of Butterfield's colours and painted decoration, while renovating the house and restoring the park.

A north-facing view of the library, "the perfect embodiment of mid-Victorian culture." Since this photograph was taken in 1990, the house has been sold and most of its original contents dispersed, although Lady Coleridge's drawings after Michelangelo seen here over the chimneypiece and the majority of the library books remain.

Kelmscott Manor

— GLOUCESTERSHIRE —

KELMSCOTT Manor is the embodiment of the Romantic vision that lay at the heart of the Arts & Crafts movement. William Morris called it "a sweet simple old place" and, on first discovering the old stone farmhouse in a peaceful hamlet near Lechlade, was entranced by its spell. Here he could indulge his nostalgia for a preindustrial age and his romance with nature and the beauty of weathered old buildings and hand-wrought craftsmanship. "Everywhere there was but little furniture, and that only the most necessary and of the most simple forms," he wrote in his utopian novel *News from Nowhere* (1890). The book bore on its frontispiece an image of Kelmscott Manor and contained lyrical descriptions of the house and its setting on low-lying meadowland beside the Thames. From 1871 until his death in 1896, Morris rented Kelmscott as a summer retreat, tolerating his wife's affair with Dante Gabriel Rossetti, who came to live here too.

The house was built in about 1600 by Thomas Turner, a yeoman farmer whose family owned the place for more than three centuries. Of mellow Cotswold limestone, with stone-tiled roofs and wooden gutters, the original house has a simple U plan, its gabled, mullion-windowed front approached through a garden secluded behind high stone walls. Two ranges to the rear contained the kitchen and pantry and a pair of parlours. At right angles to the front is a tall cross wing of about 1665, with pedimented classical windows set high up in its attic gables.

The third Thomas Turner became rich and married well. His addition of ca. 1665 contained a spacious new parlour with a best chamber above, their chimneypieces carved with his newly granted coat of arms. These rooms were redecorated in the early eighteenth century; the parlour, with wainscoting and pilasters of that date, is now known as the White Drawing Room. The best chamber was hung with cut-down seventeenth-century Brussels or Antwerp tapestries depicting the life of Samson. Their texture and faded colours added greatly to the warmth and atmosphere of the chamber, which the Morrises used as their sitting room.

The main entrance leads into the hall, which Morris used as a dining room and furnished with simple country furniture. Divided from the kitchen by a screens passage, the hall has changed since it was recorded in an inventory of 1611. During his lifetime, Morris had the house looking deliberately quite

[OPPOSITE] *The entrance front of Kelmscott Manor, a farmhouse built around 1600 that became the embodiment of William Morris's philosophy and way of life. The gabled cross wing on the right was added in ca. 1665.*

[OPPOSITE] *The Tapestry Room, originally the best chamber, above the parlour in the 1665 wing; the Morrises used it as their sitting room. The beautifully faded tapestries depicting the life of Samson gave "an air of romance that nothing else would quite do," wrote Morris.*

[RIGHT] *William Morris's bedroom, with wallpaper in the Daisy pattern. The hangings and pelmet on his beloved four-poster bed were designed by May Morris, the latter bearing a poem by her father in medieval script. The coverlet was embroidered with a pattern of wildflowers by Jane Morris and Augusta de Morgan in 1894–95.*

Spartan. Faithful to his philosophy for old buildings, he left the paintwork untouched and made minimal changes. Indeed, the interior decoration was largely the work of his wife, Jane, who introduced wallpapers from Morris & Co. and commissioned Philip Webb to design tiles for the fireplace in the Green Room.

Morris's bedroom was situated in the old part of the house that preserved "the peculiarity of being without passages, so that you have to go from one room into another." It was hung with one of his earliest wallpaper designs, Daisy, and furnished with his beloved four-poster bed, a hybrid made up of Elizabethan and Jacobean panelling, cornices, and newel posts, about which he wrote the poem *For the Bed at Kelmscott* in 1891. His daughter May designed the bed hangings and pelmet, the latter bearing a poem by her father in medieval script. Jane Morris worked the coverlet with Augusta de Morgan in 1894–95, embroidering it with a beautiful pattern of wildflowers and fauna.

After Morris's death in 1896, his wife moved here permanently, acquiring the freehold in 1913, a year before her death. She brought to Kelmscott the furnishings from their Hammersmith home, and in the 1920s May added the contents of her house, so that Kelmscott became much fuller than it had been during Morris's lifetime, including pieces designed by Philip Webb for Red House in Kent, which he had built for the Morrises in 1860, as well as a collection of Georgian and Regency furniture.

Photographs and engravings by artists such as F. L. Griggs contributed to Morris's own depictions in *News from Nowhere* to enshrine Kelmscott's Romantic reputation. By 1921, when A. E. Henson photographed the house for two articles in *Country Life*, it had already assumed something of its present identity as a place devoted to the memory of William Morris, and the way of life he espoused. His interest in unpretentious vernacular forms, "the strange and quaint garrets amongst the great timbers of the roof, where of old time the tillers and herdsmen of the manor slept," struck a chord with *Country Life*, whose articles included photographs of the old wooden staircase, and of the roof structures in the attic, where the simplicity of the servants' rooms has been maintained.

May Morris lived at Kelmscott until her death in 1938, and the rooms are very much as she furnished them, with handwoven wall hangings, fabrics and wallpapers by Morris, needlework by his wife and daughters, and books published by the Kelmscott Press. Portraits of Jane Morris by Rossetti hang in the house, and in the Garden Hall is an embroidery she worked to Morris's design depicting her as Queen Guinevere.

May left the house, unmodernised but still with its most important contents, to Oxford University. In 1962 the university passed it on to the Society of Antiquaries, which initiated a programme of repairs by Peter Locke of Donald Insall Associates and conserved the contents. Since 1992 Kelmscott has been open to the public on a regular basis and, more recently, Hal Moggridge has re-created the garden.

[OPPOSITE, CLOCKWISE FROM TOP LEFT] *The Tapestry Room, with a table designed by Philip Webb in ca. 1860.*

Jane Morris's bedroom, decorated with Morris & Co.'s famous Willow Pattern.

The fireplace in the Green Room, which Jane Morris opened up and decorated with tiles designed by Morris and Webb.

The Panelled Room, the spacious parlour on the ground floor of the 1665 wing. William Morris left it painted white, as it probably always had been. The chimney-piece is carved with Thomas Turner's coat of arms. The chairs are upholstered in Peacock and Dragon.

[RIGHT] *The house from the west. The left-hand wing contains the Green Room with Jane Morris's bedroom above; the service wing is on the right.*

[ABOVE] *The detail of the original main staircase suggests that the house was built in the early 1600s, which documents support.*

[RIGHT] *A pair of chairs by Ernest Gimson in the servants' garrets, which Morris found filled with "bunches of dying flowers, feathers of birds, shells of starlings' eggs, cadis worms in mugs." He loved "the great timbers of the roof, where of old time the tillers and herdsmen of the manor slept." Arts & Crafts furniture and textiles are now displayed in these attic rooms, where the air of simplicity has been maintained.*

Wightwick Manor

— STAFFORDSHIRE —

WIGHTWICK Manor is one of the best surviving examples of the late Victorian medieval revival and a glowing memorial to the circle of William Morris. Built and furnished for an industrialist who was passionate about traditional craftsmanship, it has since been enriched by the addition of many fine Arts & Crafts and Aesthetic movement artefacts, as well as an outstanding collection of Pre-Raphaelite art. In 1937 Wightwick became the first completely furnished house to be acquired by the National Trust, under its new Country Houses Scheme.

Although it takes its name from an old manorial family (whose Jacobean house was remodelled as staff accommodation), Wightwick is not so much a country house as a large villa, built on the edge of Wolverhampton for the director of a paint and varnish manufacturer. Samuel Theodore Mander was a typical patron of Arts & Crafts designers: wealthy, liberal, devout, public-spirited, and highly educated. He and his Canadian wife (whose name, bizarrely, was Flora Paint) were deeply influenced by the works of Ruskin and Morris. They commissioned the Cheshire architect Edward Ould, and the original part of their new house was completed in 1888. A mix of tile-hung

[OPPOSITE] *A detail of the Great Parlour, showing painted roof timbers, wall panels hung with Morris & Co. wool fabric printed with J. H. Dearle's 1893 Diagonal Trail design, and C. E. Kempe's plaster frieze depicting the story of Orpheus and Eurydice, which was possibly inspired by one at Hardwick Hall.*

[BELOW] *The entrance front, showing the late Victorian interest in timber-framed buildings. "No style of building will harmonize so quickly and so completely with its surroundings and so soon pass through the crude and brand-new period," wrote the architect Edward Ould in his book about the half-timbered buildings of Herefordshire, Shropshire, and Cheshire, published in 1904.*

and half-timbered gabled ranges, it formed an L plan around a tower of hard, bright-red brick and was surrounded by formal gardens, extended first by the artist Alfred Parsons in 1899 and then by Thomas Mawson.

Before half-timbering became widely popularised under the influence of R. Norman Shaw and W. E. Nesfield, it had enjoyed a revival in the north-east, largely thanks to the work of John Douglas of Chester. Ould had been a pupil of his and became an authority on the subject. In 1893 he doubled the house in size. This more successful and scholarly east wing attempted a convincing re-creation of a timber-framed building, incorporating details copied from Tudor houses such as Little Moreton Hall in Cheshire and Ockwells in Buckinghamshire. Interestingly, despite the obvious delight in craftsmanship, this careful re-creation of a historic style and arrangement of intricately carved oak, moulded terra-cotta, sandstone, brick, and tiled elements for Picturesque effect was in opposition to Arts & Crafts principles.

The spine of the house is a long corridor leading from the porch, with the drawing room, morning room, and former dining room (now library) opening

[LEFT] *The walnut-panelled Great Parlour, which shows the influence of R. Norman Shaw in its reinterpretation of a Tudor hall, complete with screens, minstrels' gallery, exposed painted roof timbers, and a huge inglenook fireplace. The brass chandeliers were made by W. A. S. Benson for Holman Hunt and brought here in the late 1930s. Beneath the gallery hangs one of Burne-Jones's finest works,* Love Among the Ruins, *introduced by the National Trust from the Bearsted Collection at Upton House. The Victorian arrangement of the room as an informal living hall was reinstated in 1992–95.*

[RIGHT] *A settle designed by G. F. Bodley and painted by Kempe, acquired for Wightwick in 1959.*

off it to the south. The corridor then turns left into the grander-scaled later wing, which is dominated by a double-height living hall known as the Great Parlour, one of the finest late-Victorian rooms in England. Beyond it lie the dining room and billiard room, with beautifully modelled plaster friezes and ceilings by L. A. Shuffrey, above which are five guest bedrooms.

The National Trust has been able to recapture the spirit of certain rooms by reversing later alterations to the furnishings. The Manders did not employ Morris & Co. to decorate the house, but bought wallpapers, fabrics, upholstered furniture, and woven carpets from their London showroom. Most of the stained glass, hand-knotted carpets, embroideries, de Morgan lustreware, and other ceramics were bought later from Morris's more expensive ranges by their son, Sir Geoffrey, and his second wife, Rosalie. It was they who turned Wightwick into a shrine to Morris, introducing more furniture and Kelmscott Press books, and decorating other rooms with Morris papers and fabrics. They were also among the first serious collectors of Pre-Raphaelite art, leaving Wightwick with remarkable works by Rossetti, Holman Hunt, Burne-Jones, and Ford Madox Brown, among others.

Despite the differences in spirit and quality of the external architecture, the largely Jacobean-style interiors are quite harmoniously integrated. This may owe something to the involvement throughout of the stained-glass maker and architectural decorator C. E. Kempe. His input is particularly notable in the Great Parlour, where he was responsible for the polychrome decoration of the roof timbers, stained-glass windows, and delightful gesso overmantel and plaster frieze. Tiles by de Morgan, light fittings and other metalwork by W. A. S. Benson, Flemish tapestries, Morris carpets and textiles, Eastern rugs, and Oriental porcelain combine to create a richness of pattern, colour, and texture typical of the "artistic" eclecticism of late-nineteenth-century taste.

The drawing room in the earlier wing contains further examples of this juxtaposition of antique and Victorian pieces, including an Italian Renaissance chimneypiece inset with de Morgan tiles. And at every turn, without and within, the eye is caught by appropriate inscriptions painted onto lintels and carved into walls—quotes from Shakespeare, Walter Scott, Robert Herrick, John Ruskin, or the Bible that capture the spirit of this romantic house.

[OPPOSITE] *The celebrated portrait of Jane Morris that was begun by Rossetti but completed by Madox Brown. Acquired in 1937, it was among the first purchases for the house by Sir Geoffrey and Lady Mander. It hangs above a fine walnut-and-rosewood piano in the drawing room.*

[ABOVE] *The oak room, with its original arrangement of interconnecting bedroom, dressing room, and writing room, as reinstated in 1993. The folding bed belonged to the poet A. C. Swinburne and came* *from the Pines in Putney, along with the cupboard, both similarly carved and with painted panels by H. Treffry Dunn. The Morris hand-knotted carpet, purchased in 1961, is exceptionally fine.*

[BELOW] *A view of the night nursery, redecorated in ca. 1908 and restored in 1991. The Minton tiles date from the 1880s, and the printed frieze was designed by sporting artist and illustrator Cecil Aldin. The floor is covered in green linoleum and the walls painted in green distemper.*

[LEFT] *A view from the gallery into the bay window of the Great Parlour, with stained glass by C. E. Kempe.*

[OPPOSITE] *The library, created out of the original dining room in 1893, with books reflecting the Manders' interest in science, religion, history, and politics. The wallpaper shows Morris's Larkspur design of 1888, and the stained-glass windows, introduced by Sir Geoffrey and Lady Mander, are by Ford Madox Brown and Burne-Jones.*

Blackwell

— CUMBRIA —

BUILT in 1898–1900 as a holiday home for the Manchester brewer Sir Edward Holt, Blackwell is a masterpiece of great subtlety and artistic imagination by the Arts & Crafts architect M. H. Baillie Scott. Hermann Muthesius described it in *Das englische Haus* (1905) as "one of the most attractive creations that the new movement in house-building has produced," and it is regarded as a pivotal work in the architect's career. There are references to C. F. A. Voysey in some of the vernacular detail; much of the internal decoration belongs to a late flowering of the Art Nouveau style, while the clean, unadorned lines of the exterior and the play with abstract space look forward to modernism.

A key aspect of this commission was the opportunity it gave Baillie Scott to explore his ideas free of the constraints that a permanent residence would have imposed. The house is orientated and designed to take maximum advantage of its spectacular situation, perched high above Lake Windermere with views to the Coniston Fells. The exterior, of whitewashed roughcast

[OPPOSITE] *The great hall, with a small room projecting above the inglenook. The fireplace is surmounted by interlocking blocks of local stone and slate and flanked by Delft tiles. Baillie Scott wrote in his book* Houses and Gardens, *"The house, however warm, without a fire, may very reasonably be compared to a summer day without the sun."*

[BELOW] *Blackwell from the former tennis courts, showing how the house is subtly integrated with its gardens and terraces on the fellside site. The plain, roughcast render gives it a vernacular feel, in contrast with the richness of the interior decoration, but the effect of the clean, white lines and pared-down ornament is also strikingly modern.*

with roofs of Westmorland slate, has a simplicity suited to a rural retreat. Cylindrical chimneys, prominent gables, and stone-mullioned windows evoke the architecture of Lakeland farmhouses, but Blackwell also feels strikingly modern.

The interior, by contrast, is richly decorated with plasterwork, wallpaper friezes, stained glass, metalwork, and carved stone and wood of the finest craftsmanship in an ecstatic celebration of the local flora and fauna. As a result, Blackwell feels wholly at ease with its natural surroundings and in tune with the Arts & Crafts movement that was already flourishing in the Lake District. "It was especially desired," wrote Baillie Scott, "that the Mountain Ash should form the subject of the decoration. . . . In the carved trees, which appear in the staircase screen and on the hall ingle, birds' nests are interwoven in the branches and birds flutter amongst the leaves and fruit. In the brackets to the lower beams and in the bosses to the ceiling various local plants are represented. One is entwined with bryony, another shows the blooms of the wild guelder-rose, while the bloom and berries of the hawthorn and the wild rose are among the features of the carving."

Blackwell signifies an important moment in European domestic building, when architects began to reconsider the way houses were used. The flowing, open plan revolves around a large, double-height hall, a place where the family could congregate at the heart of the house, with an inglenook hearth and adjoining window seat representing warmth, solidity, and comfort. This emphasis on the hearth, with the inglenook fireplace as a theme running through the house, reflects the influence of Norman Shaw, as does the "Old English"–style half timbering on the wall of a small room above the inglenook. There is a certain complexity about the way the hall is compartmentalised, with areas of lower ceiling representing different functions within the single space. The billiard room occupies one end, doing away with the Victorian tradition of segregating the male domain. The dining room is in a separate room beyond. Everywhere light, space, colour, and texture are carefully orchestrated to create a sense of drama. The climax comes in moving from the warm, oak-wainscoted hall into the brilliantly lit White Drawing Room, one of Baillie Scott's finest interiors and an intensely feminine room. Here, capitals, frieze, ceiling, and stained glass flow with naturalistic decoration in a delicate Art Nouveau style. The room has a great feeling of modernity and exemplifies Muthesius's claim that Baillie Scott was "the first to have realised the interior as an autonomous work of art."

After years as a girls' school, Blackwell was still remarkably intact but faced with an uncertain future. The Lakeland Arts Trust purchased it in 1999, restored and refurnished the house, and in 2001 opened it to the public as a branch of the Abbot Hall Art Gallery and Museum in nearby Kendal.

The south front, with Lake Windermere and the Coniston Fells in the background. Blackwell is one of several large Arts & Crafts houses built in this area at a time when growing numbers of tourists were discovering the Lake District.

[ABOVE] The window bay in the
White Drawing Room, one of
Baillie Scott's finest interiors. This
intensely feminine room spans the
width of the house at its western
end, overlooking the lake from
two bay windows. Its naturalistic
decoration represents a late flowering
of the Art Nouveau style.

[OPPOSITE, CLOCKWISE FROM TOP
LEFT] The east end of the great hall,
designed as a billiard room. The glowing
peacock wallpaper frieze by Shand Kydd
was added in 1906; it has been carefully
conserved. The hanging light shades of
beaten copper were discovered in storage,
restored, and rehung above the original
position of the billiard table.

A stained-glass window in the
White Drawing Room decorated with
stylised birds.

The exquisite White Drawing Room, with
motifs of local wildflowers and plants in
the decorative scheme. The oriel window
over the stone fireplace has stained glass
depicting swaying fronds and hidden birds.

One of the wrought-iron window catches
seen throughout the house, each pair
slightly different from the others.

374

TIM RICHARDSON

THE LANDSCAPES AND GARDENS OF
THE ENGLISH COUNTRY HOUSE

THE affinity between the English and the practice of gardening has long been noted by foreign visitors, from the courtier-diarists of the seventeenth and eighteenth centuries and Vincent van Gogh, who marvelled at the beauty of the front gardens of suburban south London in the 1870s, right up to the modern-day tourists who arrive in droves to visit great gardens such as Sissinghurst (see page 477) or Chatsworth (see page 474), or the Chelsea Flower Show. In many ways, gardening has emerged as the domestic artform of Britain, playing a role similar to that of cookery in France. This pronounced horticultural urge is usually ascribed at least in part to the favourable climate of these islands, where it is possible to grow an exceptionally wide range of plants from all parts of the world with, in addition, a gratifyingly long flowering season. But there is more to it than that. Without dipping too far into the realms of speculative psychology, there does seem to be something in the mindset of the British that makes gardening attractive to them. It has something to do with a deeply engrained respect for private property—"every Englishman's home is his castle," as the saying goes—and the tradition of entertaining at home, as opposed to in some public or semi-public space.

❡ In the realm of the country house, the garden has generally been deemed to be of considerable importance, both as a productive space supplying vegetables, fruit, and cut flowers for the house, and as a venue for entertainment and leisure. It has also been used as a means of expressing fashionable taste, or asserting social or dynastic status. Indeed, the health and attractiveness of the garden and wider estate have consistently been seen as a kind of barometer for the fortunes of the resident family, as well as functioning as a piquant way for them to express their own distinctive attitudes to agriculture, politics, and the culture as a whole. In this sense, the gardens of country houses can be read as autobiographies of the families that owned them.

❡ A strong tradition of country house and garden visiting dates back to the eighteenth century, when large estates had set days of the week when they were open to the public. Even today some 80 percent of visitors to National Trust properties say that the garden is the main reason for their interest. It is clear that gardens are peculiarly important in this culture.

❡ The earliest archaeological evidence of gardens in Britain dates from the 1st century A D and the time of the Roman occupation. These followed the standard Roman model of open courtyards decorated with mosaics and formal pools, together with a larger walled area reserved for the cultivation of vines, flowers, herbs, and fruit trees, perhaps with a colonnaded perimeter walkway (as at the Roman villa at Fishbourne in Sussex). Before the Romans, and for a number of centuries after their departure, there is scanty evidence of gardening except in the sense of the raising of crops near settlements to provide food. One area of exception is that of medicine: monasteries grew medicinal herbs as well as culinary ones, alongside fruit and vegetables for the table.

℃ After the Norman Conquest in 1066, there are records of areas of land being enclosed at great estates for the purposes of hunting deer and wild boar—for example at Henry I's Woodstock in Oxfordshire in the early twelfth century. Medieval manuscript illuminations indicate that closer to the house were small, enclosed gardens filled with climbing roses and other flowers, as well as fruit. Such a garden was sometimes referred to as a *hortus conclusus* and was traditionally associated with the Virgin Mary. There was probably some Islamic precedent for these small, enclosed gardens, which may have been retreats reserved chiefly for women. Documents suggest that trees were planted, partly for decorative effect, and there is evidence of the English liking for expanses of green turf or lawn developing at this time. Stewponds (for fish) would have had some decorative appeal and were very often joined up and transformed into large lakes in later centuries. Trellised fences, arbours, and tunnels were a particularly popular feature of the medieval garden, and by the fifteenth century clipped topiary and small parterres of box hedging ("knots") had become fashionable.

℃ These ideas were elaborated during the reign of Henry VIII, specifically at the royal palaces of Hampton Court, Nonsuch, and Whitehall in the 1530s and '40s. One novelty here was the addition, among the topiary, of painted wooden heraldic devices atop tall wooden poles. The later sixteenth century saw the introduction of formal Italian features such as grottoes and, a little later, elaborate water tricks and optical effects.

℃ By the late seventeenth century, a more strident and monumental approach to landscape design had emerged, derived from the precedent of André Le Notre in France. The London-based team of George London and Henry Wise realised numerous large-scale parterre gardens with extending axial rides or avenues. One peculiarly English aspect of this was the fashion for parterres made entirely of cut turf and fine gravel or sand, popularised through Europe as the "parterre à l'Angloise."

℃ The English had always opted for a slightly more naturalistic manner of formal gardening than their European contemporaries (except the Dutch), and the writings of John Evelyn were influential in this respect: in his *Sylva* of 1664 he recommended planting for aesthetic as well as economic reasons. This distinctive attitude became more entrenched in the last decades of the seventeenth century, when England's increasingly close links with Holland culminated in the importation of William of Orange as monarch in 1688, to replace James II. While certain formal features, such as mounts, parterres, statuary, and gridded plantations of trees, endured, and some "Dutch" ideas (notably straight canals and decorative ironwork) were borrowed, in both Dutch and English gardens at this time a looseness of planning was introduced to wooded areas, which now incorporated serpentine walks and unadorned grassy clearings, and a generally much more relaxed, bucolic flavour. Productive areas such as orchards were now integrated into the aesthetic programme of the garden, as was the natural topography. The impression of "wandering" through episodic spaces as opposed to "wondering" at set-piece features such as fountains, increasingly came to characterise English gardens in the early eighteenth century.

❦ Joseph Addison, writing in *The Spectator* in 1712, is usually credited as the populariser of this idea of mixing ornament and utility on an estate, but in reality he was elucidating a fashion that had been growing for several decades. As the prime mover in the Whig propaganda machine, which supported first William of Orange and then the House of Hanover, Addision sought to use landscape gardening as an emblem of new Whiggish attitudes to agriculture, and a badge of loyalty to the cause. But it was never quite the "revolution" he espoused: the landscape garden developed slowly as more formal features were dropped or reinterpreted. (The designer Charles Bridgeman—responsible for Stowe, Claremont, Grimsthorpe, and many other notable gardens—was perhaps the prime mover in this respect.) The connection between house, garden, and wider landscape was encapsulated in the feature known as a ha-ha: a ditch, invisible at a distance, which kept animals away from the house but created the impression of unbounded landscape.

❦ The importance of classical pastoral poetry and the experience of the Grand Tour helped ensure that English gardens were often replete with classical symbolism and small buildings that echoed classical precedent. Alexander Pope's garden at Twickenham, with its celebrated grotto, reflected these preoccupations, as well as contemporary scientific interests such as optics and geology. His friend William Kent, designer of gardens such as Rousham and Chiswick (see page 475), perhaps did more than anyone to further the cause of landscape design in this episodic mode. Symbolism could be used to advance any point of view, including political ideas, and in this sense Lord Cobham's mammoth project at Stowe was certainly the most strident and ambitious. Here, features such as the Temple of British Worthies were formed as a rebuke directed at the venal, nepotistic mainstream Whig regime under the first minister Robert Walpole by an enraged and superannuated Whig dissident. Many of the best gardens of the period were made by Whig grandees who had been forcibly "retired." John Aislabie, Whig Chancellor of the Exchequer at the time of the South Sea Bubble financial scandal, made his garden in exile at Studley Royal in Yorkshire after being incarcerated in the Tower of London. Tory garden makers such as Lord Bathurst and Lord Bolingbroke, supported by poets including Pope, Swift, and Gay, sought to formulate a landscape-garden riposte to Addison and his Whig cronies after they had been sidelined from government when the aggressively Whiggish Elector of Hanover was crowned George I in 1714.

❦ By the 1730s and '40s, it was de rigueur to design garden buildings inspired by models other than Greek or Roman, and a dazzling variety of "Chinese," rustic, Gothick, and other structures were now to be found within fantastical garden realms such as Painshill, where the owner briefly employed a live hermit to reside in his hermitage (he was sacked for drunkennesss). In some gardens from the 1740s, notably Stourhead, the landscape paintings of Claude, Poussin, and Gaspard were the inspiration for the principal vistas. Now, after years during which the eighteenth-century landscape garden was considered essentially a green environment, the past decade saw the extent and importance of flowers for colour and scent beginning to be properly understood again (and in some case reinstated).

℄ By the 1750s, the vogue for symbolic or political landscape gardening had diminished, and the second half of the eighteenth century was dominated by the misleadingly yeoman-like figure of Lancelot "Capability" Brown, who effectively exerted a landscape monopoly in England over a period of some three decades. Brown espoused a pastoral landscape style that was devoid of meaning but proved irresistible to large numbers of landowning families, charmed by the formula of lakes, rolling pasture, clumps of trees ("punctuation," Brown called them), dramatic entrance drives, and multiple vistas from the house and other key points on the estate. Many of the surviving formal gardens of the seventeenth century and earlier were lost to Brown's pastoral steamroller, though he displayed sensitivity and restraint on occasion.

℄ There followed in the 1780s and '90s a brief but intense fashion for the Picturesque—that is,

landscape gardens predicated on ideas of fear, excitement, and the danger of natural surroundings. The wild topography of the Wye Valley or North Yorkshire, for example, was exploited to create landscape gardens that thrilled visitors and perhaps reminded them of journeys across the Swiss Alps. Hermitages, grottoes, mock castles, and alpine bridges added to the experience at places such as Hawkstone Park and Hackfall Wood.

℄ At the turn of the century, Humphry Repton succeeded in his desire to become Brown's successor as the prime landscaper of England, with his famous "before-and-after" Red Books made for clients, with movable watercolour flaps. What Repton added to Brown's formula was a return to formality around the house—that is, flower gardening within fencing, with some decorative ornament in the form of statuary or fountains. Regency gardens, such as that at the Royal Pavilion in Brighton, also featured large island beds for shrubs and flowers, and decorous expanses of smooth lawn.

℄ From the 1830s, the taste for Picturesque gardening declined at country houses, to be replaced by a more formal emphasis on Italianate gardening, as espoused most skilfully by Charles Barry. There was also a fashion for a more generally historicist look, loosely based on either English models (Jacobean or Caroline, for example) or French parterre gardening. The latter led to the fashion for "carpet-bedding" with annual flowers that can still be seen in British public parks today. Hand in hand with these formalist preoccupations went a veritable obsession with exotic plants from abroad: fruit trees for the glass-house, rhododendrons from China for dells and valleys, pines from the Americas, and alpine plants for large rockeries.

℃ The later decades of the nineteenth century saw a penchant for a Romantic look, ostensibly based on the seventeenth-century precedent of such celebrated houses as Montacute (see pages 8 and 13). Massive, old yew topiaries, sundials, and decaying stonework were all fetishised at this time by designers who allied themselves first with the Aesthetic and then the Arts & Crafts movements. *Country Life* played a key role in promoting this particular look around 1900–10, when its sometime gardens editor Gertrude Jekyll emerged as a prime protagonist, latterly in tandem with the young architect Edwin Lutyens. Their partnership was vaunted then and since for its fine balance between architecture and horticulture. But Jekyll had other interests: she reprised her knowledge of painterly colour theory for flower gardening, suggesting that certain colour combinations would evoke certain emotions in the onlooker. Her prescriptions regarding flower colour were to prove of enduring interest, despite their technically challenging nature; it is a moot point how many others have been able to achieve the results she had in mind. Perhaps an even more important figure at this time was William Robinson, a journalist who espoused a version of the "wild garden" in which he suggested that the gardener might ornament natural scenes by the judicious addition of other plants, including exotica.

℃ The cult of the cottage garden also grew out of the observations of Jekyll and others, and was certainly of more lasting importance than technical colour theory. The idea of an ancient English vernacular gardening style, although largely fabricated by writers and watercolourists such as Helen Allingham, found an enthusiastic audience among the enlarging middle classes, particularly in the south. And the garden architecture of Arts & Crafts designers such as Lutyens, Philip Webb, and M. H. Baillie Scott was appropriated by speculative house builders and used for new garden suburbs and estates. Features such as crazy paving, wishing wells, rose standards up to the front door, and small rockeries became de rigueur in these gardens, as did a cottagey approach to planting. Influential through their journalistic writings were mid-century gardeners such as Vita Sackville-West and Margery Fish, who promoted a deceptively relaxed attitude to horticulture (deceptive because they and their followers were obsessed with gardening), an approach that has in many ways endured until today.

℃ The country house garden of the mid- to late twentieth century was in many ways much reduced in scope compared with what went before. The Second World War marked the death knell of the servant culture at larger houses, and owners were obliged to garden for themselves or with a much-reduced staff. It has to be said that many garden owners grasped the opportunity with both hands, and a strong culture of gentry gardening emerged, defined at first by a connoisseurial interest in plants (epitomised by gardeners such as Bobby James at St. Nicholas in Yorkshire), and later by a renewed interest in flower gardening (led by Rosemary Verey in the 1970s and 1980s) and historical formalism (promoted by Sir Roy Strong and others). Sculpture and other modern interventions have been used to good effect at gardens such as Antony and Kiftsgate, while a vibrant example has been set by garden-makers such as Charles Jencks in Scotland, where he created the ebulliently land-formed Garden of Cosmic Speculation in the 1990s. The influx of new planting ideas from Holland and Germany since the late 1990s—the "New Perennials" movement—has led to a new emphasis on form and structure in British gardens, in the shape of decorative grasses particularly. Britain's receptiveness to new ideas is illustrated by the creation of a number of groundbreaking gardens in this spirit in recent years, from the regeneration of the Barry-designed Italianate Trentham gardens in Staffordshire by Piet Oudolf and Tom Stuart-Smith, to the wildest garden style of all—that of Dutchman Henk Gerrittsen at Waltham Place in Berkshire.

Pages 376 and 385: Jasmine, ca. 1830,
Hamilton Weston Wallpapers

Voewood

— NORFOLK —

SEA breezes, bathing, a benign climate, and the new craze for golf and tennis attracted the leisured classes to the area of North Norfolk christened "Poppyland" around the turn of the nineteenth century. Of the Arts & Crafts holiday houses that sprang up along this coastal stretch, none is more extraordinary than Voewood, which stands a little inland on the edge of the market town of Holt. One of the most original Rogue houses of the English Arts & Crafts movement, Voewood is also the finest domestic work of Edward Schroeder Prior.

The form of the house—a truncated H with the wings spread apart at 120 degrees to the central range—is a supreme example of the "butterfly plan," which was conceived by Richard Norman Shaw, with whom Prior had trained. Voewood is the most successful of a notable group of these "sun-trap" houses built on the East Anglian coast in the early 1900s.

The skewed and restless lines of Prior's design, its ingenious plan and

[OPPOSITE] *The "cloister" room with a mosaic by Annabel Grey. Now enclosed, this was originally an open loggia between the dining room and the terrace overlooking the sunken gardens.*

[BELOW] *The entrance front, facing northwest on one of the "butterfly" wings.*

[ABOVE] *The inglenook fireplace in the hall, lined with Delft tiles and surmounted by* The Spirit of the Industrial Evolution *by Simon Finch and Roger Ackling (2005). With its massive fireplace, open-timbered roof, and gallery, this double-height space at the centre of the house is clearly inspired by the medieval great hall.*

[OPPOSITE, CLOCKWISE FROM TOP LEFT] *The open corridor on the south side of the hall, which gives access to the dining room and kitchen quarters in the east wing. Above it is a gallery, originally open*

lively mannerisms, are distinctive characteristics of this strange, ruggedly beautiful architectural mosaic, which seems almost literally to have been forged from the ground on which it stands. It is hard to believe, looking at the picturesque ensemble today, that just over a century ago the site was a windswept turnip field. It was built between 1903 and 1905 for the Reverend Percy Lloyd, although he never actually lived here. Instead he let it out, and then, from 1914 until 1998, Voewood was occupied by a succession of institutional establishments. Only since becoming a private home again has the house, for the first time in its life, been furnished and arranged in a manner that lives up to its architecture.

Many of the ideas that Prior explored at Voewood were rooted in the traditions of the medieval builders whose work he had explored in his book *A History of Gothic Art in England*, published in 1900. Prior believed that the way a building is constructed is as important as its design, and that it should be an honest expression of the functional relationship between construction, materials, and place. And so the exterior ripples with the materials of the local vernacular: greyish flints and dun pebbles embedded into

but glazed-in shortly after it was built to reduce draughts on the first floor.

The sitting room, furnished to evoke the atmosphere of a game lodge. Geometric-weave fabrics and animal skins, Roman blinds printed with birds, and a collection of pods, gourds, skulls, snakeskins, shell pictures, and tribal instruments reflect the owner's strong interest in Africa.

The dining room has a particularly strong Arts & Crafts flavour, with its rug specially commissioned to a design by Voysey, Gimson-inspired chairs, oak dining table, and Moroccan light fittings inset with coloured glass.

The kitchen, with its array of junk-shop finds and inherited china; the ducks were roadkill sent to the local taxidermists.

walls; thin, red bricks and tile strips defining openings and used as friezes; tawny carstones forming cross stitches and random flecks of gold. Colour and texture are celebrated in a Ruskinian manner, with no attempt to hide the roughness and imperfections of the materials and workmanship. As the late Roderick Gradidge observed, the spiralling, diapered, and zigzag patterns give the house the quaint appearance of being covered with a very old Fair Isle pullover.

Prior's commitment to "economy of materials" is reflected in the manner of construction: sand and gravel from the site were mixed into local lime for mortar and used as aggregate for the mass concrete that forms much of the structure. Flints and pebbles were extracted from the ground; the carstone came from nearby Sandringham; and bricks and tiles were made locally by hand. Prior dispensed with the "unnecessary expense" of a contractor and instead entrusted the job of superintending the building works to the young architect Randall Wells.

The full, daring impact of the plan is revealed on the south front, where the gabled central range and embracing diagonal wings form one symmetrical composition with the sunken formal gardens. At the centre, an octagonal-columned loggia serves to integrate the two, and on each side the wings, with their additional loggias and canted, Dutch-gabled ends, are fused with the flanking garden walls. The organic relationship between house, garden walls, and attendant buildings is one of the wonders of Voewood.

Inside, the complexity of the plan results in many differently shaped rooms, and two awkward V-shaped spaces that Prior used for staircases. But light floods in from all directions and there is a sense of space and modernity, which is emphasised by the relatively plain finishes of plaster, polished concrete, and oak.

The owner, Simon Finch, a rare books and art dealer, has restored the original internal spaces and redecorated and furnished Voewood in collaboration with the textile designer Annabel Grey. Good Arts & Crafts pieces are combined with 1950s objects, Pop art, and tribal artefacts; junk-shop curiosities reflect an eye for the quirky, and a bolder, modernist note is struck by the Eames and de Stijl chairs and an art collection ranging from Jean Cocteau and John Piper to works by Pop and contemporary British artists. These eclectic tastes work well in the Arts & Crafts interiors and resonate with the idiosyncracies of Prior's architecture.

A view from the southwest, showing the chimneys with diagonally set spiralled shafts that are among the most powerful elements of Voewood's design. They recall the chimneys of some of the great sixteenth- and seventeenth-century houses of East Anglia, but instead of using rubbed and moulded bricks, Prior achieved the same effect much more economically by laying tile bricks in lime mortar around fireclay flue pipes without any cutting or rubbing.

391

Great Dixter

— SUSSEX —

GREAT Dixter, enveloped by its famous gardens, is one of the most alluring and admired of early-twentieth-century manor house restorations. The result of a collaboration between the architect Edwin Lutyens and the owner Nathaniel Lloyd, it was conceived, in true Arts & Crafts spirit, as a total work of art. Buildings and gardens flow into one another; new work respects the existing building forms and traditions of craftsmanship; and the furnishings, including antiques specially made for the house, enhance the feeling of antiquity. Seen against the beautiful landscape of the Sussex Weald, the whole composition possesses those romantic and aesthetic qualities that *Country Life* celebrated in its influential early articles; it is a dream of Old England.

Nathaniel Lloyd was a typical patron. A wealthy businessman and master printer with antiquarian interests, he was able to retire young and devote himself to rural pursuits and the restoration of his newly acquired manor house. The dilapidated property had been on the market for ten years when

[OPPOSITE] *A stencil decoration on the landing to designs by Nathaniel Lloyd.*

[BELOW] *The entrance front, showing the close-studded timber framing of the porch, which, along with everything to its right, is what survives of the fifteenth- and sixteenth-century house. Everything to the left (the east wing) is by Lutyens, with kitchen and service quarters below, bedrooms and day nursery above.*

he bought it in 1910—the house, farm buildings, and immediate grounds all for £6,000. Great Dixter unleashed Lloyd's enthusiasm for architecture: in middle age he embarked on an architect's training, encouraged by Lutyens, and also became a respected authority and writer on architectural subjects. At every stage he was closely involved in the restoration, sourcing salvaged materials, making drawings of local details for Lutyens to copy, and designing many of the internal fittings himself.

The recent discovery of correspondence between Lutyens and Lloyd has thrown new light on the project, which Nikolaus Pevsner described as "one of his [Lutyens's] most successful domestic jobs, combining sensitivity to the old with quite some daring, discreetly concealed." Lutyens wrote in May 1910 that he wanted "to make the old house sing out," while ensuring that the whole complex composed well. Meanwhile, Lloyd was determined to "provide the necessary accommodation of a modern house" while doing no more "than was absolutely necessary to secure the ancient structure." The result, a modified and scaled-down version of the initial scheme, was one of Lutyens's most archaeological country house remodellings: "Nothing has been done without authority, nothing has been done from imagination; there has been no forgery," wrote Lloyd.

The earliest surviving part of the medieval house is the great hall of ca. 1450, one of the largest surviving timber-framed halls in England. Entered through the porch shown on page 393, it has a splendid hammer-beam roof incorporating armorial shields of the Etchinghams, Dalyngrigges, and Gaynesfords, families associated with Richard Wakehurst, who built the house. In 1595 it was acquired by John Glydd, who subdivided the hall, the parlour, and the chamber above it known as the solar, and reduced the old house in size, while making some additions of his own. Then, for the next three hundred years, Great Dixter was little touched, so that when Lawrence Weaver wrote about the house for *Country Life* in 1913, he was able to describe it as "one of the most important and perhaps the earliest timber house in Sussex." A key element of the renovation was to restore the original proportions of the three medieval rooms. Evidence showed that the great hall had been lit by two large bay windows, and these Lutyens reinstated. In the parlour to its east (the drawing room), he replaced the original stone chimneypiece, which had become mutilated.

The need for more accommodation was answered by Lloyd's purchase of

[ABOVE] *The main staircase, added by Lutyens to an unknown model.*

[BELOW] *The corner of the Porch Bedroom, with a radiator case doubling as a washstand made from an old chest. Many examples of this resourceful adaptation of wooden coffers survive in the house.*

[OPPOSITE] *The great hall, dating from the 1450s, its unusual roof construction comprising hammer beams alternating with tie beams. Lutyens's original proposals for a new fireplace in the middle of the south wall had to be dropped when evidence was revealed of a former bay window here (which he reinstated). The Lloyds used this great space as a living hall.*

a condemned sixteenth-century farmhouse from near Benenden, just across the border in Kent. Carefully dismantled, this timber-framed structure was re-erected to the southeast of the manor house, with a new east wing seamlessly connecting the two houses. Lutyens exercised considerable restraint in his work at Great Dixter, though the dramatic, sweeping tiled roofs punctuated by dormers and soaring chimneys are unmistakably his. He distinguished his work from the original fabric with great subtlety, using different, but still traditional, materials of the local vernacular: brick and tile hanging instead of the existing timber framing.

The hall of the Benenden house became the master bedroom, with its bed, a copy of a fifteenth-century one in the Palazzo Davanzati in Florence, raised up on a dais at one end. Known as the Yeoman's Hall, it has been a summer sitting room since the 1940s. Lutyens designed some of the simple oak furniture and fittings in the house, including the staircases, and adapted old farm buildings as loggias and summerhouses. The gardens, with their famous topiary yews, he laid out with considerable input from Nathaniel and Daisy Lloyd. Their son, the renowned horticulturalist Christopher Lloyd, took over in the 1950s, and thereafter Great Dixter acquired considerable fame for its gardens. Christopher's prodigious knowledge and continuous experiments with planting were charted weekly in his gardening column for *Country Life*, which he wrote for forty-three years. He died in 2006, but Great Dixter has continued to attract increasing numbers of visitors, its seductive blend of ancient building fabric and beautiful plantings a celebration of two quintessentially English preoccupations: a warm nostalgia for the past and an abiding love of gardening.

[RIGHT] *The chamber above the parlour, its kingpost truss roof partly original, partly reinstated. The carved stone chimneypiece must be a slightly later addition, judging by the heraldry on the spandrels. Known as the solar, this room was used as a library, with bookshelves designed by Lutyens. Nathaniel Lloyd designed the lamp standards, and his son Christopher commissioned the contemporary furniture by Rupert Williamson.*

[OPPOSITE] *The view from the northeast, showing Lutyens's brick and weather-tiled additions east of the great hall, the lower buildings in the foreground comprising the kitchen and service quarters.*

Eyford House

— GLOUCESTERSHIRE —

THE architect Guy Dawber has been described as "the Lutyens of the West," although he never fully achieved the fame he deserved. Deriving inspiration from the indigenous architecture of the Cotswolds, he produced not only an influential book, *Old Cottages, Farmhouses and Other Stone Buildings of the Cotswold Region* (1905), but also a number of fine houses, of which Eyford is probably the most ambitious and the best. Commissioned by John Cheetham in 1911, this elegant essay in provincial classicism shows how well Dawber assimilated the character of the smaller Queen Anne and early Georgian houses that belong to the Cotswolds valleys. He combined his "simple and quiet manner" with lively touches of Baroque detail to produce a house that has architectural presence without being too grand.

Dawber got to know the area in the 1880s, when he was clerk of works at Batsford Park, George and Peto's house for the 1st Lord Redesdale. He established a practice at Moreton-in-Marsh and learned how to create, in the lovely golden-toned limestone of the Cotswolds, buildings that blended in with their natural setting and looked as if they had always been there, without sacrificing practicality or modern comforts. At Eyford, Dawber had the advantage of working with an already mellowed ashlar stone, salvaged from its 1870s predecessor (which had, in turn, replaced a seventeenth-century house built by the Duke of Shrewsbury). For the roof, he used stone from the local quarry, slated in the traditional manner.

The house stands high up on a wooded slope of the north Cotswolds hills, looking down over a park watered by the Ey. Seventeenth-century landscaping altered this brook to create ornamental lakes and a cascade, beside which, in a summerhouse in the 1670s, John Milton is reputed to have begun *Paradise Lost*. Eyford's beautiful setting provided the key to Dawber's design, which included not just the house and its balustraded terraces, but an entire ensemble of pleasure gardens, a walled kitchen garden, and a formal, semicircular herb garden, as well as several ornamental pavilions.

The main rooms face south and are decorated in a restrained manner, with handsome chimneypieces and plasterwork, probably by H. H. Martyn of Cheltenham. The stair hall, which is asymmetrically positioned, is more ornately treated and has slender, finely detailed Ionic columns. More recently, a series of murals by Penelope Reeve has added a delightful contemporary layer.

[OPPOSITE] *Eyford House, commissioned in 1911, is redolent of a late-seventeenth-century house in the provincial English Baroque manner. The entrance front faces north to a circular stone summerhouse on a rise, which is seen on alignment with the front door through receding pairs of pillars beyond the forecourt. The Arts & Crafts garden was also to Dawber's design.*

399

[LEFT] *Looking towards the drawing room from the hall, which is more ornately treated and has a gracious staircase decorated with swags and urns.*

[OPPOSITE] *The dining room (originally the Garden Hall) with Venetian scenes painted by Penelope Reeve in 2004.*

Nymans

— SUSSEX —

[OPPOSITE] *A view into the little Book Room that opens off the north end of the Garden Hall.*

THERE is a dreamlike quality about Nymans, emphasised by the fact that much of it is only half there. Unroofed gables and plant-draped walls pierced with empty mullions and tracery rise over the gardens, haunted still by the ghosts of an imagined world. For even before the devastating fire of 1947, the house was not all it seemed: what appeared to be a building of late medieval provenance was in fact an "exquisite example of pastiche" dating from the 1920s, the invention of Lt. Col. Leonard Messel and his wife, Maud. Nymans belongs to the early-twentieth-century manor house revival—that nostalgic, creative chapter in the story of the English country house so evocatively recorded in the early articles of *Country Life*.

The story of the Messels at Nymans begins a generation earlier, when Ludwig Messel, a German stockbroker, bought a Regency house here in 1890 and employed Ernest George to extend it. The resulting pile, which his son Leonard inherited in 1915, was far from the sort of place that he and his wife coveted. Their dream was for a mellow, gabled old West Country manor house "where their oak furniture would find a congenial setting against rough plaster walls and beneath fatly moulded ceilings." But they were also keen gardeners, and here on the Sussex Weald the soil was ideal; furthermore, Nymans was close enough to London for Leonard to continue stockbroking in the city. So they decided to keep it and, with the help of the architects Norman Evill and Walter Tapper, transformed the house and garden into the place of their dreams. Their own input was considerable. Maud was the daughter of *Punch* political cartoonist Linley Sambourne and herself an artist; inspired by such houses as Great Chalfield in Wiltshire and Brede Place in Sussex, she did many of the preliminary sketches herself.

They began in 1923 with the west wing—the part later resurrected after the fire. This Evill designed to suggest an early-fifteenth-century manor house, with a porch partly modelled on the one at Great Chalfield, traceried windows and upper lights reminiscent of those at Brede Place, and other features derived from the local vernacular. While building they uncovered parts of a much earlier structure, confirming knowledge that there had long been a house at Nymans.

The west wing opens onto a beautifully planted forecourt, which is entered through a stone-arched doorway overlooked by an octagonal dovecote. It is

[ABOVE] *The Garden Hall, the centrepiece of the restored west wing, as refurnished by Lady Rosse in the 1960s to re-create its atmosphere in her parents' day, before the fire of 1947.*

difficult to believe that all this is less than a century old. The interior, dominated by the Garden Hall, looks again very much as it did in the Messels' day, with tapestry wall hangings, antique rugs on flagstoned floors, faded textiles and cushions, lime-washed walls, and old oak furniture.

The Messels wanted Nymans to look as if it had evolved over centuries, so next they recast the main part of the Regency house and the Victorian tower as an early Tudor wing. For this they employed the Gothic revival architect Walter Tapper, who worked mostly on churches but had restored

[ABOVE] *The south front of Walter Tapper's "early Tudor" wing with, at right angles to it, the fourteenth-century-style "great hall." On the far left is Norman Evill's west wing, restored after the fire of 1947.*

nearby Penshurst Place. This now-roofless wing contained the long drawing room and the panelled library, whose irreplaceable collection of botanical books also perished in the fire. Tapper also remodelled a Victorian billiard room as a fourteenth-century-style great hall, forming a wing projecting to the south.

With their eclectic taste and creative talents, the Messels conjured up a convincing patina of age and "well ordered waywardness," simulating with disarming subtlety the "elusive quality" of timeworn things. The rooms were designed around their collections of old furniture, faded textiles, and salvaged architectural pieces, their atmosphere heightened with candles in mirrored sconces and the scent of flowers. As John Cornforth pointed out in his June 5, 1997, article in *Country Life*, the tonal links between the interior and the garden were an essential part of the character of Nymans.

Following Leonard's death in 1953, the National Trust took on Nymans as one of its first garden properties, the west wing being rebuilt and used by the family. One of the Messels' sons was the famous theatre designer Oliver Messel, and their daughter Anne, a great beauty who married the 6th Earl of Rosse and was the mother of Lord Snowdon, also inherited her parents' artistic and gardening skills. After her mother's death in 1960, Lady Rosse re-created with great flair and imagination the atmosphere of the rooms in the west wing as they had been before the fire, and she also oversaw the gardens. In 1997, five years after Lady Rosse's death, the trust opened the ground-floor rooms to the public, providing visitors with a fuller picture of the extraordinary creativity and vision that inspired the Messels to turn Nymans into such a romantic place.

Eltham Palace

— MIDDLESEX —

STEPHEN and Virginia Courtauld had Eltham for less than a decade, but in that short time—1933 to 1944—they created one of the most unusual and glamorous houses of the interwar period. It is neither wholly modernist nor traditional, its complexity reflecting the history of the site as a medieval royal palace as well as the couple's enthusiasm for the diversity of styles then in vogue, from Romantic medievalising and Renaissance revival, to the sleek aesthetic of the ocean liner.

Eltham's principal interest today lies in its outstanding Art Deco interiors, surviving examples of which are particularly rare in England. They are all the more remarkable here, given that from 1945 to 1992 the house was in institutional use, its contents all dispersed. But key decorative elements survived, as, crucially, did *Country Life*'s photographs of 1937, an inventory of 1939, and the architects' original drawings. This information, supported by extensive research by Treve Rosoman and Dr. Michael Turner, made it possible for English Heritage to carry out a faithful restoration in 1996–99. Colours, paints, papers, and veneers were restored; loaned items were combined with newly made replicas of original textiles, rugs, and important furniture; and significant paintings from the Courtaulds' art collection were reproduced. Open to the public since 1999, Eltham appears again as it did

[OPPOSITE] *A detail of the dining room, with replicas of the original furniture reproduced by Neil Stevenson using the* Country Life *photographs of 1937 and the inventory dated 1939.*

[BELOW] *The entrance front seen from the north, with the medieval hall adjoining as part of the right-hand wing. The two towers help to balance the change of levels and unavoidable mix of styles. Above the entrance arcade can be seen the preserved gables of the Tudor lodging.*

during its brief period of domestic occupation: the epitome of smart, stylish 1930s opulence.

The Courtaulds' fortune came from the family textile manufacturing business, though Stephen himself trained as a brewer (his brother, Samuel, founded the Courtauld Institute of Art in 1930). Highly cultivated, Stephen Courtauld combined a love of Old Masters with sophisticated international modern tastes. His natural reserve was a foil to the vivacity of his half-Italian wife, Ginie, who had a snake tattooed on her leg and kept a pet ring-tailed lemur called Mah-Jongg in a heated cage decorated with bamboo murals. The Courtaulds leased Eltham from the Crown in 1933, attracted by the prospect of creating a home that would function like a villa: close to the cultural epicentre (Westminster is just six miles away), yet suitable for weekend entertaining, and with twenty acres to indulge their passion for gardening.

The medieval palace of Eltham dates back to 1305, when the Bishop of Durham built an important manor house here, choosing the site for its astonishing views over London. It was developed as a royal palace from the fourteenth to the sixteenth centuries, and then largely destroyed during the Civil War. The one survival was Edward IV's great hall of 1475–79, under whose magnificent hammer-beamed roof Henry VIII met Erasmus and Thomas More in 1503. The architects Seely and Paget incorporated this building into their V-plan design for the Courtaulds' new house, adding an orangery and squash court at its far end. They used a soft, rose-tinted brick and Clipsham stone to harmonise with the medieval masonry, but designed the exterior in a style described as "Wrenaissance" that appears almost determinedly discordant with the Gothic glory of the great hall. Writing in *The Times* in 1936, G. M. Young compared it to "an admirably designed but unfortunately sited cigarette factory."

The Courtaulds financed the restoration of the great hall and dressed it up in their own version of the medieval, with damask wall hangings, antique furniture, and even a minstrels' gallery. It could not be more of a contrast to the interiors of their new house, where an eclectic fusion of work by several leading designers combined Art Deco, Swedish Modern, and Italianate influences in a series of carefully orchestrated contrasts of colour and mood. The entrance hall, designed by the Swedish architect Rolf Engströmer, might be the foyer to a 1930s liner, with its round-ended clerestorey, Art Deco furnishings, and Australian black bean panelling inlaid with marquetry scenes. Fronted by an arcaded, semicircular porch, it links the two splayed wings at their inner angle, the drawing room and dining room opening off it on opposite sides. These rooms were designed by the fashionable Mayfair decorator Marchese Peter Malacrida, the drawing room in a Renaissance style to complement the Courtaulds' collection of Old Master paintings. The dining room, lined with bird's-eye maple Flexwood, is the height of sophisticated 1930s glamour, with its floor and chimneypiece of black marble, concealed lighting in a recessed silvered ceiling, and pink leather-upholstered chairs.

Stephen Courtauld's interest in woods from different countries is reflected

The entrance hall, designed by Rolf Engströmer as a modern living hall, with a concrete dome lit by glass pavement lights. The marquetry figures of a Roman and Viking, flanked by scenes of Venice and Stockholm, are by Jerk Werkmäster, symbolising the Mediterranean and Scandanavian cultures. The circular rug is an exact copy of Marion Dorn's original, and the chairs, made by Neil Stevenson of Rugby, are replicas of the ones Engströmer designed for the room.

[ABOVE] *The east side overlooking the moat, with the hinge of the V plan emphasised by one of the three copper-roofed towers that give the house the flavour of a French chateau and also recall the tapering cupolas of Eltham's Tudor silhouette.*

in the lavish use of veneers and marquetry throughout the house, from his "Indian mahogany"–panelled library, where sliding vertical panels to his own design displayed and protected his collection of Turner watercolours, to the inlaid decoration of black bean, maple, sycamore, and aspen. His literary interests are reflected in a series of inscriptions and other whimsical pieces of iconography scattered throughout the house.

But it is the Courtaulds' respective bedrooms that reveal most about their tastes and personalities: his restrained and sparsely furnished with a hand-printed Sanderson wallpaper in muted greens over a dado of silvery-gold Colorado aspen; hers luxuriously decorated by Malacrida, with an en-suite bathroom lined in onyx and gold mosaic. Virginia's bedroom is oval, with curved sliding doors and walls lined with pinkish-brown maple Flexwood punctuated with sycamore-veneered pilasters inlaid with delicate Swedish Rococo-style patterns. Concealed cornice lighting, a fitted carpet, and a polished metal electric fire contributed to its modern comforts. The house was equipped with all the latest conveniences, from underfloor heating and piped music, to electric picture lights, a centralised vacuum-cleaning system, and even a coinbox telephone in the hall.

Eltham's brief heyday ended in 1944, when the Courtaulds gave up their lease. They eventually settled in Rhodesia, where they built a national art gallery and concert hall and supported racial equality. The restoration of Eltham Palace is a fitting tribute to the style and patronage of this glamorous, unconventional couple.

[OPPOSITE, CLOCKWISE FROM TOP LEFT] *Virginia Courtauld's onyx-lined bathroom, with a marble copy of the* Psyche of Capua *in the gold-mosaicked apse over the bath.*

Virginia Courtauld's oval bedroom, designed by the Mayfair decorator Marchese Peter Malacrida. The bedhead is slightly recessed, leaving a ledge for lamps, with low bedside commodes on each side. The walls are lined with maple Flexwood and weathered sycamore inlaid with various coloured woods.

Looking from the dining room to the entrance hall through the original lacquered doors, decorated by Narini with exotic animals in white composition on a black ground, and Greek influences in the key pattern and vase.

The dining room, designed by Malacrida in "a smooth, European form of abstracted Classicism." This room is one of the triumphs of English Heritage's restoration, with replicas of the original furniture and reinstated concealed lighting in the recessed ceiling, now resilvered in aluminium leaf.

The Manor House, Hambleden

— BUCKINGHAMSHIRE —

[OPPOSITE] *The garden front, with the early-nineteenth-century bay-windowed drawing room addition on the right.*

AN early-seventeenth-century manor house tucked into one of the secluded valleys of the Chilterns, the Manor House at Hambleden was redecorated by John Fowler in one of his most interesting country house schemes of the 1950s. Carried out in collaboration with Lady Hambleden, who still lives here, it remains one of the best surviving examples of Fowler's work of the period.

In the nineteenth century, a large part of this beautiful, beech-hung valley was owned by the Smiths, Viscounts Hambleden, whose family firm was the famous booksellers founded by W. H. Smith. They bought the Greenlands estate at Hambleden in 1868 and expanded their property to include the manor of Ewden and the picturesque village of Hambleden itself, to which William Henry Smith II, an eminent Conservative politician, added pretty estate cottages and a school. He also enlarged Greenlands, the mid-nineteenth-century Italianate mansion that remained the family seat until the Second World War.

The Manor House at Hambleden was in different ownership until 1923, when the 2nd Viscount Hambleden bought it from Major Frank Scott-Murray, whose family had owned it since 1815. Prior to this, in the late eighteenth century, it had been the home of the 6th Earl of Cardigan, whose son led the Charge of the Light Brigade at Balaclava in 1854. Dated 1603, the house has a richly textured exterior of knapped flint and local red brick, with a parade of gables on each main front and diagonally set chimneystacks rising up through its red-tiled roof. The gables on the west front retain their original windows, mullioned and transomed in moulded brick plastered over and stone-washed to resemble masonry; the sash windows on the lower floors were introduced in 1748. This is the date inscribed on the rainwater pipes, and it is taken to indicate the year that the interior was Georgianised, when the front rooms acquired their raised and fielded panelling, and the present staircase, with its moulded balusters and shaped tread-ends, was installed.

The present owner, the daughter of Count Bernardo Attolico di Adelfia of Rome, married the 4th Viscount Hambleden in 1955, and at that time they decided to restore the Manor House as a home. More historic and picturesque than Greenlands, it was also more compact and conveniently adaptable to modern living. Fowler was commissioned to mastermind the interior redecoration in 1956, and the result has been described by John Martin Robinson in *Country Life* as "one of the most successful ensembles of its type to have been achieved in England in the past forty years: comfortable, faultless in scale, colour, and texture." It was, he emphasised, a particularly successful example of the way Fowler could achieve simple, harmonious effects by adapting and reusing existing elements without sacrificing the highest standards of execution from the craftsmen and painters he employed. For example, in the bow-windowed drawing room, added by the 6th Earl of Cardigan in the Regency period, Fowler bleached some red velvet curtains, previously hung at Greenlands, to a colour that would harmonise with the walls, adding a new silk trim to match. The walls he painted a strong pink, assuring his client that they would soon fade to a soft apricot tone, which indeed they did. Lady Hambleden bought the large Aubusson carpet around which this room is furnished. She also commissioned the pair of pier glasses in carved frames to complement the two gilt Rococo console tables and an enormous gilded Chippendale picture frame that dominates one wall.

In contrast to the elegant Regency drawing room, some of the Georgian rooms are relatively small and low-ceilinged. Fowler introduced clear, striking colours to brighten them up, and Lady Hambleden has since refreshed some of them. He restored the Georgian character to the stair hall by removing the dark panelling, which he dismissed as "Victorian and vulgar," and painted the walls and joinery his favourite grey-blue. By taking away a dividing wall between the stairs and the garden lobby, he created a more spacious inner hall.

Fowler's skill with colour is seen to particular effect in Lady Hambleden's sitting room, where vibrant yellow glazed walls offset a handsome Regency chimneypiece of grey marble and richly coloured fabrics. For the dining room, he devised two summery shades of yellow and installed a modern bolection-moulded chimneypiece, introducing among the furnishings a set of white-painted chairs that look as if they might have come from an Italian garden pavilion.

Since the 1950s, the Manor House has benefited from other phases of improvement, including additions by the architect Sir Martyn Beckett, a family friend. He designed the domed conservatory for use as a summer dining room, which was added to the garden front in 1961, and also reorganised the services and domestic quarters. Subsequent additions to his design included the billiard room and a trellised swimming pool pavilion. John Fowler returned to the Manor House in 1977, a week before his death. He told Lady Hambleden what a joy it was to find that, unlike so many other houses he had worked with, this one remained almost exactly as he had decorated it twenty years before.

[RIGHT] *The Regency drawing room, which was added to the house when the 6th Earl of Cardigan lived here, and redecorated with verve by John Fowler and Lady Hambleden in a fusion of English and Italian taste. The chandelier was designed by Fowler and made in Venice.*

[OVERLEAF] *The sitting room, which was remodelled in about 1748 and redecorated by John Fowler in the 1950s. Family furniture from Greenlands combines well with Lady Hambleden's own pieces, many bought in antique shops and markets.*

[LEFT] *The staircase, dating from the Georgian remodelling of the interior, ca. 1748. John Fowler re-Georgianised the stair hall and painted the walls and joinery his favourite grey-blue.*

[OPPOSITE, CLOCKWISE FROM TOP LEFT] *The entrance hall, paved with diagonally laid Portland stone flags. Lady Hambleden redecorated the hall in 1992, replacing Fowler's pale grey scheme with a more cheerful yellow. Through the open door is a glimpse of the porch, which Fowler painted Mediterranean blue, creating a wonderful contrast with the red brick walls of the exterior.*

The billiard room added by Sir Martyn Beckett, which Lady Hambleden decorated with a tentlike interior.

The dining room, panelled in 1748 and with a colour scheme devised by John Fowler.

An attic bedroom decorated by Fowler in blue-and-white matching chintz and wallpaper, with simple painted furniture.

Arundel Park

— SUSSEX —

Claud Phillimore's Arundel Park of 1958–62, for the 16th Duke and Duchess of Norfolk, was one of the largest English classical houses of its era and the first to attempt a modern interpretation of a Palladian design. It belongs to a group of significant dower houses built in the twentieth century, several of which Phillimore designed. The home of Lavinia, Duchess of Norfolk, until her death in 1995, Arundel Park is now let to tenants, but these photographs show it as it was during her lifetime.

The idea of building a house within the grounds of Arundel Castle was the late duchess's. It appealed because of the greater degree of comfort and privacy offered in comparison to the family's ancestral seat, where she and her husband had brought up their family, and which they continued to use when necessary. The duchess chose a site at the south end of the park and devised the initial concept: a compact central block flanked by pavilion wings, the inspiration for which was Ditchley Park in Oxfordshire, where she had stayed with her friends Ronald and Nancy Tree before the war. The Norfolks had not yet decided on an architect when, by serendipity, the duchess met Phillimore on a visit to the Midhurst Hospital, where he was recovering from TB. It transpired that he had spent his convalescence dreaming up his "ideal house"—a three-part Palladian design adapted for modern living. And so they duly appointed him to design Arundel Park.

The exterior of the main part of the house is more Regency than Palladian in style, with oversailing eaves, tall, tripartite windows on the garden front, and a rhythm of segmental bows and arches. These curving forms are echoed by the concave shape of the entrance front, the alignment of which reflects the contour of the hillside. On the roof is a balustraded viewing platform with a glazed cupola—more seventeenth-century in feel, and with nautical references, too, in its resemblance to an "admiral's walk." The sea is just a few miles away, and the house reflects this in other details, such as the "portholes" in the lower links to the pavilion wings.

Though Phillimore's work was not generally as scholarly or original as that of contemporaries such as Francis Johnson and Raymond Erith, Arundel Park is one of his more interesting schemes. In particular, it demonstrates his skill at handling internal arrangements and detail, the aspect of buildings that interested him most. He managed to make the interior feel compact and

[OPPOSITE] *The view from the dining room looking through to the drawing room, showing the rooms as they appeared when Arundel Park was the dower house of Lavinia, Duchess of Norfolk. The inspiration for the double doors came from those in the Cube Rooms at Wilton House, Wiltshire, which were replacements of Inigo Jones's originals by Richard Westmacott of 1826.*

comfortable, while also conveying a certain note of grandeur. Architectural detail is sparing, and there is a Soanian quality about the way unadorned arches and recesses are used for spatial effect. This is particularly felt in the top-lit stair hall, which rises the full height of the house beneath a plaster vault. The stone staircase has a handsome wrought-iron balustrade that was made by Sussex craftsmen to a design incorporating the Norfolk cypher and coronet.

Other specially made architectural elements include the doors to the principal ground-floor openings, which have distinctively shaped gilded panels and central circular mouldings inspired by the doors to Inigo Jones's Cube Rooms at Wilton House in Wiltshire, and ormolu fittings made in Paris. Salvaged pieces were also introduced: the drawing room and sitting room chimneypieces, for example, and the mid-eighteenth-century front door, which came from Norfolk House in St. James's Square, London (demolished in 1938).

The house was furnished and decorated in a collaboration between the duchess and the leading country house decorator John Fowler, who often worked with Phillimore. Dating from 1962, Fowler's interior designs were conceived around furniture and paintings from the family collection. The focus of the drawing room was a set of three magnificent architectural *capricii* by Canaletto, which were commissioned for Norfolk House in 1750. Other objects in this room, such as the smaller pieces of French and English furniture, also came from Norfolk House. Fowler covered the walls with a duck-egg blue silk, which faded beautifully to greeny blue; he had the pale carpet specially woven for the room in Spain.

Both bow-ended, the drawing room and dining room on the garden front interconnect through double doors that can be opened up for entertaining. Fowler decorated the dining room in a green French flock wallpaper with an unusually small pattern, and glazed the arched alcoves and oval recesses to enhance their display of china and Greek vases. A bronze and ormolu Regency chandelier contributed to the French Empire character of this elegant room. The duchess's sitting room doubled as a library, with bookcases in arched recesses on the end walls. Here, Fowler introduced a striped red flock wallpaper, although this was later removed when the room was redecorated.

These photographs provide a valuable record of Fowler's work at Arundel Park, for since the duchess's death many of the contents have been returned to the castle or inherited by her daughters, and, inevitably, elements of the decoration have changed.

The concave entrance front, faced with pink-washed stucco, the portholes in the lower links inspired by the house's proximity to the sea.

[ABOVE] The stair hall, flagged with Portland stone and painted a stone colour dubbed "Thames mud" by John Fowler, who went to a great deal of trouble to get it right. The wrought-iron balustrade was made by local craftsmen and incorporates the Norfolk cipher and coronet.

[OPPOSITE] The drawing room, decorated by John Fowler. The room was designed around three capricii by Canaletto, which, along with smaller pieces of French and English furniture such as the marquetry side tables by Topino and chairs by Jean Adel L'Ainé, came from Norfolk House in London. The sofas and chairs are upholstered in Hollyhock, a chintz design by Lee Jofa.

424

Bellamont

— DORSET —

BELLAMONT is a delightful, teasing confection that exudes the spirit and architectural enthusiasms of its owners, Anthony and Harriet Sykes. In some ways Mr. Sykes is the modern gentleman amateur architect in the eighteenth-century tradition: well versed in stylistic detail and decoration, steeped in family history and genealogy, and energetically involved. The house is as much his creation as that of architect Anthony Jaggard, with whom he collaborated on the initial design in the early 1990s. Since then, Bellamont has continued to evolve and is still undergoing changes as Mr. Sykes initiates further embellishments, many of his own making. To mark the millennium, he commissioned Stuart Martin to design the octagonal dining room that projects from the canted bay on the south front overlooking the park. It opens into a small formal garden with axial canals, enclosed by defensive-looking screen walls with square turrets and a similarly castellated topiary hedge. Since these photographs were taken in 2001, a warren of inner and outer "baileys" has been added to the entrance front, and a Gothick pavilion erected on the north side of the forecourt.

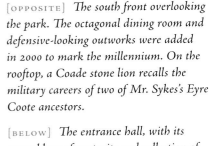

[OPPOSITE] *The south front overlooking the park. The octagonal dining room and defensive-looking outworks were added in 2000 to mark the millennium. On the rooftop, a Coade stone lion recalls the military careers of two of Mr. Sykes's Eyre Coote ancestors.*

[BELOW] *The entrance hall, with its assemblage of portraits and collection of arms inspired by the Picture Staircase at Blair Castle. The eighteenth-century Portland stone chimneypiece came from an Irish house. The large portrait is of the 11th Duke of St. Albans and his sisters.*

A romantic vision of pink-washed stucco set amidst the Dorset Downs, Bellamont is Anglo-Irish in inspiration, combining the air of an Irish Georgian country house with that of an English Regency castle. The entire building—the five-bay pedimented central block, lower three-bay wings, turrets, and outworks—is castellated in the manner of Nash, and there is something, too, of the pattern-book designs of Batty Langley. The influences come in part from houses associated with Mr. Sykes's forbears: the general form and massing echo his mother's former family home, Jeffrey Wyatville's West Park in Hampshire (now demolished). The castellated parapets suggest Alscot Park in Warwickshire, the great Gothick house where Mr. Sykes was partly brought up, and then there is the name itself, Bellamont, which recalls Bellamont Forest at Cootehill in Country Cavan, an Irish Palladian seat of Mr. Sykes's maternal forbears, the Cootes. This feeling for ancestral associations is also expressed in the repertoire of heraldic detail that adorns the exterior and enlivens the interior decoration. The Coade stone imperial lion cresting the central chimneystack and the motto "Coute que Coute" on the pediment refer to General Sir Eyre Coote I and Sir Eyre Coote II (forbear of Gen. Colin Powell), who held important military posts in India and Jamaica in the eighteenth and early-nineteenth centuries. Inside, swans rise from the staircase newel posts and gilded coots adorn walls and mirrors.

The principal feature of the interior is the gallery-like room along the south side, intended to evoke the period around 1830. One long, uninterrupted space, it functions as a modern, open-plan family living room. But at first glance it might be a traditional drawing room, the generous, grandly decorated space unified by a richly moulded cornice. The effect is highly theatrical. Closer inspection reveals that the columns are trompe l'oeil and that the pairs of Thomas Hope–inspired panelled doors are studded with heraldic disks made of fiberglass painted gold.

The cubic entrance hall feels stylistically more mid-eighteenth century (the owner's favourite period), with later Soanian flashes in details such as the plain rounded arches. It was inspired by the Picture Staircase at Blair Castle in Scotland, the whole composition—with its assemblage of family portraits, trophies, arms, and busts—being partly a tribute to the military achievements of the Eyre Coote generals. Trompe l'oeil columns continue up the staircase, which has gutsy balusters in the manner of William Kent, mirrored in trompe l'oeil on the wall. The wings contain staff/service rooms, a kitchen and two studies on the east, and a flat on the west. Mr. Sykes stresses that Bellamont is not a pastiche—that he has chosen architectural elements he likes and assembled them in an original manner. True to the spirit of the place, the barn standing above the house is conceived as an eye-catcher, with a triumphal-arch façade surmounted by a gilded turret clock.

The entrance front, with castellations inspired by Alscot Park in Warwickshire. It has changed dramatically since this photograph was taken, with the addition of castellated inner and outer "baileys," and a Gothick-style pavilion. The parkland plantings have also matured considerably, in particular the avenue of Norway maple.

[ABOVE] The octagonal dining room on the south side. Since this photograph was taken the room has been "tented" with blue and white mattress ticking.

[RIGHT] The early-eighteenth-century-style staircase, with swans (the Sykes family crest) on the newel posts.

[ABOVE] The marble and "Sicilian jasper" chimneypiece in the drawing room section of the main living room, framed by trompe l'oeil Corinthian pilasters from a wallpaper design by Dodds & Gibbs.

[OPPOSITE] The principal long living room on the south side, which is made up of three compartments: at one end an informal TV sitting room/library, the drawing room with chimneypiece and canted bay in the centre, and a kitchen at the other end, all unified by a richly moulded plaster cornice.

IN 1816 President Jefferson's advice on designing a new house was relayed to the owner of Bremo in Virginia: "Palladio he said 'was the bible.' You should get it and stick close to it." From Palladio's *Four Books of Architecture*—usually the English edition by Leoni—came plans, elevations, and proportions. Numerous other English pattern books provided motifs such as panelling, doors and doorcases, cornices, chimneypieces, and joinery of all kinds, including staircases. Such details were also the stock in trade of the many English craftsmen who came to work in the colonies, sometimes bringing their own pattern books or engravings and often simply working from memory.

❧ In Charleston, South Carolina, artisans advertised themselves as "just arrived from London." In May 1751 Dudley Inman, "carpenter and joiner from London," announced he would "give designs of houses, according to modern taste." John Landridge, another carpenter and joiner from London, advertised his "neat chimneypieces."

❧ Like enterprising, prospering colonists around the world, the Americans liked to be abreast of the latest fashions from the mother country. Drayton Hall, the grand southern plantation house on the Ashley River outside Charleston, was begun in 1738 and has a richly carved two-tier chimneypiece taken from William Kent's *Designs of Inigo Jones* published in 1727, just eleven years before. Welsh red sandstone and Portland limestone were shipped from Britain for the floor of the portico.

❧ The Virginia plantation owner William Byrd of Westover was educated in England and lived in the style of an English country gentleman, with a large library including thirty architectural books. The handsome swan-pedimented stone doorcase, following a design in William Salmon's *Palladio Londiniensis* (1734), was probably ordered from England by Byrd for the house he planned to build—there is no natural stone in the region and carved stone was imported in many forms, notably tombstones. It was added to the present house, built by his son, William Byrd III, in the 1750s. Byrd III embellished Westover's parlour with a monumental marble chimneypiece also ordered from England.

❧ Mount Airy, dramatically set on a plateau above the broad Rappahannock River, was built in 1748–58 for John Tayloe and has a pedimented stone centrepiece modelled on Plate 58 in James Gibbs's *Book of Architecture* showing "a design for the house of a Gentleman in Dorset." The dining room was hung with prints of "twenty-four of the most celebrated . . . English Race-Horses," all in gilt frames. Mount Airy's five-part composition, consisting of the main block connected to dependencies by curved hyphens, is America's purest expression of eighteenth-century Anglo-Palladianism.

❧ One widely used London pattern book was William Pain's *British Palladio* of 1786. This was evidently the source for many details at Belle Grove in the Shenandoah Valley, built for Isaac Hite, who married Nelly, sister of James Madison, the principal author of the United States Constitution and future president. From Pain came the delightful rams' head capitals in the parlour, as well as cornices, doorcases, and the two-tier fireplaces still early Georgian in style. Scores of other American houses of the Federal period display both interior and exterior details taken from Pain's several pattern books. Pain's *Practical House Carpenter* was published in Boston in 1796 and in Philadelphia in 1797.

℄ In his expansion and embellishment of Mount Vernon, George Washington relied on several English pattern books. Exterior details were taken from Batty Langley's *The City and Country Builder's Assistant and Workman's Treasury of Designs* (1740). On the interior, a plasterwork ceiling follows a design in William Pain's *Builder's Companion and Workman's General Assistant* (3rd edition, 1769), and the Rococo chimneypieces are from Abram Swan's *British Architect* (1758).

℄ Another fascinating group of links between English and American houses is to be found in Annapolis, Maryland. Here, the Chase-Lloyd House, completed in 1771, has unusual and distinctive octagonal panels in the doors and window shutters, and even octagonal-pattern glazing—motifs found in certain English houses of the 1750s and '60s, the Rococo moment in English architecture. These details, including a divided stair with scrolled soffits, were added to the house by the English-born architect and artisan

William Buckland, who had an impressive library of English pattern books.

℄ Just as English country gentry resorted to towns such as Bury St. Edmunds for concerts, dances, and plays, and to find suitors for their children, rice planters of South Carolina, bored with country life, would spend midwinter in Charleston enjoying rounds of parties and horse racing. Eliza Lucas, living on her father's plantation outside Charleston, wrote in May 1740, "the people live very genteel and very much in the English taste." Governor James Glen of Charleston wrote in 1751, "Plate begins to shine upon their sideboards, and in proportion as they thrive they delight to have good things from England."

℄ By the early nineteenth century America had its own pattern book, *The American Builder's Companion* (1806) by Asher Benjamin, who produced as many as seven pattern books. Nicholas Biddle is mainly responsible for promoting the use of Greek orders and Greek moulding profiles, drawing from English sources such as Stuart and Revette's *Antiquities of Athens*. An example is to be found at the Governor's Mansion in Virginia, where the capitals on the portico are based on the Temple of the Winds in Athens, illustrated in Stuart and Revette.

℄ A good example of continuing English influence in the nineteenth century is to be found at Cedar Hill in Rhode Island, a delightful gingerbread Gothic house dating from 1872–77. This has a distinctive family resemblance to the gabled rectories and mansions illustrated in William Wilkinson's *English Country Houses*, first published in 1870, a copy of which belonged to the architect of the house, William R. Walker.

❧ A new wave of English influence followed in the 1920s, sparked by American participation in the First World War. Windsor Farms, a garden suburb on the edge of Richmond, Virginia, is described in the lavish sales brochure of 1926 as "hauntingly reminiscent of old England." Two demolished English country houses were rebuilt here: Elizabethan house Warwick Priory and medieval Agecroft Hall. The first houses on the estate were Tudor style, with half-timbering inspired by Anne Hathaway's cottage at Stratford-on-Avon. All the streets in Windsor Farms were given English names such as Berkshire, Oxford, and Sulgrave.

❧ The all-important exchange of plants went two ways. Of special interest is the twelve-year correspondence between the English gardener Peter Collinson, who lived in Peckham near London, and the prominent Virginia planter John Custis. Collinson sent double Dutch tulips and Guernsey lilies, the double-blossomed peach, horse chestnuts, carnations, and auriculas, as well as crown imperial lilies, blue and white hyacinths, yellow asphodel, white moley, and double yellow pilewort. Custis returned dogwoods and flowering bay. Later Collinson sent half a cone of the cedar of Lebanon—the other half went to a friend in Pennsylvania.

❧ A volume on American husbandry published in London in 1775 relates that the meals served to country gentlemen's families in Pennsylvania closely followed contemporary fashion in England: "Coffee tea and chocolate of the best sorts, sugar (cheaper than in England), with bread and butter make a superior breakfast"; for dinner and supper there was a quantity of game, fish, poultry, meat, and venison. Fruit was held to surpass the best in Europe—melons, cucumbers (grown in open fields), apples, cherries, peaches, nectarines, gooseberries, currants, strawberries, and raspberries. As in England the wine commonly drunk was Madeira, which, being fortified, always travelled well. The 1797 inventory of the estate of Francis Lightfoot Lee, owner of Menokin in Virginia, lists one pipe of Madeira wine, a dozen ditto wine bottles, and thirteen bottles of Mal[msey], the sweetest of the Madeiras. While there was also some port and various spirits, there was far more Madeira than anything else, and the Madeira was certainly the most highly valued.

❧ Thomas Jefferson's tour of English houses, parks, and gardens with John Adams is as interesting for what they criticised and rejected as for what they admired. Adams, in his sweeping final words, wrote, "It will be long, I hope, before Ridings, Parks, Pleasure Grounds, Gardens and ornamented farms grow so much in fashion in America. . . . Nature has done greater Things and furnished nobler Materials there. The Oceans, Islands, Rivers, Mountains, Valleys, are all laid out on a larger scale."

❧ Jefferson, used to the grand, natural scenery of Virginia, was repeatedly critical. At Stowe he noted, "the straight approach is very ill" and "the Corinthian arch has a very useless appearance" and formed "an obstacle to a very pleasing distant view." At the famous ornamental farm of the Leasowes, he wrote, "the waters small . . . architecture has contributed nothing," though at Blenheim (see page 479) he allowed, "the water here is very beautiful and very grand" but added "the gravelled walks are broad—art appears too much."

℃ Another interesting point that emerges is the very strong sense that Americans had for historical sites even at this date. At Worcester, stirred by the scene of Cromwell and Parliament's final victory, Adams wrote, "And why do Englishmen so soon forget the Ground where Liberty was fought for? Tell your neighbours and your Children that this is holy Ground, much holier than that on which your Churches stand. All England should come in Pilgrimage to this Hill, once a Year."

Pages 432 and 437: Uppark Yellow Bedroom, ca. 1850,
Hamilton Weston Wallpapers

Henbury Hall

— CHESHIRE —

HENBURY Hall is England's twentieth-century Villa Rotonda: a breathtaking addition to the Anglo-Palladian tradition of Colen Campbell's Mereworth Castle and Lord Burlington's Chiswick House. Evocative of a classical temple in an Arcadian landscape, it might have been the inspiration for a painting by Claude Lorrain, but it was in fact built in the mid-1980s and has an interior equipped with the best modern technology. Few recent examples of the classical revival have proved so ambitious and scholarly in scope, or made such a confident statement about the role of the country house in late-twentieth-century Britain.

The house stands in a park of one hundred acres on the edge of the Peak District, surrounded by a substantial agricultural and sporting estate. The site is not a new one: it was last occupied by an eighteenth-century pile which, savaged by alterations and wet rot, was demolished by Sir Vincent de Ferranti, father of the present owner, in 1957.

The de Ferranti family came to England from Venice around 1800 and established an industry based on electrical supply, building the world's first high-voltage alternating current power station at Deptford in 1885. A former chairman of the company, Sebastian de Ferranti inherited Henbury in 1980. At first he considered building a house in the modern style and approached the Japanese architect Yamasaki, but the eighteenth-century setting, with the wider landscape rolling gently up to the Cheshire hills, seemed to cry out for something more harmonious. The site is an elevated one with views out over wooded parkland to lakes and landscaped vistas, and the freestanding form of the villas of the Veneto, with their equal faces and distinctive silhouette, suggested the perfect model for such a commanding spot.

De Ferranti is an exacting patron with strong ideas about architecture, and it is his conviction that a building is better conceived by an artist than an architect. Thus a key influence in the early stages of Henbury's evolution was a 1982 oil painting by the late topographical artist Felix Kelly, who also designed a number of buildings with a great feeling for the Romantic. Kelly's architectural *capriccio* showed a Palladian rotunda as it might have been interpreted by the bold and original hand of Sir John Vanbrugh, the great master of the English Baroque.

[OPPOSITE] *A view from the magnificent saloonlike space of the hall on the* piano nobile, *looking into the morning room through one of the doorcases designed in the manner of William Kent.*

[OVERLEAF] *Henbury Hall from the south. The dome was inspired by the ovoid domes of Baroque Rome rather than Palladio's perfect hemispheres, and this gives it a more dramatic silhouette, while the pattern of the leadwork was copied from the dome at Mereworth. The porticoes, as in Felix Kelly's painting, have four, instead of the Palladian model of six, Ionic columns, and a distinctive Venetian window arrangement.*

De Ferranti also collaborated with the architect Julian Bicknell, to whom Kelly introduced him in 1983. As well as making careful studies of Mereworth, Chiswick, and other Palladian villas, of which Henbury is a scaled-down version, they also looked to Vanbrugh's celebrated Baroque masterpiece, Castle Howard, where the architect and artist had recently been working. The resulting design, with its pedimented porticos and ovoid dome, combines the form of a Palladian villa with the Baroque spirit of Castle Howard's Temple of the Four Winds.

Henbury is built of brick and concrete, clad with a warm-toned French limestone, the crisp external detail cast in reconstituted stone from models carved by the supreme English master carver Dick Reid of York. The roofs are covered in Macclesfield stone slabs, and the dome is encased in lead. The house is cubic in plan and similar in height and profile to Palladio's Villa Capra, known as Villa Rotonda, near Vicenza, commissioned in ca. 1556. But the plan is very different, the principal space being a magnificent axial hall running through the centre of the house on the *piano nobile*, in the manner of a Venetian palazzo. This great saloon is articulated as three spaces, with the centre rising fifty feet up into the dome, the flanking sections groin-vaulted. The whole floor feels vast and filled with light, which reflects on the floor of inlaid limestones and floods in from above and through the Venetian windows at each end. Doorcases in the manner of William Kent add to the elegant grandeur, offset by leading interior decorator David Mlinaric's muted shades of grey, white plasterwork, and green columns and pilasters painted to resemble scagliola.

The house is entered through a heavily quoined and pedimented doorway in the rusticated plinth of the north portico. This leads into a low, Doric-screened hall, from which the staircase rises up into the north end of the principal hall. The drawing room and dining room on each side are planned so as to incorporate part of the volume of the east and west porticos, their decoration by Mlinaric creating a striking contrast to the subdued palette of the hall.

In the corners on each side of the hall are the library and morning rooms at the south end, with steps leading straight into the park, and an oval, cantilevered staircase and butler's pantry at the north end. The floor above

[ABOVE] *The light-filled central hall, which runs through the core of the house from north to south on the* piano nobile.

[BELOW] *The oval, cantilevered staircase on the northwest corner, showing the rippling pattern created by the shaped undersides of the cantilevered steps.*

[OPPOSITE] *A view from the study/library, through doorcases carved by Dick Reid of York, to the morning room on the east side of the hall.*

accommodates the master bedrooms (with their bathrooms and dressing rooms), which open off a gallery encircling the central dome. There are also three further bedrooms with dressing rooms.

The resurgence of Henbury has touched every corner of the estate, so that all the ancillary buildings relate well to the landscape and reflect the architectural sensibilities of the owner. The former stables survive, with a small walled garden enclosed at one end and the tenants' hall converted into offices and staff accommodation. Kelly designed the delightful *cottage orné* gamekeeper's cottage as an eye-catcher in the tradition of an eighteenth-century garden folly, and his Chinese bridge adorns the extensive pleasure gardens. There is a pool house conceived in the manner of a Baroque grotto, with a fernery and a cascade, and in the park, which has been greatly improved and relandscaped, figures of Greek gods carved by Simon Verity embellish the walks.

Despite its villa precedents and relatively small size, Henbury is not so much a rustic retreat as a proper country house—a place of cultivated taste that makes a grand architectural statement at the centre of a landed estate. As John Martin Robinson observed in *The Latest Country Houses* (1984), it combines "the romantic vision of amateurs, inspired by the English eighteenth century, and the recent scholarly revival of Palladianism as the style best suited to the design of a 'gentleman's house' in the late 20th century."

[LEFT] *The dining room, decorated by David Mlinaric, with a rich, red Fortuny damask woven in Italy. The gilding and vibrant patterns in this room create a striking contrast to the muted tones of the hall. The furniture is mostly eighteenth century, as is the marble chimneypiece and giltwood mirror above it, the latter from Venice, where the chandelier was also made.*

[OPPOSITE] *A view from the dining room looking through double oak doors into the central hall, with the drawing room beyond.*

Ashfold House

— SUSSEX —

THIS exquisite essay in contemporary classicism concentrates the elegance and rationality of its eighteenth-century antecedents into the perfect, compact modern villa. Designed by the architect John Simpson for his parents in 1985, Ashfold stands in the walled garden of a former house near Cuckfield, from where it enjoys unspoiled views over eighteenth-century parkland towards the South Downs.

Simpson had built little at the time of Ashfold's creation, and Alan Powers has described it as "a manifesto work by a younger architect who, like Quinlan Terry (see p. 461), had rebelled against the modernist orthodoxy of architecture schools and emerged from the struggle with a messianic fervour." Because of the nature of the commission, there was not the usual pressure to complete the house within a strict time frame, and the project evolved slowly, every element beautifully crafted and thought out in the minutest detail. Ashfold was eventually completed in 1991, and since then Simpson has become widely regarded as one of the most original and intelligent of the current generation of British classicists. His works range from the Queen's Gallery at Buckingham Palace (2002) and the Carhart Mansion in New York (2005) to large-scale urban master plans and green field houses.

[OPPOSITE] *The view across the upper part of the hall, showing the sarcophagus and urn design that fronts each side of the gallery.*

[BELOW] *The garden front, derived from Sir John Soane's London house in the way the drawing room projects out from the wall plane.*

[LEFT] *The staircase, framed by one of the arches that open off each side of the hall. The stairs are built of timber, painted and detailed to resemble stone.*

[OPPOSITE] *The drawing room, which runs the full length of the south front. On each side of the windows are boxes into which the shutters fold back, flush with the walls. This ingenious arrangement differs from the traditional one of shutters folding back into deep window reveals. The lower parts of the curtains are attached to the shutters and move with them. The sofa and chaise longue were designed by the architect of the house, John Simpson.*

The architectural sophistication of the house belies the fact that it was built on a relatively tight budget. Ashfold possesses a subtlety of proportion, ingenuity of plan, and austere beauty of detailing that give it a gravitas beyond its stature. It also pays homage to Sir John Soane in the way surface detail is pared down to a minimum, and through some of its architectural forms and the adventurous handling of internal space.

The entrance front, suggesting an abstracted triumphal arch, is redolent of Soane's own country house, Pitzhanger Manor in Ealing, while the garden elevation, with the drawing room projecting some three feet from the wall plane to play tricks with the perceived boundaries of the building, is clearly derived from the front of Soane's London house at 13 Lincoln's Inn Fields, now part of the Sir John Soane Museum.

Inside, the plan echoes Pitzhanger in the way that the central hall rises two storeys, with archways opening off it on each of its four sides. There is a sense of space and drama here that one would not normally expect of a building with a square plan reduced to such relatively small dimensions. This is also felt on the staircase beyond the left-hand arch, which is lit by the upper part of a bowed window bay accommodating a breakfast room in the restricted area behind the stair. Still more exciting is the spatial complexity of the upper level of the hall, where a gallery fronted on each side by a sarcophagus and urns commands views across the void out into the landscape beyond. The feeling of scale and openness is remarkable for such a compact building.

Everything is meticulously designed to integrate seamlessly the provision of modern technology. Servicing and control equipment is cleverly concealed behind hinged doors flush with the wall planes; candle sconces incorporate the security system's sensors, and throughout the house are disguised closets and hidden doors.

The drawing room runs across the garden front, with windows on three sides. On the south front, where they repeat the recurring arch motif, the windows are floor length, opening the room out onto the terrace. Instead of heavy double glazing, Simpson devised an ingenious system of internal shutters that fold back into the walls when not in use. His finesse of detail is evident, too, in the furniture he designed for the house, including the Roman-style chaise longue and sofa seen in this room.

[ABOVE LEFT] *The view from the front door, looking across the central hall into the drawing room.*

[LEFT] *The view into the kitchen through one of the doors hidden in the reveals of the stair arch. Ashfold demonstrates Simpson's skill at updating traditional forms to respond to contemporary requirements and modern technology.*

[OPPOSITE] *The entrance front, which echoes Sir John Soane's Pitzhanger Manor in Ealing with its abstracted triumphal-arch form.*

Baggy House

— DEVON —

RARELY does the opportunity arise in England to build an exciting new modernist house in a spectacular coastal setting. Baggy House, which gained planning consent because it replaced an existing dwelling, is an exhilarating cliff-top villa that rises triumphantly to the challenge.

Built between 1992 and 1994 to the design of Anthony Hudson, it could not be more different in appearance to its predecessor. That building had started life as the Victorian holiday home of the founder of *The Birmingham Post* and ended up as a marine hotel with Art Deco additions. The present owners, who have modernist leanings, investigated options for its conversion, but these threatened to be prohibitively expensive so instead they took their architect's advice to demolish and start again.

Gavyn Davies, a London banker, and his wife, Sue Nye, had been searching for the perfect place to build a summer holiday house, and this peninsula on the North Devon coast seemed to answer their dreams. Their brief was straightforward: the house should take maximum advantage of the dramatic situation and have plenty of flexible space to accommodate their family and friends. Otherwise, Mr. Hudson was given a virtually free reign.

His response to the challenge of creating a thoroughly up-to-date house that resonated with the magnificent coastal landscape was to fuse modernist forms and an innovative plan with elements of the Devon vernacular. Thus, the clean, geometric lines, cantilevered forms, and wide expanses of glass associated with houses by Le Corbusier and Frank Lloyd Wright are combined with the battered walls, slate roofs, and small, deeply set windows of the West Country's indigenous cob buildings. The surface resembles a traditional whitewashed render but in fact comprises an externally insulated skin with an acrylic coating on the Dryvit system.

Baggy House stands on the south side of Baggy Point, a rocky promontory that juts out into the Bristol Channel to form the southern headland of Woolacombe Bay. Viewed from its long eastern approach, the flank of the house is a striking vision of intersecting, white, buttressed wall planes randomly pierced by small openings beneath a jagged roofline, anchored by a massive battered chimney. There is a sense of solidity and confidence about the way it confronts the elements in this wild setting, bounded to the south and west by cliffs, sea, and surf, and to the north by a wind-cropped hill.

[OPPOSITE] *A detail of the west side, showing the copper-roofed canopy over glazed screens, which are lowered in summer to create an open veranda overlooking the small bay named after the nearby village of Croyde.*

[OVERLEAF] *Baggy House seen from its long easterly approach, showing the combination of modernist forms and references to the Devon vernacular.*

453

The suggestion of ancient defensive structures combined with Cubist forms recalls C. R. Mackintosh's iconic Hill House in Helensburgh of 1904, which looks back to Baronial architecture and forward to modernism.

Baggy House is conceived as a frame from which to contemplate the seascape, with the play of planes and voids, light and colour, and textures of contrasting materials all integral to its composition. The open, flowing plan and complex relationship of rooms were inspired by Adolf Loos's Muller House in Prague, while Islamic architecture informed the way hierarchies of circulation and alignments to sun and wind are observed, and the importance given to the surface treatment of materials.

The house is entered through a deliberately modest-feeling wall: dimly lit, slate-floored, and with a low, lead-clad ceiling, suggestive in scale and atmosphere of a traditional Devon house. The sense of solidity is enhanced by the column of local granite, roughly hewn to resemble a prehistoric standing stone from nearby Exmoor. To the left is the kitchen, sleekly finished in glass, timber, and stainless steel; the playroom lies below, and ahead, the study and garden. The dramatic transition from the dark, enclosed hall to the light-flooded rooms above is achieved by ascending the staircase, which rises in a delicious curve as if sculpted out of cob, bathed in a shaft of natural light.

The principal living spaces are on split levels linked by steps. The sitting room at the top is dominated by a tapering column of maple wood, turned by a local organ maker to a polished smoothness that contrasts with the stone stele below. This supports the ceiling and serves as a vertical marker, fulfilling both a structural and aesthetic role. Steps lead down to the dining area, which in turn leads to the external terraces. The central living space is enclosed by glazed screens, which can be lowered in summer to create an open pavilion commanding spectacular views over Bideford Bay.

Baggy House celebrates the best Arts & Crafts tradition in its simple, finely crafted detail and use of traditional materials such as oak (for the sitting-room floor and panelling), creamy limestone (in the dining room), and copper (forming the canopy to the living room/pavilion), already developing a beautiful patina as the house weathers. Work by contemporary designers and craftsmen includes the hand-painted silk curtains in the dining room by Louise Woodward, and furniture by Michael Young.

The family quarters occupy a long, low, cottagelike wing to the rear, which again reflects the influence of Devon longhouses. Sheltered and private, the vaulted master bedroom sits into the hill, with an oriel window framing southwesterly views out to Hartland Point. The guest bedrooms are above the main living spaces, reached by a narrow glass staircase that rises partly within the chimney stack and over the top of the kitchen, allowing light to stream down through several levels.

Pliny's description of his Laurentine villa was a guiding inspiration: "lightly washed by the spray of the spent breakers . . . [with] folding doors or windows . . . enjoying the bright light of the sun reflected from the sea." Two millennia later, Baggy House realises the same powerful image.

[OPPOSITE] *A view of the sitting room, with tiny, randomly set openings suggesting those of cob buildings, and the traditional forms of an open fireplace and panelling updated for the 1990s.*

[ABOVE] *Louise Woodward's hand-painted curtains in raw silk and the roughly textured cast-glass top of Anthony Hudson's table frame the view from the dining room.*

[BELOW] *The west front in summer, with its glazed screens lowered to create a veranda or open pavilion.*

[OPPOSITE, CLOCKWISE FROM TOP LEFT] *The breakfast corner in the kitchen viewed through a "porthole" from the entrance hall.*

A view of the sitting room, showing the pivotal maple wood column and some furniture by contemporary designers: a coffee table and chaise longue by Michael Young and a chair by Tom Dixon.

The entrance hall, with the monolithic granite stele that resembles a standing stone.

One of the guest bathrooms, with slate and zinc finishes and a small opening like a porthole.

Merks Hall

— ESSEX —

MERKS Hall belongs to a generation of country houses now more than twenty years old that dared to challenge the modernist aversion to classical ornament. Indeed, its architect, Quinlan Terry, has carved out an international reputation designing buildings that adhere faithfully to the classical tradition, yet are also relevant to the modern age. The owners were attracted to the site for its established landscape—there had once been a Georgian house here, although its successor was a "health centre–style" eyesore of 1961. The present house swept this away, responding to the setting with a wonderful sense of place. It was built in 1982–86, a time when growing prosperity and a new aesthetic vision made such statements of confidence seem once again possible.

The house is visible from afar on its ridge above Great Dunmow, although the entrance front does not come into view until the drive has wound through farmland and park, and then turned suddenly up a short, steep slope to emerge at the corner of an octagonal forecourt. Only then is it seen, diagonally across the forecourt, framed by a pair of large, square gate piers surmounted by stone pyramids.

This is the most richly ornamented of the three show façades, and it

[OPPOSITE] *The entrance front, with the contrast of a richly treated frontispiece against the plainer brick façade and a balustraded belvedere recalling English Baroque houses of the seventeenth century. The proportion of the orders is Palladian, the cornice of the upper Ionic order so large that it serves as the main cornice to this front. The setting of the round-headed first-floor windows into deep canted reveals is a typical Baroque detail that gives a greater impression of depth.*

[BELOW] *The south-facing garden front, of handmade local brick with stone dressings. In contrast to the more opulent entrance front, the other three sides of the house are relatively austere, with late-eighteenth-century-style sash windows cut directly into the walls.*

reflects Terry's love of the Baroque. With its contrast of spirited frontispiece and plain brick flanks, it is reminiscent of houses such as Aldby Park in Yorkshire, which derived their detail from seventeenth-century Dutch architecture as brought to England by Sir Roger Pratt and Hugh May.

Pratt's influential Coleshill House in Berkshire (1649–60, demolished 1950s) is recalled in a number of other features at Merks Hall, notably the form of the hipped roof with its balustraded belvedere (a favourite feature of Terry's) and delightful domed lantern. However, whereas Coleshill had emphatic chimney stacks, Merks Hall appears to have none, for its flues are hidden in the brick piers at the corners of the balustrade. The gate piers recall a pair designed by Pratt that still survives at Coleshill.

[LEFT] *The stair hall with its elegant imperial staircase and cantilevered steps of the same Portland stone as the floor. The only major nontraditional feature in the construction of the house was the use of a steel joist instead of columns to support the stair hall ceiling.*

[RIGHT] *The sitting room on the south front, with Portland stone paving continuing from the stair hall.*

The garden front has a similar urn-topped pediment but, designed to be seen from afar, it is bolder and plainer, as is the east front, with the exception of a first-floor Palladian window. The plan is similar to Terry's Waverton in Gloucestershire of 1979, though more expansive despite the lack of wings. A double square, it is dominated by a large, top-lit central stair hall with a handsome imperial staircase, and the rooms flow into one another without the need for corridors. The east range comprises the drawing room and dining room, the former with Baroque-pedimented doorcases, the latter with a stone chimneypiece boldly carved with serpentine forms.

Terry remodelled the existing swimming pool to resemble an orangery, linking it to the new house through a conservatory-style breakfast room, and he completed the ensemble with a pair of garages and kennels in sympathetic style. The house has now changed hands, but these photographs show it as it was when occupied by the original owners.

[RIGHT] *One of the sitting room's three sash windows, descending to the floor to allow access onto the garden terrace. Their upper parts slide up into a space above the lintel.*

Wakeham

— SUSSEX —

THIS innovative house by the contemporary Robert Adam represented an exciting new direction in modern classicism when it was built on the South Downs a decade ago. Its architect—a leading designer of new country houses, although no relation to his famous eighteenth-century namesake—wanted to demonstrate that energy efficiency and environmental sustainability could be made compatible with the simple, elegant language of classicism.

The circumstances of the commission were exceptional, too, for the project was initiated by the present owner's late mother, the Honorable Brenda Carter, who was a pioneer in the field of solar energy. She and her son Harold, who built and owns Wakeham, collaborated on the plans with the architect and a solar heating expert before her death in 1993.

The house, which was built in 1999 on the site of an earlier building, is deceptive in its method of construction, for although it appears to be of stone, in fact only the door and window surrounds are. The rest is timber framed with a stone-coloured render, the result being a more highly insulated building of materials that were locally sourced. Compact beneath its hipped roof, Wakeham is square in plan with a projecting central entrance bay, the ground floor comprising just three main spaces: a two-storey hall/living area at the centre, flanked on each side by a study/sitting room and kitchen/dining room. Four small bedrooms and three bathrooms open off a U-plan gallery above.

On the north (entrance) front, window openings are kept to a minimum to prevent heat loss, whereas more than half of the south elevation is glazed. The main entrance is flanked by deeply rusticated bands, the vertical emphasis of which is continued by the twin "wind towers" that rise from the roof, serving as combined ventilation shafts and chimneys. Unlike Palladian villas, Wakeham has its portico on the garden front, where glass and steel are combined with a slender classical order redolent of buildings by the great nineteenth-century Scottish architect Alexander "Greek" Thomson. In his article on Wakeham in *Country Life* (June 21, 2001), David Watkin suggested that this double-height portico has something of the Baroque vigour of the one fronting Hawksmoor's Christ Church in Spitalfields of 1714, and also that there is an echo of C. N. Ledoux's "startling cubic villas or 'maisons de

[OPPOSITE] *The south front of Wakeham, with its double-height portico. The slender stainless-steel columns, with lotus leaf capitals reminiscent of the Tower of the Four Winds in Athens, suggest the work of the nineteenth-century architect Alexander "Greek" Thomson (as seen, for example, inside St. Vincent Street Church in Glasgow).*

campagne,' often with belvedere towers" in Wakeham's fusion of modernist purity and picturesque classical forms.

The windows on the garden front allow the sun to warm the slate floor that runs from the portico through to the hall, where white walls reflect the heat. Counteracting this are the deep eaves, which provide an element of shade in hot weather. As solar heating is passive, there is minimal need for mechanical equipment. Warm air circulates freely from the hall to the main living rooms and up to the bedrooms, before emerging naturally through the ventilation shafts in the roof. Cool air can also be drawn in through hidden ducts and discharged in the same manner. The house functions more organically than a conventionally heated building, with different rooms being used at different times, depending on the weather.

Robert Adam has said of Wakeham that he wanted "to enable technology to be humanised and to allow the classical tradition to develop." In experimenting with solar energy and natural convection within this architectural framework, he has shown that he is not afraid to use classicism in novel ways.

Corfe Farm

— DORSET —

THERE is a satisfying symmetry about concluding with this brand-new house near Bridport, for it takes us back, via Lutyens and the English manor house revival, to some of the earlier houses in the book. Designed for a local brewer, Corfe Farm demonstrates how vernacular building traditions can be relevant to modern ideas: "I wanted to show how the simplicity of medieval construction can be expressed in a clean, modern way," says the architect, Stuart Martin, who has created here a house that is also highly contextual and ecologically sensitive, heated by fuel from its own farmland and built of sustainable local materials.

The design for Corfe Farm, which was built in 2006–07, evolved partly in response to the setting—a beech-hung coombe opening out to the south towards the Marshwood Vale—and partly as the result of a decision to reinstate on its original footprint the form of the previous house, which had been badly butchered and was considered not worth keeping. Thus the central, south-facing block, which reused the old masonry, has the appearance of a typical stone-mullioned Dorset farmhouse. It is here that the principal rooms are located: a sitting room and dining room, both treated more

[OPPOSITE] *The view from the northwest, with Preswood Copse behind. The double-height window and chimney stacks were inspired by Lutyens. The roofs are covered in handmade Goxhill tiles and the wings clad with unpainted oak that will weather to a silvery grey.*

[BELOW] *The south-facing range, rebuilt on the footprint of the previous house and treated in a more traditional manner to distinguish it from the wings. The disposition of the original windows has been repeated, with one sole survivor incorporated at the centre of the first floor (the others, with mullions and bronze leaded lights, are copies). The architrave and bracketed cornice to the door were modelled on those of a neighbouring eighteenth-century farmhouse.*

traditionally, with raised and fielded panelling and compartmented ceilings, and a master bedroom suite above.

A parallel range and flanking wings are clad with unpainted oak and fitted out in a more contemporary style. These form a courtyard on the north side, with a broad, almost churchlike entrance (a deliberate reference to many Arts & Crafts houses) leading into a transverse, double-height hall. Mr. Martin wanted to ensure that the internal joinery was of the robust quality of structural woodwork, and so the cantilevered landing and staircase are of oak carpentry pegged in the traditional manner.

The wings accommodate bedrooms and bathrooms for each of John and Lucille Palmers' four daughters, and, on the ground floor of the west wing, the kitchen and family room. Here, on the southwest corner, the idea of an Elizabethan hall has been reinterpreted for open-plan modern living, with a spectacular double-height window inspired by Lutyens's design for the music room window at Plumpton Place in Sussex. The involvement of Mr. Martin at every stage has resulted in a house in which architecture, internal fittings, and decoration are all beautifully integrated.

[RIGHT] *The linear hall, which runs along the north side of the house under one of the two parallel pitched roofs. The cantilevered landing and staircase are of oak, pegged in the traditional manner, the latter with polyhedron finials modelled on a Tudor pew end.*

[OPPOSITE] *The living room at the south end of the kitchen, its window inspired by a Lutyens design and also evoking Elizabethan houses such as Hardwick Hall, one of Stuart Martin's favourite buildings. Throughout the house, modern servicing has been hidden in cupboards or within walls, allowing the internal spaces to remain clean and calm.*

1	Angeston Grange
2	Arbury Hall
3	Arundel Park
4	Ashfold House
5	Baggy House
6	Beckside House
7	Bellamont
8	Belton House
9	Berrington Hall
10	Birtsmorton Court
11	Bishops Court
12	Blackwell
13	Bolesworth Castle
14	Brodsworth Hall
15	Castle Godwyn
16	The Chanter's House
17	The Chantry
18	Chastleton House
19	Chavenage
20	Claydon House
21	Corfe Farm
22	Cothay Manor
23	Cronkhill
24	Daneway
25	East Barsham Manor
26	Eastnor Castle
27	Eltham Palace
28	Eyford House
29	Farnborough Hall
30	Great Dixter
31	Heaton Hall
32	Henbury Hall
33	Honington Hall
34	Hovingham Hall
35	The Ivy
36	Kelmarsh Hall
37	Kelmscott Manor
38	Knepp Castle
39	Lodge Park
40	The Manor House, Hambleden
41	Merks Hall
42	Milton Manor
43	Nether Lypiatt
44	Newby Hall
45	Newe House
46	Nymans
47	Oakly Park
48	Owlpen Manor
49	Parnham House
50	Renishaw Hall
51	Sandon Hall
52	Southill Park
53	Stepleton House
54	Stokesay Castle
55	Sutton Place
56	Trafalgar
57	Trerice
58	Tyntesfield
59	Voewood
60	Wakeham
61	Wightwick Manor
62	Wrotham Park

Glossary

AMORINI: an Italian term used to describe small winged babies accompanying Cupid.

ARCHITRAVE: the moulded frame around a rectangular opening.

ARTS & CRAFTS: a widely influential late-nineteenth-century English movement whose aim was to re-establish the skills of craftsmanship threatened by mass-production and industrialization. In architecture, the appreciation of vernacular buildings was central. The father of the Arts & Crafts movement was William Morris, who was inspired by the writings of John Ruskin.

ART DECO: an opulent decorative style of the 1920s and 1930s characterized by geometric forms and bold lines.

ART NOUVEAU: a decorative style that flourished at the turn of the nineteenth century, characterized by intricate linear designs and sinuous curves and inspired by the natural world.

BALDECHINO: a canopy over an altar, usually supported by four columns.

BAROQUE: an architectural style first developed in late-sixteenth-century Italy characterized by spatial dynamism and the manipulation of mass, rhythm, and silhouette in architectural composition (the word Baroque is derived from the Portuguese for an irregularly shaped pearl). It flourished in England from ca. 1692 to ca. 1722.

BOLECTION: a moulding projecting beyond the face of a panel or frame.

BOULLE: inlaid decoration of tortoiseshell, yellow metal, and white metal in cabinetwork.

BOTHY: hut (from Gaelic *bothan*).

CAPRICCIO (plural: *capricii*): a painting of an architectural fantasy, where buildings and archaeological remains are depicted together in fantastical combinations.

CAROLINE: used to describe the period spanning the reigns of the Stuart kings Charles I (1625–49) and Charles II (1660–85), which includes the Civil War and Restoration periods.

CARSTONE: a firmly cemented ferruginous rock found in the British Isles.

CARTOUCHE: a shaped tablet enclosed in an ornate or ornamental frame.

CASTELLATED: having battlements like a castle.

CHAMFER: a beveled edge—the surface formed when a square angle is cut away obliquely.

COOMBE: a deep narrow valley; or a valley or basin on the flank of a hill.

COTTAGE ORNÉ: a small house or cottage that consciously imitates the careless rustic style of the vernacular, a concept popularized by the Picturesque movement.

[OPPOSITE] *The kitchen garden at Chatsworth House, Derbyshire.*

[PAGE 472] *The stables at Seaton Delaval Hall, Northumberland.*

[LEFT] *Early 1970s decoration by David Hicks in the drawing room at Britwell Salome, Oxfordshire.*

[ABOVE] *The 3rd Earl of Burlington's Chiswick House, Middlesex.*

[BELOW] *A detail of a seventeenth-century Mortlake tapestry in the hall at Wassand Hall, Yorkshire.*

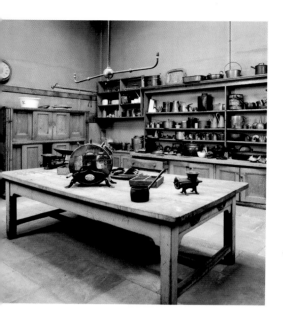

CROCKET: an ornament common in Gothic architecture, usually in the form of curved and bent foliage on the edge of a gable, spire, or pinnacle.

CRUCK: one of a pair of curved timbers that curve inwards from the outer walls to support a ridge beam and form a principal roof support in primitive timber-framed construction.

DADO: the finishing (often decorated or with paneling) of the lower part of a wall in a classical interior.

DECORATED: of or relating to a medieval English Gothic style of architecture characterized by its tracery, which flourished from ca. 1290 to ca. 1360.

DISTEMPER: a type of paint in which the pigments are mixed with an emulsion of egg yolk, with size or egg white as a vehicle. Generally used as a form of whitewash, it was also used for painting scenery and murals.

DOUBLE PILE: a house plan whereby two ranges of rooms are placed back to back.

DOVECOT: a small, compartmentalized raised house or box for domestic pigeons.

DOWER HOUSE: a moderately large house on an estate that is occupied by the widow of the late owner.

EDWARDIAN: the period coinciding with the reign of Edward VII, 1901–10.

EGG AND DART: a carved ornamental design in relief consisting of an egg-shaped figure alternating with a figure resembling an arrowhead.

ELIZABETHAN: the period coinciding with the reign of Elizabeth I, 1558–1603.

ENFILADE: an interconnected group of rooms usually arranged in a row with each room opening onto the next.

FEDERAL STYLE: a style of architecture and decoration in the United States following the American Revolution.

FELL: a high barren field or moor.

FERME ORNÉE: a farm building that has been ornamented to disguise its functional character.

GEORGIAN: the period spanning 1714–1810, coinciding with reigns of the Hanoverian kings George I, II, and III (though George III did not die until 1820). It was followed by the Regency period (qv).

GOTHIC: a medieval style of architecture characterized by pointed arches that in England succeeded the Norman style in the mid-eleventh century and is generally divided into three periods: Early English, Decorated, and Perpendicular. It underwent several revivals in later centuries.

GOTHICK: a fanciful and essentially decorative eighteenth-century style of architecture and ornament derived from the Gothic.

GREEK REVIVAL: an architectural style that began in the late eighteenth century and became fashionable in the early nineteenth century, based on archaeological discoveries of ancient Greece.

HAMMER BEAM: a horizontal bracket projecting at wall-plate level, part of a form of truss roof where the roof is supported by large projecting brackets, creating a much more open effect than previously.

HIGH VICTORIAN: the term used to describe a later nineteenth-century style of architecture that was very eclectic and ornate, combining elements of Gothic Revival, Italianate, and Romanesque architecture.

JACOBEAN: the period coinciding with the reign of the Stuart king James I, (1603–1625).

[ABOVE LEFT] *The kitchen at Brodsworth Hall, Cheshire (see page 328).*

[ABOVE RIGHT] *Moggerhanger, Bedfordshire.*

[BELOW LEFT] *The Queen of Scots dressing room at Chatsworth House, Derbyshire.*

[BELOW RIGHT] *The White Drawing Room at Houghton Hall, Norfolk.*

JACOBETHAN: the term coined by John Betjeman to describe the English Revival style made popular from the 1830s, which derived from the English Renaissance (1550–1625), with elements of Elizabethan and Jacobean.

LINENFOLD PANELING: a form of carved paneling with a representation of vertically folded linen.

MODERN MOVEMENT: the dominant movement in twentieth-century architecture that developed out of nineteenth-century industrial innovations and that is characterized by a rejection of ornament, simplicity of design, and emphasis on the mantra "form follows function."

MODILLION: an ornamental block or bracket under the corona of the cornice (found in the Corinthian and Composite orders).

NEOCLASSICAL: an architectural style that flourished in ca. 1760–90 based directly on archaeological evidence of Greek and Roman design, rather than Renaissance interpretations.

OGEE: a pointed arch formed of two concave arcs above the two convex arcs below.

ORIEL: a large bay window projecting from a wall and supported by a corbel or bracket.

ORMOLU: a golden or gilded brass or bronze used for decorative purposes (as in mounts for furniture).

OXFORD MOVEMENT: an affiliation of High Church Anglicans, mainly members of the University of Oxford, who argued against the increasing secularisation of the Church of England. It was also known as the Tractarian Movement after the publication of *Tracts for the Times* (1833–1841).

PALLADIAN: the architectural style based on the work of Andrea Palladio (1508–1580), whose influence was to spread worldwide. It flourished in England in the eighteenth century.

PARTERRE: a formal garden laid out in geometrical patterns, with planting beds, box hedges, and paths.

PERPENDICULAR: of or relating to a medieval English Gothic style of architecture in which vertical lines predominate, and which began in the late fourteenth century.

PRODIGY HOUSE: a term used by Sir John Summerson to describe the great Tudor and Stuart houses e.g. Burghley and Audley End, built generally of brick with stone dressings and characterized by having widespread symmetrical plans, their elaborate frontispieces with great, glittering expanses of glass in big windows, turrets, balustraded parapets, and ranks of ornate chimneys.

PIANO NOBILE: an Italian term for the first floor above ground level on which the principal rooms were located.

PICTURESQUE MOVEMENT: the Picturesque is an aesthetic quality between the sublime and the beautiful which was adopted in architecture and landscape design according to the theories of Richard Payne Knight and Uvedale Price in the 1770s. The movement was characterized by irregularity of design, variety of texture, and an emphasis on the relationship of the building and its landscape.

POTAGER: a kitchen garden.

QUEEN ANNE: the period coinciding with reign of Queen Anne, 1702–14.

QUOINS: dressed stones at the corners of a building, alternately long and short.

REGENCY: the period coinciding with the time that George IV was Prince Regent, 1811–20.

[ABOVE] *The double cube room at Wilton House, Wiltshire.*

[LEFT] *The entrance to the inner court at Sissinghurst, Kent, from the walled garden.*

[BELOW] *The south front of Castle Howard, Yorkshire.*

477

[ABOVE] *The dining room at Belvoir Castle, Leicestershire.*

[RIGHT] *A detail of Thomas Carter's chimneypiece in the drawing room at Syon House, Middlesex.*

[BELOW] *The Gothick library at Milton Manor, Oxfordshire (see page 124)*

REREDOS: a screen or partition behind an altar, usually made of ornamental wood or stone.

RESTORATION: the period beginning in 1660 when, following the Civil War, the monarchy was restored under Charles II.

ROCOCO: an eighteenth-century style of decoration originating in France, essentially an interior style characterized by ornamentation and fanciful forms.

ROGUE: a term used to describe works by certain Victorian Gothic Revival architects whose designs were not marked by scholarship, but attempted to combine the medieval and the modern.

SCAGLIOLA: an imitation marble used for floors, columns, and ornamental interior work.

SCREENS PASSAGE: the entrance passage between the great hall and the kitchen quarters in medieval (and some later) house plans, created by a screen, which was often decorated.

SETTLE: a wooden bench with arms, a high solid back, and an enclosed foundation that can be used as a chest.

SKITTLES: English ninepins played with a wooden disk or ball.

SOANIAN: in the manner of the architecture of Sir John Soane (1753–1837).

SPANDREL: the sometimes-ornamented space between the exterior curve of an arch and its enclosing rectangle.

SPIRELETTED: decorated with slender spires.

STATE APARTMENT: a suite of rooms intended for the display of magnificence and in which to entertain visitors of importance. A notable feature of Baroque house plans.

STRINGCOURSE: a continuous horizontal moulding on the exterior of a building.

TRACTARIAN: see Oxford movement.

TREFOIL: an ornament or symbol in the form of a stylized trifoliate leaf, often found in Gothic tracery.

TUDOR: coinciding with the reign of the Tudor monarchs, 1485–1603.

VICTORIAN: coinciding with the reign of Queen Victoria, 1837–1901.

VILLA RUSTICA: a term used by ancient Romans to describe a villa in open countryside usually centered around a working farm and agricultural estate.

VOLUTE: a spiral scroll-shaped ornament forming the chief feature of the Ionic capital.

VOUSSOIR: one of the wedge-shaped blocks of stone forming an arch or vault.

WHIG: one of the two political parties (the other being the Tories) active in England between 1678 and 1868. Whigs tended to be more liberal-minded and culturally enlightened.

WRENAISSANCE: the architectural revival in the early twentieth century of the manner of Sir Christopher Wren. See for example Eltham Palace (p. 407).

Bibliography

Alexander, Jonathan, and Paul Binski. *The Age of Chivalry: Art in Plantagenet England, 1200–1400.* London: Royal Academy of Arts, 1987.

Aslet, Clive. *The American Country House.* New Haven: Yale University Press, 2005.

—. *The English House: The Story of a Nation at Home.* London: Bloomsbury, 2009.

—. *The Last Country Houses.* New Haven: Yale University Press, 1985.

Aslet, Clive, and Alan Powers. *The National Trust Book of the English House.* London: Penguin Books, 1985.

Clark, Kenneth. *The Gothic Revival: An Essay in the History of Taste.* London: John Murray, 1996.

Colvin, Howard. *A Biographical Dictionary of British Architects, 1600–1840.* New York: Facts on File, 1980.

Cooper, Nicholas. *The Jacobean Country House.* London: Aurum Press, 2006.

—. *Houses of the Gentry, 1480–1680.* London: Paul Mellon Centre, 1999.

Cornforth, John. *The Country Houses of England 1948–1998.* London: Constable, 1999.

—. *Early Georgian Interiors.* London: Paul Mellon Centre, 2005.

—. *English Interiors 1790–1848: The Quest for Comfort.* London: Barrie & Jenkins), 1978.

—. *The Search for a Style: Country Life and Architecture 1897–1935.* New York: W. W. Norton & Co., 1989.

Cornforth, John, and John Fowler. *English Decoration in the 18th Century.* London: Barrie & Jenkins, 1974.

Crook, Joe Mordaunt. *The Greek Revival: Neo-Classical Attitudes in British Architecture, 1760–1870.* London: John Murray, 1972.

Curl, James Stevens. *Victorian Architecture.* Devon: David & Charles, 1990.

Darley, Gillian. *Villages of Vision.* London: Architectural Press, 1975.

Davey, Peter. *Arts and Crafts Architecture.* London: Phaidon Press, 1997.

Davis, Terence. *The Architecture of John Nash.* London: Studio Books, 1960.

Downes, Kerry. *English Baroque Architecture.* London: Sotheby Parke Bernet Publications, 1987.

Elliott, Brent. *Victorian Gardens.* London: Batsford Ltd., 1990.

Franklin, Jill. *The Gentleman's Country House and Its Plan, 1835–1914.* London: Routledge & Kegan Paul, 1981.

Girouard, Mark. *Elizabethan Architecture.* New Haven: Yale University Press, 2009.

—. *Life in the English Country House: A Social and Architectural History.* New Haven: Yale University Press, 1994.

[ABOVE LEFT] *The King's Bed at Knole, Kent.*

[ABOVE RIGHT] *A pair of gate lodges at Cranborne Manor, Dorset.*

[BELOW LEFT] *The north portico at Blenheim Palace, Oxfordshire.*

[BELOW RIGHT] *Mapperton House, Dorset (voted England's Finest Manor House in 2006).*

—. *Robert Smythson and the Elizabethan Country House*. New Haven: Yale University Press, 1985.

—. *The Victorian Country House*. New Haven: Yale University Press, 1985.

Gradidge, Roderick. *Dream Houses: The Edwardian Ideal*. New York: George Braziller, 1980.

Greensted, Mary. *The Arts and Crafts Movement in the Cotswolds*. London: Alan Sutton Publishing, 1999.

Hall, Michael. *The Victorian Country House*. London: Aurum Press, 2009.

Harris, Eileen. *The Country Houses of Robert Adam*. London: Aurum Press, 2008.

Harvey, John. *Mediaeval Gardens*. Portland, Oregon: Timber Press, 1982.

Hill, Oliver, and John Cornforth. *English Country Houses: Caroline 1625–1685*. London: Country Life, 1966.

Hill, Rosemary. *God's Architect: Pugin and the Building of Romantic Britain*. New Haven: Yale University Press, 2009.

Hussey, Christopher. *English Country Houses 1715–1840* (3 vols.). London: Country Life, 1955.

—. *The Life of Sir Edwin Lutyens*. Woodbridge, England: Antique Collectors' Club, 1985.

Jenkins, Simon. *England's Thousand Best Houses*. London: Penguin Books, 2004

Kornwolf, James. *M. H. Baillie Scott and the Arts and Crafts Movement: Pioneers of Modern Design*. Baltimore: Johns Hopkins University Press, 1972.

Lacey, Stephen. *Gardens of the National Trust*. London: Anova Books, 2005.

Mander, Nicholas. *Country Houses of the Cotswolds*. London: Aurum Press, 2008.

Middleton, Robin, and David Watkin. *Neoclassical and 19th Century Architecture* (2 vols.). New York: Rizzoli International Publications, 1993.

Mowl, Timothy. *Elizabethan and Jacobean Style*. London, Phaidon Press, 1993.

—. *Gentleman and Players: Gardeners of the English Landscape*. Stroud, England: Sutton Publishing, 2000.

—. *William Kent: Architect, Designer, Opportunist*. London: Pimlico, 2007.

Mowl, Timothy, and Brian Earnshaw. *Trumpet at a Distant Gate: The Lodge as Prelude to the Country House*. Boston, David R. Godine, 1985.

Musson, Jeremy. *The Country Houses of Sir John Vanbrugh*. London: Aurum Press, 2009.

—. *The English Manor House*. London: Aurum Press, 2008.

—. *How to Read a Country House*. London: Ebury Press, 2005.

Robinson, John Martin. *The Regency Country House*. London: Aurum Press, 2009.

Pevsner, Nikolaus. *Staffordshire*, Pevsner Buildings of England. New Haven: Yale University Press, 1974.

—. *Somerset: South and West*, Pevsner Buildings of England. New Haven: Yale University Press, 1958.

Pevsner, Nikolaus, and Alan Brooks. *Worcestershire, The Buildings of England*, Pevsner Architectural Guides. New Haven: Yale University Press, 2007.

Pevsner, Nikolaus, and Ian Nairn. *Sussex*, The Buildings of England. London: Penguin UK, 1999.

Powers, Alan. *The Twentieth Century House in Britain*. London: Aurum Press, 2004.

Quest-Ritson, Charles. *The English Garden: A Social History*. Boston: David R. Godine, 2004.

—. *The Arcadian Friends: Inventing the English Landscape Garden*. London: Bantam Press, 2007.

Richardson, Tim. *English Gardens in the Twentieth Century*. London: Aurum Press, 2005.

Ridley, Jane. *The Architect and His Wife: A Life of Edwin Lutyens*. London: Chatto and Windus, 2002.

Robinson, John Martin. *Georgian Model Farms: A Study of Decorative and Model Farm Buildings in the Age of Improvement, 1700–1846*. Oxford: Oxford University Press, 1984

—. *The Latest Country Houses, 1945–83*. London: The Bodley Head, 1987.

—. *The Wyatts: An Architectural Dynasty*. Oxford: Oxford University Press, 1980.

Stamp, Gavin. *Edwin Lutyens Country Houses*. New York: The Monacelli Press, 2009.

Stroud, Dorothy. *The Architecture of Sir John Soane*. London: Studio, 1961.

—. *Henry Holland: His Life and Architecture*. London: Barnes, 1966.

Summerson, John. *Architecture in Britain 1530–1830*. New Haven: Yale University Press, 1989.

—. *Inigo Jones*. London: Paul Mellon Centre, 2000.

—. *The Life and Work of John Nash, Architect*. Cambridge, Mass.: 1981.

Thacker, Christopher. *The History of Gardens*. Berkeley: University of California Press, 1979.

Thurley, Simon. *The Royal Palaces of Tudor England: Architecture and Court Life, 1460–1547*. London: Paul Mellon Centre, 1993.

Tinniswood, Adrain. *The Arts & Crafts House*. London: Mitchell Beazley, 2005.

Wade-Martens, Susanna. *The English Model Farm: Building the Agricultural Ideal*. Oxford: Windgather Press, 2002.

Watkin, David. *Athenian Stuart: Pioneer of the Greek Revival*. London: Unwin Hyman, 1982.

—. *The Life and Work of C. R. Cockerell*. London: Zwemmer, 1987.

—. *The English Vision: The Picturesque in Architecture, Landscape and Garden Design*. London: Harper & Row, 1982.

—. *Radical Classicism: The Architecture of Quinlan Terry*. New York: Rizzoli International Publications, 2006.

Wood, Margaret E. *The English Medieval House*. New York: Harpercollins, 1983.

Woolgar, C. M. *The Great Household in Late Medieval England*. New Haven: Yale University Press, 1999.

Worsley, Giles. *The British Stable*. London: Paul Mellon Centre, 2005.

—. *Classical Architecture in Britain: The Heroic Age*. London: Paul Mellon Centre, 1995.

—. *Inigo Jones and the European Classicist Tradition*. London: Paul Mellon Centre, 2007.

Contributors & Acknowledgements

MARCUS BINNEY is an architectural historian and author known for his work in the British conservation movement. He is president and co-founder of SAVE Britain's Heritage. His books include *In Search of the Perfect House: 500 of the Best Buildings in Britain & Ireland* (2008), *Town Houses: Urban Houses from 1200 to the Present Day* (1998), and *Lost Houses of Scotland* (1980).

TIM KNOX is director of Sir John Soane's Museum in London. Formerly architectural historian, and then head curator, of the National Trust, he regularly lectures and writes on art, architecture, and the history of collecting. His publications include numerous country house guidebooks, and articles in *Apollo* and *Country Life*.

JEREMY MUSSON is an architectural historian and journalist, and author of several books, including *Up and Down Stairs: The History of the Country House Servant* (2009), *The Country Houses of Sir John Vanbrugh* (2008) and *How to Read a Country House* (2006). He was architectural editor at *Country Life* magazine from 1998 to 2007, and presenter of the BBC2 TV series *The Curious House Guest* about the history and lives of country houses in 2005–6.

TIM RICHARDSON is an independent garden historian and landscape critic, and the author of several books including *English Gardens in the 20th Century* and *Arcadian Friends:*

Inventing the English Landscape Garden. He is a trustee of the Garden History Society and serves on the gardens advisory panel of the National Trust.

JOHN MARTIN ROBINSON is an architectural historian and the author of several books on British architecture, including *The Regency House* (2005), *Heraldry in Historic Houses of Great Britain* (2000), and *The Oxford Guide to Heraldry* (1990).

GEOFFREY TYACK is a fellow of Kellogg College, University of Oxford, and director of the Stanford University Centre in Oxford. He has lectured and published widely on the history of the English country house and his written several articles in *Country Life*. Other publications include *Sir James Pennethorne and the Making of Victorian London, Oxford: An Architectural Guide*, and the *Blue Guide to Oxford and Cambridge*. He has recently finished a new edition of *The Buildings of England: Berkshire* and is currently working on the life and work of the architect John Nash.

ACKNOWLEDGEMENTS

I must express my thanks to all owners of the houses included in the book.

I would also like to acknowledge my debt to the authors of the *Country Life* articles that provided the main source of information for this book: Clive Aslet, Chris Brooks, Nicholas Cooper, John Cornforth, Marcus Field, Mark Girouard, John Goodall, Ruth Guilding,

Michael Hall, Richard Haslam, Richard Hewlings, Charles Hind, Christopher Hussey, Gervase Jackson-Stops, Sally Jeffery, Tim Knox, Katherine MacInnes, Philip Mainwaring Johnston, Harry Mount, Jeremy Musson, Gordon Nares, Arthur Oswald, Stephen Ponder, Alan Powers, Arthur T. Quiller-Couch, Alistair Rowan, Malcolm Reynes, John Martin Robinson, Henry Avray Tipping, Geoffrey Tyack, David Watkin, Lawrence Weaver, Annabel Westman, Antony Woodward, Christopher Woodward, and Giles Worsley.

I would also like to thank the following who have given me considerable help or accommodated me during the writing of this book: Justin Hobson and Helen Carey of the Country Life Picture Library and Camilla Costello, formerly of the Country Life Picture Library; Dominic Walters, picture editor, *Country Life*; John Goodall, architectural editor, *Country Life*; Katherine Boyle; Katharine Goodison; Robert Dalrymple and Nye Hughes; Jim Lewis; Alexandra Tart, Charles Miers, and Maria Pia Gramaglia of Rizzoli; Douglas and Richenda Miers. MM

PHOTOGRAPHIC CREDITS

All photographs are © Country Life (www.countrylifeimages.co.uk) except for the following:

© Clive Boursnall: 454–55

© English Heritage Photo Library: 328, 330–31, 332, 333, 476 (top left)

© Derry Moore: 154, 155

482

484